CW00330494

THE WORLD'S TEN
MOST EVIL MEN

THE WORLD'S TEN MOST EVIL MEN

FROM TWISTED DICTATORS TO CHILD KILLERS...

NIGEL CAWTHORNE

JOHN BLAKE

Published by John Blake Publishing Ltd,
3 Bramber Court, 2 Bramber Road,
London W14 9PB, England

www.johnblakepublishing.co.uk

First published in paperback in 2009

ISBN: 978 1 84454 745 6

All rights reserved. No part of this publication may be reproduced,
stored in a retrieval system, or in any form or by any means, without
the prior permission in writing of the publisher, nor be otherwise
circulated in any form of binding or cover other than that in which it is
published and without a similar condition including this condition
being imposed on the subsequent publisher.

British Library Cataloguing-in-Publication Data:

A catalogue record for this book is available from the British Library.

Design by www.envydesign.co.uk

Printed in the UK by CPI William Clowes Beccles NR34 7TL

3 5 7 9 10 8 6 4 2

© Text copyright Nigel Cawthorne 2009

Papers used by John Blake Publishing are natural, recyclable
products made from wood grown in sustainable forests.
The manufacturing processes conform to the environmental
regulations of the country of origin.

Every attempt has been made to contact the relevant copyright-holders,
but some were unobtainable. We would be grateful if the appropriate
people could contact us.

CONTENTS

INTRODUCTION   VII

CHAPTER ONE: OSAMA BIN LADEN   1

CHAPTER TWO: ROBERT MUGABE   25

CHAPTER THREE: COLONEL MENGISTU HAILE MARIAM   45

CHAPTER FOUR: RADOVAN KARADZIC   65

CHAPTER FIVE: CHARLES TAYLOR   99

CHAPTER SIX: IAN BRADY   115

CHAPTER SEVEN: CHARLES MANSON   141

CHAPTER EIGHT: PETER SUTCLIFFE   167

CHAPTER NINE: DENNIS NILSEN   207

CHAPTER TEN: JOSEF FRITZL   227

FURTHER READING   243

INTRODUCTION

There are so many evil people in the world that it was hard to limit the scope of this book to just ten of them. And when I say 'evil', I don't just mean bad or misguided, or even misunderstood; I'm talking about people whose principal aim is to make life a living hell for the rest of us. Some, like Osama bin Laden and Charles Manson, may want to drag the entire world into bloodshed and chaos. Others, such as Robert Mugabe, are content to draw only their own people into the abyss. Colonel Mengistu Haile Mariam and Charles Taylor inflicted murderous misery on two nations apiece, while Radovan Karadzic was happy to order the extermination of others who were not like him.

Ian Brady tortured and murdered defenceless children in an attempt to break down the moral constraints that the rest of us rely on to get through life. Peter Sutcliffe killed vulnerable women for his own sexual gratification and then claimed that he was doing the work of God, while Dennis Nilsen killed because he could not stand to be alone – something we all must face, from time to time.

History is littered with truly evil characters. The twelfth-century Mongol leader Genghis Khan once stated: 'I have committed many acts of cruelty and had an incalculable number of men killed, never knowing what I did was right, but I am indifferent to what people think of me.' It is estimated that he killed up to a quarter of the world's population during his lifetime. Outside the cities he conquered, he built pyramids of heads before completely destroying the internal fabric, but his evil did not stop there: when he died on the shore of Lake Baikal in 1227, he left orders that, if anyone gazed on his coffin, the next one would be theirs.

The evil deeds of Adolf Hitler are almost too infamous to recount. He started World War II, which resulted in the deaths of up to 60 million. There are no reliable estimates of the number of wounded or displaced, or those who endured other terrible privations. Hitler was also responsible for the systemic murder of some six million Jews, along with gypsies, Slavs, homosexuals and political allies, as well as direct enemies of Germany.

And it's not just limited to men. In the 1860s, a million died during one woman's attempt to make herself the Empress of South America. She was an Irish prostitute named Eliza Lynch, who was the mistress of Francisco Solano López, the President of Paraguay. To further her lover's ambitions, she pushed him into simultaneously declaring war on Brazil, Argentina and Uruguay in 1863. In the six-year battle that ensued, Paraguay was completely destroyed. When Lynch eventually fled the country not a single male over the age of nine was left alive.

For the purposes of this book, I was confined to write about evil people who are, at the time of writing, still alive. There are more than enough of them. You may disagree with my choice – you are, of course, free to come up with your own list. I have not presented my own selection in any particular order (I think it would be tasteless to come up with a Top Ten). Again, you are free to rank them.

Nigel Cawthorne
Bloomsbury, London 2009

CHAPTER ONE

OSAMA BIN LADEN

On the morning of Tuesday, 11 September 2001, four US airliners were hijacked. Two of the planes, filled with passengers, were deliberately crashed into the Twin Towers of the World Trade Center in New York, starting fires that eventually destroyed the 110-storey buildings. A third was crashed into the Pentagon in Arlington, Virginia, across the Potomac River from Washington, DC. On board a fourth plane, believed to be heading for the White House, the passengers fought back against the hijackers. As a result, the aircraft crashed into a field in Pennsylvania, some 75 miles southeast of Pittsburgh. In all, some 3,000 people lost their lives.

A few hours after the Twin Towers collapsed, the Bush administration concluded that Osama bin Laden and his al-Qaeda organisation were to blame, though bin Laden has actually never been formally indicted for the attacks. Soon the British government also came to the decision that bin Laden was to blame. Although bin Laden appears on the FBI's Ten Most Wanted list, this is for the bombing of the US Embassies in Dar es Salaam, Tanzania, and Nairobi, Kenya, in 1998 when over 200 were killed. The wanted poster does, however, state: 'In addition, bin Laden is a suspect in other terrorist attacks throughout the world' and also mentions that he is 'considered armed and extremely dangerous'. And there is a price on his head: 'The Rewards For Justice Program, United States Department of State, is offering a reward of up to $25million for information leading directly to the apprehension or conviction of Usama Bin Laden. An additional $2million is being offered through a program developed and funded by the Airline Pilots Association and the Air Transport Association.'

At first, bin Laden denied involvement in the attacks, referring to them through an aide as 'punishment from Allah'. Later, he took responsibility for 'inspiring' the events of September 11 although according to him, the attacks were down to the US for supporting Israel. Then, on video tape aired on the Arabic TV station Al-Jazeera on 29 October 2004, bin Laden admitted that al-Qaeda had decided that they 'should destroy towers in America' because they were 'a free people... and we want to regain the freedom of our nation.'

Finally, in another video tape released through Al-Jazeera on 23 May 2006, he admitted: 'I am the man responsible for the recruitment of the 19 people who carried out the attacks.' This came two weeks after Zacarias Moussaoui, a would-be hijacker captured during flight-training two weeks before 9/11, was sentenced to life without the possibility of parole on four counts of conspiracy.

'Brother Zacarias Moussaoui has no connection whatever with the 11 September operation,' said bin Laden, adding that Moussaoui's confession was, 'null and void, because it was extracted under pressure.'

Al-Qaeda, the terrorist organisation run and trained by Osama bin Laden, has also been responsible for attacks in the Yemen, Riyadh, Bali, Jakarta, Tunisia, Casablanca and Istanbul, as well as inspiring bombings in Madrid and London. It is linked to other terrorist groups across the Islamic world, and under the inspiration of bin Laden, it has declared a *jihad* or 'Holy War' against the US and the West itself. No one can say how many deaths bin Laden has been responsible for; what we can be sure of is that he has promoted hatred and bloodshed on a global scale and the death toll that can be laid at his door will continue to accumulate with the passing years.

Osama bin Laden was born with a silver spoon in his mouth. He was one of more than 50 children of one of Saudi Arabia's richest families. His father, Muhammed Awad bin Laden, was a wealthy businessman with close ties to the Saudi royal family. Originally from Yemeni, Muhammed bin Laden moved to Saudi Arabia as a youth, when he began a construction company. Soon, he became so successful that he could lend money to King Faisal, who issued a royal decree awarding all future construction projects to bin Laden's company. As a result, the bin Ladens became the richest non-royals in Saudi Arabia with a company grossing US$5 billion a year.

Muhammed bin Laden married 22 times. Born in Riyadh on 10 March 1957, Osama was his sixteenth child and his only son by his tenth wife Hamida, a Syrian thought to be more cosmopolitan that his other Wahhabi wives. Soon after Osama was born, his parents divorced and his mother married Muhammad al-Attas. The couple had four children, and the young Osama lived in the new household with three stepbrothers and one stepsister.

Although he was raised a devout Sunni Muslim, from 1968 to 1976 Osama bin Laden was educated at an élite secular school in Jeddah, where the pupils wore a Western-style school uniform. Reports on his further education are confused: he himself claims to have studied Economics and Business Administration at King Abdul Aziz University. Formal biographies say he earned a degree in Civil Engineering in 1979, or a degree in Public Administration in 1981, but other sources state that, though he was reportedly 'hard-working', bin Laden dropped out of university during the third year before sitting his degree. The implication is that his main interest was religion and he spent his time 'interpreting the Koran and *jihad*', as well as doing charitable work. It seems that, along the way, he dropped the liberal Sunni beliefs of his mother and became a hard-line Wahhabi, a puritan sect dominant in Saudi Arabia that stresses a literal belief in the Koran and the establishment of a Muslim state based solely on Islamic Sharia law.

In 1974, at the age of 17, bin Laden married his 14-year-old cousin Najwa Ghanem, a Syrian, in Latakia. She went on to become the mother of some 11 of his children including Saaden bin Laden, a stalwart of al-Qaeda. Saaden is thought to have been responsible for the suicide bombing of a synagogue in Tunisia on 11 April 2002, which killed 19 and wounded 30. He is also thought to have been behind another suicide bombing in Riyadh on 12 May and a further attack in Morocco just four days later. Besides Najwa, Osama bin Laden is reported to have married three other women, as permitted under Muslim law, and he has fathered up to 24 children.

While bin Laden attended university in 1979, several crucial events occurred on the world stage. In February of that year the US-backed Shah of Iran was ousted following an Islamic Revolution under the leadership of the Ayatollah Khomeini. Meanwhile, the Communist government in Kabul called on the Soviet Union for support in their fight against regional groups, who became known collectively as the *mujahideen* – which means 'those who engage in *jihad*'. By the end of that year, Soviet helicopters, tanks and two motorised rifle divisions were in action in Afghanistan.

After leaving college, bin Laden travelled to Afghanistan to join the Palestinian scholar Abdullah Azzam, who was recruiting international volunteers and raising funds for the *mujahideen*. The Afghan jihad was backed by American money and had the blessing of the governments of Saudi

Arabia and Pakistan. According to Middle Eastern analyst Hazhir Teimourian, bin Laden received security training from the CIA, who also provided money and weapons to the *mujahideen*. America saw the struggle in Afghanistan as part of the Cold War. US politicians, including National Security Advisor Zbigniew Brzezinski, saw no danger in Muslim fundamentalism. Rather, they regarded the fundamentalists as allies in the global struggle against Communism and the Soviet Union.

In 1984, Azzam and bin Laden set up the Maktab al-Khidamat organisation using bin Laden's family fortune. Also known as the Afghan Services Bureau, it funnelled money, arms and Muslim fighters recruited around the Arabic world into the Afghan war. MAK was run through Peshawar, where it maintained a close liaison with the Pakistan's Directorate of Inter-Services Intelligence and the CIA. The organisation also opened recruitment and fund-raising centres in Arab and Western countries, including 33 such centres in the US.

By 1988, bin Laden had split from Maktab al-Khidamat. While Azzam continued to provide material support for Afghan fighters, bin Laden sought a more active role. One key dispute was over Azzam's insistence that Arab fighters recruited from abroad should be integrated into Afghan fighting groups, while bin Laden believed that they should form their own separate fighting force. This was to be the beginnings of al-Qaeda (which means 'the base' although the name did not emerge until much later).

Armed with modern weapons supplied by the Americans and with highly motivated fighters, the *mujahideen* were more than a match for the Red Army. Afghanistan turned into the Soviet Union's Vietnam and Moscow began to withdraw its troops. The last Soviet soldier left Afghanistan in February 1989.

Around that time bin Laden also came under the influence of Ayman al-Zawahiri, head of the Egyptian

Islamic Jihad. Although Azzam was a believer in global jihad, he felt that the first priority should be to set up an Islamic government in post-war Afghanistan. Al-Zawahiri, in contrast, favoured using the assets of the MAK to overthrow governments in Muslim countries deemed to be too un-Islamic. In November 1989, Azzam died in a car bombing, for which the EIJ were under suspicion. With the death of Azzam, many MAK members moved over to bin Laden's new organisation.

That month, al-Qaeda gained another key recruit. Also in November 1989, Ali Mohamed, a former Special Forces sergeant stationed at the Special Warfare Center at Fort Bragg, North Carolina, left military service and moved to Santa Clara, California. He travelled to Pakistan and then Afghanistan, where he became involved with bin Laden's plans. The following year, on 8 November 1990, the FBI raided the New Jersey apartment of Mohammed's associate El Sayyid Nosair and discovered Special Warfare Center manuals, books on bomb-making and evidence of terrorist plots, including plans to blow up New York City skyscrapers. Nosair was eventually convicted in connection with the 1993 World Trade Center bombing. Bin Laden contributed $20,000 towards his defence.

Though the Red Army has withdrawn from Afghanistan, the civil war continued, but after the collapse of the Soviet Union in 1991, the government in Kabul fell and the *mujahideen* took over. They were a disparate group, made up of numerous local factions, however, and the result was anarchy. Order was restored when the Taliban, an army of religious students under the ultra-pious former *mujahideen* fighter Mullah Mohammad Omar, took over in 1994.

Bin Laden had left the country long before. In 1990, he returned to Saudi Arabia, a hero of *jihad*: it was said that he and his Arab legion had brought down the mighty superpower of the Soviet Union – though, in fact, foreign fighters made only a minor contribution to the struggle. However, after spending his time among fundamentalists who were happy to lay down their lives for Islam, bin Laden rallied against the corruption of the Saudi government and that of his own family.

In August 1990, Iraq invaded Kuwait, posing an immediate threat to Saudi Arabia. Bin Laden met the Crown Prince and offered his Arab fighters to King Fahd to defend Saudi Arabia. Instead, King Fahd accepted the support of the US and NATO, meaning foreign, non-Muslim troops would be stationed on Saudi territory. Bin Laden was appalled. Their presence, he argued, defiled the sacred soil of the 'land of two mosques', meaning the holy cities of Mecca and Medina. His vocal criticism of the Saudi monarchy provoked government attempts to silence him.

Aided by ex-Green Beret Ali Mohammed, bin Laden moved to Sudan in 1992. This was at the invitation of the Islamic scholar and leader of Sudan's National Islamic Front Hassan al-Turabi, following an Islamist coup d'état. There, bin Laden set up legitimate businesses, including a tannery, two large farms and a road construction company. The Sudanese leaders were delighted that the wealthy Saudi was investing in their fledgling Islamic state, but when Saudi Arabia pressured Pakistan to get rid of the *mujahedeen* living along the border with Afghanistan, bin Laden reportedly paid for the 480 Afghan veterans to come and work for him. With their assistance, he set up camps to train insurgents, while continuing his verbal assaults on King Fahd. On 5 March 1994, Fahd retaliated by personally revoking his citizenship and sending an emissary to Sudan to seize bin Laden's passport. Bin Laden's family also cut off his allowance amounting to around $7million a year.

By then, bin Laden had already begun his global *jihad*. In 1992 he sent an emissary named Qari el-Said with $40,000 to Algeria to aid the Islamists there and to warn them not to compromise with the impious secular government. In the civil war that resulted, an estimated 150,000–200,000 Algerians have died. Civilians have been massacred, and journalists and politicians assassinated.

On 29 December 1992, al-Qaeda set off bombs outside two hotels in Aden, Yemen. The target was American soldiers, on their way to take part in Operation Restore Hope, in support of the United Nation's famine relief programme in Somalia. In fact, the US soldiers were billeted elsewhere. However, two people were killed – an Australian tourist and a Yemeni hotel worker – and seven more, mostly Yemenis, severely injured. This was justified by al-Qaeda theoretician and co-founder Mamdouh Mahmud Salim, aka Abu Hajer al Iraqi, by reference to two medieval *fatwas*, which ruled that killing innocent bystanders was OK because if they were good Muslims, they would go to paradise... and if they weren't, it didn't matter.

As a result of the attack in Yemen, Sudan was placed on the State Department's list of countries sponsoring terrorist activities. At the time, the US government believed that bin Laden's followers were trying to obtain the components to build nuclear weapons and, with Sudan's National Islamic Front, they began to work developing chemical arms.

On 26 February 1993, a car bomb was detonated below the North Tower of the World Trade Center in New York City. The 1,500-lb device was intended to knock Tower One onto Tower Two, bringing both towers down and killing up to 250,000 people. As it was, the towers shook and swayed, but the foundations held. On that occasion only six people were killed and 1,042 injured. The blast caused nearly $300million of damage to property.

The attackers had received funding from al-Qaeda member Khalid Shaikh Mohammed. Their leader was Khalid's nephew Ramzi Yousef. He had been trained in a camp in Afghanistan and has been linked via co-conspirators to El Sayyid Nosair in New Jersey, where the bomb was assembled. In tapped telephone conversations, 'al-Qaeda' was mentioned. After the attack on the World Trade Center, it is alleged that Yousef took part in an attempt to assassinate Benazir Bhutto, then Prime Minister of Pakistan, in the summer of 1993. Then, with his uncle Khalid and Afghan-war veteran Wali Khan Amin Shah, Yousef planned to assassinate Pope John Paul II, or perhaps US President Bill Clinton, during a visit to the Philippines, crash a plane into the CIA headquarters at Langley, Virginia, and blow up 11 airliners on their way from Asia to the United States, killing around 4,000 passengers. Again, the plot was funded by bin Laden.

Yousef began making bombs, which he planned to conceal under the seats of the aircraft. On 1 December 1994, one such bomb was tested by placing it under the seat of the Greenbelt Theater in Manila. It went off, injuring several theatregoers. A second bomb was tested on 11 December when Yousef placed it under the seat of Philippine Airlines Flight 434 from Manila to Tokyo, with a stopover in the city of Cebu. He got off at Cebu, his seat taken by 24-year-old Japanese businessman Haruki Ikegami. Four hours later, the bomb went off, blowing Haruki in half and injuring ten other passengers. It blew a large hole in the cabin floor and damaged the rudder control. The crew made an emergency landing at Okinawa, saving the lives of the 272 other passengers and 20 crewmembers. By then, Yousef had made the FBI's Ten Most Wanted list. He was arrested in an al-Qaeda safe house is Islamabad and extradited to the US. At his trial, he admitted: 'Yes, I am a terrorist and am proud of it.'

The judge described him as an 'apostle of evil' and sentenced him to life imprisonment without possibility of parole with the recommendation that he should spend his entire sentence in solitary confinement.

Meanwhile, Khalid Shaikh Mohammed remained at large, eventually rejoining bin Laden, when he laid out the first plans for the 9/11 attacks. He also had contact with Richard Reid, the 'shoe bomber' who tried to blow up American Airlines Flight 63 from Paris to Miami on 22 December 2001. Reid also seems to have had contact with Zacarias Moussaoui, the one man convicted of 9/11 offences. There were also allegations that Khalid was mixed up in the murder of *Wall Street Journal* reporter Daniel Pearl in 2002 and the Bali night-club bombings that same year. In March 2003, Khalid was captured in Rawalpindi. The Human Rights Watch charity maintain he disappeared into a semi-secret prison in Jordan before reappearing in US naval base Guantanamo Bay, where he is said to have admitted, 'decapitating with my blessed right hand the head of American Jew Daniel Pearl' as well as planning attacks on London's Heathrow Airport and Big Ben.

Bin Laden, meanwhile, had established at least three terrorist training camps in north Sudan, where recruits from at least half-a-dozen countries were put through their paces. In October 1993, in nearby Somalia, US special forces attached to the United Nations' mission there made a bungled attempt to capture the general staff of warlord Mohamad Farah Aidid and found themselves involved the Black Hawk Down incident, otherwise known as the First Battle of Mogadishu. In the largest firefight since Vietnam, 19 American troops died when set upon by local militias trained by bin Laden.

Al-Zawahiri and the EIJ had also joined bin Laden in Sudan in 1992. They served at the core of al-Qaeda but also engaged in separate operations against the Egyptian government. However, in 1993, a young schoolgirl was killed in an unsuccessful EIJ attempt on the life of the Egyptian Interior Minister Hasan al-Alfi and Egyptian public opinion turned against the Islamist bombers. The police arrested 280 members and six were executed. Undeterred, in 1995, an attempt was made to assassinate Egyptian President Hosni Mubarak at a meeting of the

Organisation of African Unity in Ethiopia. The attack was led by Mustafa Hamza, a senior Egyptian member of al-Qaeda. It failed when a grenade launcher malfunctioned and Mubarak's limousine proved to be bulletproof. Sudanese Intelligence was implicated when it was found that the terrorists' weapons had been smuggled into the country via the Sudanese Embassy. Then in November 1995, EIJ made a suicide-bomb attack on the Egyptian Embassy in Pakistan, killing 16, wounding 60 and damaging buildings within a half-mile radius.

By then, according to US Intelligence sources, bin Laden had established extensive training facilities for foreign guerrillas in northern Yemen, near the Saudi border. In August 1995, he wrote an open letter to King Fahd calling for a campaign of guerrilla attacks in order to drive US forces out of Saudi Arabia. Then, on 13 November, five Americans and two Indians were killed in the truck bombing of the US-run Saudi National Guard training centre in Riyadh. Bin Laden denied involvement, but praised the attack. However, American and Saudi authorities believe he had a hand in it. Indeed, before four Saudi men accused of bombing were beheaded in Riyadh's main square, they were forced to make a public confession in which they admitted receiving communiqués from bin Laden.

In May 1996, under increasing pressure from Saudi Arabia, Egypt and the US, Sudan asked bin Laden to leave. Soon afterwards, the EIJ were expelled, following the killing of the sons of two senior EIJ members, who had been drugged and blackmailed into working for the Egyptian Intelligence Service. In a kangaroo court, the boys had been found guilty of 'sodomy, treason and attempted murder' and sentenced to death under Sharia law. Al-Zawahiri ordered their execution by firing squad and distributed video tapes of it.

Kicked out of Sudan, bin Laden returned to Taliban-controlled Afghanistan, where he forged a close relationship with Mullah Mohammad Omar. Though he had had to sell his assets in Sudan at a loss, bin Laden was still able to continue his attacks on Saudi Arabia. On 25 June 1996, members of Hizballah Al-Hijaz – Party of God in the Hijah (the western part of Saudi Arabia) – exploded a truck bomb outside the Khobar Towers compound in Dhahran, which housed foreign military personnel. Nineteen US servicemen and one Saudi were killed and 372 of various nationalities wounded. Bin Laden was seen being congratulated that day and it is thought that he was behind the attack.

On 23 August 1996, bin Laden signed and issued a Declaration of Jihad outlining al-Qaeda's goals. These were to drive US forces from the Arabian Peninsula, overthrow the Government of Saudi Arabia, liberate Muslim holy sites and support Islamic revolutionary groups around the world. He declared Saudis have the right to strike at US troops in the Persian Gulf. That same month, a secret grand jury investigation of Osama bin Laden began in New York.

In November, bin Laden was interviewed for the British TV programme *Dispatches*, during which he threatened to wage an Islamic holy war against the United States and its allies, if Washington did not remove its troops from the Gulf region. Then, in May 1997, CNN aired an interview with bin Laden, in which he condemned the US 'occupation of the land of the holy places.'

In Afghanistan, bin Laden gave financial and paramilitary support to the Taliban regime and it was during 1997 that he moved to Kandahar, the Taliban stronghold. Following this, al-Qaeda gained a measure of legitimacy under the Afghan Ministry of Defence. It established training camps in the Afghanistan and Pakistani border region, and raised money from donors who had supported the MAK during the anti-Soviet *jihad*. Ties with the Pakistani Intelligence Services were renewed.

According to the Swiss Federal Police, bin Laden funded

the 17 November 1997 massacre at Luxor, where Islamic terrorists killed 58 foreign tourists – 36 of whom were Swiss – and 4 Egyptians at the famous Luxor Temple. Another 26 were wounded. Later, the terrorists were found dead, having apparently committed suicide. Again, the Egyptian people turned against the Islamists.

In 23 February 1998, Osama bin Laden and Ayman al-Zawahiri co-signed a *fatwa* in the name of the World Islamic Front for Jihad Against Jews and Crusaders, a name al-Qaeda sometimes goes under. It said: 'To kill the Americans and their allies – civilians and military – is an individual duty for every Muslim who can do it in any country in which it is possible to do it, in order to liberate the al-Aqsa Mosque [in Jerusalem] and the Holy Mosque [in Mecca] from their grip, and in order for their armies to move out of all the lands of Islam, defeated and unable to threaten any Muslim. This is in accordance with the words of Almighty Allah, "and fight the pagans all together as they fight you all together", and "fight them until there is no more tumult or oppression, and there prevail justice and faith in Allah".'

He also issued a joint declaration with the Islamic Group, the EIJ, the Jihad Movement in Bangladesh and the '*Jamaat ul Ulema e Pakistan*' under the banner of the 'World Islamic Front', again stating that Muslims should kill Americans, including civilians, anywhere in the world.

In May 1998, bin Laden was interviewed by ABC reporter John Miller. He defended the killing of women and children on the grounds of 'reciprocity'. After all, he pointed out, America had dropped atomic bombs on Hiroshima and Nagasaki that did not differentiate between men and women, or adults and children. He defended Ramzi Yousef, saying: 'He is a Muslim who wanted to protect his religion jealously from the oppression practised by America against Islam.' And that: 'He acted with zeal to make the Americans understand that their government was

attacking Muslims in order to safeguard the American-
Jewish interests.'

Bin Laden also praised Wali Khan Amin Shah, the man
who had actually placed the bomb under the seat in the
Greenbelt Theater in Manila. He had known him in
Afghanistan and endorsed his plan to assassinate President
Clinton. Asked whether he had ordered and funded
the attacks on the US military in Dhahran and Riyadh,
bin Laden boasted that he had inspired them and called
their perpetrators 'holy martyrs'. His aim, he said, was to
fight until the Americans were driven out of all the
Islamic countries. After all, Allah had defeated the Soviet
Union, which had since fallen apart. The same future
awaited America.

'Instead of remaining United States, it shall end up
separated states and shall have to carry the bodies of its
sons back to America,' bin Laden boasted. And he had
other bleak prophecies: 'We are certain that we shall – with
the grace of Allah – prevail over the Americans and over
the Jews, as the Messenger of Allah promised us in an
authentic prophetic tradition when He said the Hour of
Resurrection shall not come before Muslims fight Jews and
before Jews hide behind trees and behind rocks.'

The Saudi Royal Family would go the way of the Shah of
Iran, he continued. They had 'sided with the Jews and the
Christians giving them free reign over the land of the two
Holy Mosques. These are grave offences that are grounds
for expulsion from the faith. They shall all be wiped out.'

Bin Laden crowed about the victory of his men over the
Americans in Somalia: the superpowers were no longer
invincible and the US soldiers merely 'paper tigers'.
According to him, all America had done during the First
Gulf War in Iraq, he said, was to have destroyed the milk
and dairy industry that was vital for infants and children,
and blow up the dams necessary for the crops that people
grew to feed their families.

'Proud of this destruction, America assumed the titles of world leader and master of the new world order,' he said. 'After a few blows, it forgot all about those titles and rushed out of Somalia in shame and disgrace, dragging the bodies of its soldiers. America stopped calling itself world leader and master of the new world order, and its politicians realised that those titles were too big for them and that they were unworthy of them. I was in Sudan when this happened. I was very happy to learn of that great defeat that America suffered, so was every Muslim.'

Asked whether he had a message for the American people, he told ABC's John Miller: 'We believe that this [the Clinton] administration represents Israel inside America. Take the sensitive ministries such as the State Department, the Department of Defense and the CIA, you will find that the Jews have the upper hand in them. They make use of America to further their plans for the world, especially the Islamic world... While millions of Americans are homeless and destitute and live in abject poverty, their government is busy occupying our land and building new settlements, and helping Israel build new settlements in the point of departure for our Prophet's midnight journey to the seven heavens.'

Muslims believe that the prophet Muhammad ascended to heaven from the site of the al-Aqsa Mosque in Jerusalem.

The following month there was a raid on a cell of an Islamic terrorist movement in Albania and two suspected employees of bin Laden were arrested. Two weeks later, two more suspected associates of bin Laden were arrested in another raid. Egyptian nationals, they were turned over to anti-terrorist officials in Egypt. All four were associated with the Islamic Revival Foundation.

On 8 June 1998, the grand jury investigation of bin Laden begun in 1996 issued a sealed indictment, charging him with the killing of five Americans and two Indians in the 1995 truck bombing of the Saudi National Guard training centre in Riyadh and, 'conspiracy to attack defense utilities of the United States'. Prosecutors said that bin Laden headed a terrorist organisation called al-Qaeda and was a major financier of Islamic terrorists around the world.

On 6 August, the EIJ sent the United States a warning: they would soon deliver a message to Americans, 'which we hope they read with care, because we will write it, with God's help, in a language they will understand.' The following day, their meaning became clear.

On 7 August 1998, car bombs went off simultaneously outside the US Embassies in Dar es Salaam and Nairobi. In Dar es Salaam, the attack killed at least 11 and injured 85; in Nairobi, some 212 people were killed and an estimated 4,000 injured. Although the targets were US government facilities, most of the victims were African civilians. The 11 killed in Dar es Salaam were Tanzanians, while about 200 of those killed at the embassy in Nairobi were Kenyans.

According to Lawrence Wright, author of *The Looming Tower: Al Qaeda and the Road to 9/11* (2006), which plots the rise of al-Qaeda, the Dar es Salaam bombing was called Operation al-Aqsa, while the Nairobi operation was named after the Holy Kaaba in Mecca, though he points out that neither had an obvious connection with the American Embassies in Africa.

Bin Laden initially claimed that these two embassies had been targeted because of the US 'invasion' of Somalia; also that an American plan to partition Sudan had been hatched in the Embassy in Nairobi, while the genocide in Rwanda had also been cooked up inside the two American Embassies. However, Lawrence Wright concludes that none of these claims made sense. Bin Laden's actual goal was, he says, 'to lure the United States into Afghanistan, which was already being called "The Graveyard of Empires"'.

In response, President Clinton froze on assets that could be linked to bin Laden. Cruise missiles were launched that hit a pharmaceutical factory in Sudan, that US Intelligence mistakenly believed was making chemical weapons, and al-Qaeda training camps in Afghanistan, where 19 were killed, though bin Laden himself escaped unharmed.

President Clinton went on television to announce the attacks, saying the camp at Khost, where al-Qaeda leaders were thought to have been meeting, was 'one of the most active terrorist bases in the world.' He added: 'I want the world to understand that our actions today were not aimed against Islam,' which he called, 'a great religion.'

However, many, including bin Laden himself, saw the attack as Clinton's way of deflecting attention from the Monica Lewinsky scandal, which was then reaching its climax. The Sudan government condemned the attack, dismissing Clinton as a 'proven liar' with 'a hundred girlfriends'. Around the world, there were massive protests against the attacks, mostly in Muslim countries. On 26 August 1998, a Muslim organisation bombed a Planet Hollywood restaurant in Cape Town, killing two and injuring 26. In Afghanistan, the Taliban also denounced the bombing. Bin Laden pledged to attack the US again, while a court under the control of the Taliban declared him 'a man without sin'. Meanwhile, back in Britain the *Sunday Times* reported that bin Laden was sending Islamic mercenaries into Kashmir to support an Islamic secession campaign there.

On 4 November 1998, Osama bin Laden was indicted by a Federal Grand Jury on charges of the murder of US nationals outside the United States, conspiracy to murder US nationals outside the United States and attacks on a Federal facility resulting in death for the embassy bombings. Evidence against him included courtroom testimony by former al-Qaeda members and satellite phone records. A reward of $5million was placed on his head. The US Attorney's office filed an indictment covering the killing of members of the American military stationed in Saudi Arabia and Somalia, as well as the murder of US embassy employees in Nairobi and Dar es Salaam in January. Then, on 7 June 1999, bin Laden made the FBI's Ten Most Wanted list. Requests for his extradition from Afghanistan fell on deaf ears, so President Clinton went to the United Nations and persuaded them to impose sanctions against Afghanistan in an attempt to force the Taliban to extradite him.

Everything went quiet until the morning of 11 September 2001 when 19 al-Qaeda terrorists hijacked four commercial passenger jet airliners. Each team of four hijackers included one member who had undergone some pilot training. They intentionally crashed two of the airliners full of passengers into the World Trade Center in New York City. One plane hit each tower, with extensive loss of life. Both buildings collapsed soon afterwards, causing extensive damage to the surrounding area.

The hijackers crashed a third passenger-laden airliner into the Pentagon. Passengers on board the fourth learnt from their mobile phones that other hijacked planes had hit the World Trade Center. Fearing the same fate, they rushed the hijackers in an attempt to seize control of the plane. In the resulting mêlée, the plane crashed into a field near the town of Shanksville in rural Somerset County, Pennsylvania. Although all those on board lost their lives, their heroic resistance at least prevented further loss of life on the ground.

Apart from the nine hijackers, 2,973 people died as an immediate result of the attacks, and a medical examiner has found that at least one person has since died of lung disease due to the resulting dust from the World Trade Center. Another 24 people remain missing and are presumed dead, bringing the total number of victims to 2,998.

All 246 on board the four hijacked planes died – no one survived. In New York, 2,603 died in the Twin Towers and on the ground. All were civilian. At the Pentagon, 125 died, some of whom were military personnel, including Deputy Chief of Staff of the Army Lieutenant General Timothy Maude, the highest ranking military officer on 9/11.

In the North Tower 1,366 people, at or above the impact, died. Hundreds were instantly killed; the rest were trapped and died when the Tower collapsed. In the South Tower, up to 600 were instantly killed or trapped above the impact. Only about 18 managed to escape from above the place where the plane hit before the Tower collapsed. At least 200 jumped to their deaths from the burning towers, dying when they hit streets and rooftops hundreds of feet below. Some of those above impact made their way upwards towards the roof in the hope of being saved by helicopter rescue, but the doors that gave access to the roof were locked. Besides, the intense heat and thick smoke would have prevented rescue helicopters from landing.

Cantor Fitzgerald L.P., an investment bank on the 101st–105th floors of the North Tower, lost 658 employees, many more than any other firm. Marsh Inc., immediately below them on the 93rd–100th floors where the plane hit, lost 295. The Aon Corporation (floors 92 and 98–105 of the South Tower) lost 175; the New York City Fire Department lost 341 fire fighters and two paramedics. New York City Police Department lost 23 staff. Thirty-seven Port Authority Police Department officers and eight private ambulance personnel were killed. The head of security at the World Trade Center, John P. O'Neill – a former assistant director of the FBI, who assisted in the capture of Ramzi Yousef – was also killed while trying to rescue people from the South Tower.

The dead included eight children: five on the plane that hit the Pentagon, three on the plane hitting the South Tower. The youngest was two years old, while the oldest passenger on board the hijacked planes was 82. In the buildings themselves, the youngest victim was 17 and the oldest was 79. Many had no resting place. New York medical examiners failed to identify the remains of more than 1,100 victims and the city has about 10,000 unidentified bone and tissue fragments that cannot be matched to the list of the dead. Bone fragments were still being found in 2006, when workers demolished the damaged Deutsche Bank Building nearby.

Bin Laden initially denied involvement. On 16 September 2001, he read out a statement that was later broadcast by Qatar's Al Jazeera satellite channel: 'I stress that I have not carried out this act, which appears to have been carried out by individuals with their own motivation.' However, he was delighted that, 'God has struck America at its Achilles heel and destroyed its greatest buildings, praise and blessing to Him.' And he dismissed the allegations being levelled at him as another example of America's hatred for Islam.

However, it was plain that Osama bin Laden was behind the attack, as he admitted later. The US demanded his extradition once again, and when the Taliban again refused to give him up, America and Britain invaded Afghanistan. By November 2001, US forces had reached Jalalabad where they discovered a video tape left by al-Qaeda members. During the course of the tape, bin Laden discusses the attack in a way that indicates he knew precisely what would happen:

We had notification since the previous Thursday
[6 September] *that the event would take place that day.*
We had finished our work that day and had the radio on.
It was 5.30pm our time... Immediately, we heard the
news that a plane had hit the World Trade Center...
After a little while, they announced that another plane
had hit the World Trade Center. The brothers who heard
the news were overjoyed by it.

He also knew in advance of the second plane:

They were overjoyed when the first plane hit the building, so I said to them: 'be patient.' The difference between the first and the second plane hitting the towers was twenty minutes. And the difference between the first plane and the plane that hit the Pentagon was one hour.

The conversation also reveals that bin Laden had more detailed knowledge of what would occur. He mentions that the Egyptian Muhammad Atta was the leader of the operation. Also, those who had not been trained to fly did not know the details of the plot and only learned of it just before they boarded the plane.

We calculated in advance the number of casualties from the enemy, who would be killed based on the position of the tower. We calculated that the floors that would be hit would be three or four floors. I was the most optimistic of them all… Due to my experience in this field, I was thinking that the fire from the gas in the plane would melt the iron structure of the building and collapse the area where the plane hit and all the floors above it only. This is all that we had hoped for.

Reacting to the tape, New York Mayor Rudy Giuliani said, '[Osama bin Laden] seems delighted at having killed more people than he anticipated, which leaves you wondering just how deep his evil heart and soul really is.'

It was only in the run-up to the 2004 Presidential election that bin Laden finally abandoned his denials and admitted al-Qaeda was responsible for the attacks. In a further tape in 2006, he boasted of being personally responsible.

Despite numerous attempts to capture him, bin Laden remains at large. Meanwhile, al-Qaeda goes from strength to strength. In April 2002, Ayman al-Zawahiri and the EIJ merged with bin Laden's group. Their tentacles spread worldwide. In October 2002, suicide bombers blew up a nightclub called Paddy's Pub in Bali and then, seconds later, detonated a huge car bomb in the street outside, killing 88 Australians, 38 Indonesians and 24 Brits. Hundreds more suffered horrific injuries and burns. Most were holidaymakers in their twenties and early thirties.

On 15 November 2003, truck bombs went off outside two synagogues in Istanbul, killing 27 people, largely Turkish Muslims, and injuring over 300 more. Six Jews were also killed in the attack. Five days later suicide bombers exploded other vehicles outside the British consulate and HSBC bank, killing 30 and wounding another 400, again largely Turkish Muslims. Al-Qaeda claimed responsibility for both attacks.

On 11 March 2004, bombs planted on commuter trains in Madrid by al-Qaeda-inspired terrorists, killed 191 and wounded 1,755. Four suicide bombers, who also drew inspiration from al-Qaeda, set off bombs in London, killing 52 and injuring 700 on 7 July 2005. On 27 July 2005, the day of the memorial service for the dead, a second group of would-be suicide bombers staged another attack. Although the intention was to cause a large-scale loss of life, this time only the detonators went off, causing one minor injury. The perpetrators were arrested and later found guilty of conspiracy to murder. Al-Qaeda is also thought to be behind the plot to detonate liquid explosives on a number of planes travelling from Heathrow airport to the United States in August 2006. No link has been discovered between al-Qaeda and the attack on Glasgow airport in June 2007, however.

Al-Qaeda has also made attacks in Iraq after the US and Britain invaded in 2003, but has since been driven out by local insurgents. Terrorists with links to al-Qaeda have also been active in Algeria, Eritrea, Somalia, Sudan, Libya, Bosnia, Chechnya, the Philippines, Palestine and the

Lebanon. On 13 July 2007, the figure set on bin Laden's head by the US government was doubled to $50million.

Although Osama bin Laden claims to be fighting in the name of Islam he has done little to help his fellow Muslims. Indeed, he seems happy to kill them – many even died in the Twin Towers. As a result of his actions, Muslims who live in Western countries have been alienated from the mainstream of society. In a number of Muslim countries, he has stirred up factional fighting with inevitable casualties. In addition, he has done nothing to help the Palestinians, whose cause he claims to support. Little of his effort has been directed at Saudi Arabia, whose rulers he says should be expelled from the faith. His endeavours there have been largely counterproductive, leaving the monarchy as secure as ever.

Bin Laden can be counted among the most evil men alive today because, at bottom, he is simply a rich boy merely indulging his millennial fantasy at the expense of other people's lives, including those of his followers. He has hijacked a religion to unleash a global *jihad* that has caused untold misery for both victims and perpetrators. In his eyes, innocent civilians can be blown apart in the name of Allah, while the lives of his young followers may be squandered in suicide attacks that seldom have any clear aim.

As New York Mayor Rudi Giuliani stated after two planes laden with passengers crashed into busy office buildings of no military significance on bin Laden's orders, killing thousands: 'This man is the personification of evil.'

CHAPTER TWO

ROBERT MUGABE

Robert Mugabe is a Jesuit-educated Marxist who cut his political teeth during a guerrilla war against white-minority rule in what was then Southern Rhodesia. In February 1980, with the negotiated settlement of the anti-colonial struggle, he became head of the first black-majority government in the newly named Zimbabwe. Within two years of assuming office, he sparked a tribal war where his Shona-speaking people crushed the Ndebele speakers in Matabeleland, leading to accusations of mass murder. Since then his rule has gone from bad to worse.

Through his land-reform policies, Robert Mugabe has turned his country, once the breadbasket of Africa, into a nation beset by famine. Economic mismanagement has seen unemployment climb to 85 per cent, though around a quarter of the population have fled the country. And, in December 2007, inflation had topped 150,000 per cent. Mugabe maintains his rule by brutally suppressing the opposition and denying his people any semblance of human rights. Fearing an insurrection among the dispossessed from the shantytowns springing up during his disastrous rule, he simply had their houses bulldozed in

Operation 'Drive Out Trash' in 2005, dumping their denizens in the countryside, where many had no chance of survival.

Despite being in his mid-80s – in a country where the life expectancy for men has dropped to 37 (34 for women) – his grip on power shows no sign of loosening. He manipulates elections by distributing food aid only to his supporters and denying the outcome when he has clearly lost. Despite his disastrous rule, Robert Mugabe takes no responsibility for the state to which Zimbabwe has been reduced since he took control. Instead he blames British colonialism, which ended over 40 years ago. As a result, Ugandan-born Archbishop of York John Sentamu has condemned him as racist and South Africa's Desmond Tutu states that he should be indicted in the International Court of Justice in The Hague for 'gross violations'.

Robert Gabriel Mugabe was born on 21 February 1924 in the village of Matibiri, near Kutama Mission in the Zvimba District northeast of Salisbury, now Harare, capital of the then Southern Rhodesia. His father, Gabriel Mugabe Matibiri, was a carpenter who abandoned his family to find work in Bulawayo in 1934, when Robert was ten. This left the child tied to his mother's apron strings.

A solitary and sickly youth, he avoided contact with other children by traipsing off to isolated grazing spots with the cows. Unlike other boys in the village, he did not scrap or play at hunting games. Instead, he would weave reeds and dry grass to make small nets, baited with feathers, moss and other nesting material. He would set these traps out down by a river, then settle down in the shade of a tree with a book, waiting for hours until a small bird or two ventured into his snares. It was his way of providing a bit of meat for the family pot.

Mugabe was raised Roman Catholic and he studied in Marist Brothers and Jesuit schools, including the exclusive St Francis Xavier College, part of the Kutama Mission.

Considered to be among Africa's top one hundred schools, it was run along the lines of an English public school. He was bookish and a swot, qualities that hardly endeared him to his fellow pupils.

After qualifying as a teacher, Mugabe left to study at Fort Hare in South Africa, where he met contemporaries such as Julius Nyerere, who became first president of Tanzania; Herbert Chitepo, who led the Zimbabwe African National Union until his untimely death (of more later); Robert Sobukwe, anti-apartheid campaigner and founder of the Pan African Congress and Kenneth Kaunda, first president of Zambia. After graduating in 1951, Mugabe went on to study at Driefontein in Johannesburg, South Africa in 1952; Salisbury in 1953; Gwelo, also in Rhodesia, in 1954; and in Tanzania from 1955–57. Along the way, and later in prison, Mugabe picked up seven academic degrees in all: a BA from the University of Fort Hare, a BSc in Economics, an LLB, an LLM and a MSc in Economics from the University of London, plus a BEd and a BA in Administration from the University of South Africa. He once boasted that he also possessed a 'degree in violence'.

From 1955–58, Mugabe taught at Chalimbana Teacher Training College in Zambia. Then he moved to Ghana, where he lectured at St Mary's Teacher Training College at Takoradi from 1958–60. It was there that he met fellow teacher Sally Hayfron, who he married in Salisbury in 1961. While in Ghana, Mugabe was influenced and inspired by Ghana's then-Prime Minister Kwame Nkrumah, of whom he claims to be a lifelong follower, though Nkrumah remains one of Africa's most respected leaders and was voted that country's man of the millennium by listeners of the BBC World Service in 2000.

Mugabe and some of his Zimbabwe African National Union Party cadres also received instruction at the Kwame Nkrumah Ideological Institute at Winneba in Ghana. Then, at the behest of the leadership of the National Democratic

Party (NDP), he quit teacher training in 1960 to return to Rhodesia as a full-time activist in nationalist politics.

The colonial government then banned the NDP. Going underground, it was renamed the Zimbabwe African People's Union (ZAPU) under Joshua Nkomo in 1962 and followed the orthodox Soviet line on national liberation. Mugabe left ZAPU in 1963 to help the Reverend Ndabaningi Sithole form the rival Zimbabwe African National Union (ZANU) with Edson Zvobgo, Enos Nkala and his old friend, the lawyer Herbert Chitepo. ZANU took a pro-Chinese Maoist line following the Sino-Soviet split. It was also influenced by the ideas of the Pan Africanist Congress, founded in South Africa in 1959, while ZAPU aligned itself with South Africa's mainstream anti-apartheid movement, the African National Congress. ZANU was also an uneasy alliance between the Ndebele and Mugabe's own Shona tribe, and it was a constant struggle to maintain cross-tribal representation.

ZANU leader Ndabaningi Sithole nominated Mugabe as the party's secretary general, but in 1964 he was arrested by the white minority government for making a 'subversive speech' and spent the next ten years in jail. During his incarceration, Mugabe returned to his books, earning his law degrees and a Bachelor of Administration through correspondence courses. While in jail, his only son Nhamodzenyika died of malaria in Ghana at the age of four. Prime Minister Ian Smith, who in 1965 had proclaimed Southern Rhodesia's Unilateral Declaration of Independence from the British over the Labour Government's sponsorship of black majority rule, refused to release Mugabe to attend the boy's funeral. This left him with a lasting resentment. His wife went into exile in London for eight years, spending her time there campaigning for the release of her husband and other detainees.

Sithole had been arrested just days before Smith declared

a Unilateral Declaration of Independence and was in prison with Mugabe, while Chitepo continued the struggle from exile in Zambia. The two detainees were released in 1974 and Mugabe fled to Mozambique, where he was reunited with his wife. On 18 March 1975, Herbert Chitepo was assassinated. A car bomb placed under his Volkswagen Beetle killed him and a bodyguard, injuring a second bodyguard. An hour later, a neighbour died from his injuries.

ZANU blamed the Rhodesian security forces. However, a commission set up by Zambian president Kenneth Kaunda to investigate Chitepo's death blamed ZANU infighting. The assassins named in the report were leading members of ZANU, one of whom went on to become a minister in Mugabe's government. Leader of the group was the former commander of the Zimbabwe African National Liberation Army (ZANLA) Josiah Tongogara, later tipped to become the first president of Zimbabwe.

Mugabe moved quickly to take over ZANU, ousting Sithole, who then formed the moderate ZANU (Ndonga) party, which renounced armed struggle and drew its support from the Ndebele. Meanwhile, the Shona, who make up two-thirds of the population of Zimbabwe, stayed with Mugabe's militant ZANU.

The guerrilla war undertaken by the armed wings of ZANU and ZAPU began to take its toll on Ian Smith's white-supremacist regime. Persuasion by South African B.J. Vorster, himself under pressure from US Secretary of State Henry Kissinger, forced Smith to recognise that white minority rule could not go on forever. On 3 March 1978, Bishop Abel Muzorewa, leader of the United African National Council (a nationalist party that had renounced violence), Ndabaningi Sithole and other moderate leaders signed an agreement with Ian Smith at Governor's Lodge in Salisbury. This paved the way for an interim power-sharing government, in preparation for elections. The elections were won by the United African National Council under Bishop Abel Muzorewa. However, international recognition did not follow and sanctions were not lifted because ZAPU under Nkomo and ZANU under Mugabe refused to participate in the elections and continued the guerrilla war as the Patriotic Front.

In 1979, a new Conservative government under Margaret Thatcher came to power in the UK. Determined to settle the problem once and for all, it set up the Lancaster House talks in London. Among others, these were attended by Bishop Abel Muzorewa, Ian Smith, Robert Mugabe, Joshua Nkomo, Edson Zvobgo and Josiah Tongogara. Eventually the parties to the talks agreed on a new constitution for the new Republic of Zimbabwe, which meant 20 seats were reserved for whites in the new parliament and prevented the new government from altering the constitution for ten years. Elections were to be held in February 1980 and this time ZANU and ZAPU would participate.

Mugabe emerged from the talks triumphant. On his return to Zimbabwe in December 1979, he was greeted by enormous crowds. With the backing of the majority Shona people, ZANU looked set to win the elections. However, within ZANU, Josiah Tongogara was still clearly a rival. On 26 December, just six days after the Lancaster House Agreement was signed, Robert Mugabe went on the Voice of Zimbabwe radio station to give, 'all the fighting people of Zimbabwe... an extremely sad message' – Tongogara was dead.

According to the ZANLA High Command's political commissar Josiah Tungamirai, he and Tongogara had been travelling at night with others in two vehicles from the Mozambique capital Maputo up to Chimoio and the border with Zimbabwe. The roads were bad and of course it was dark. Tungamirai was in the first vehicle. It passed a military vehicle abandoned at the side of the road with no warning sign. After that, he said, he could no longer see the headlights of the car following in his rear-view mirror. Turning back to see what had happened, they found Tongogara's car had run into the abandoned vehicle. He had been sitting in the front passenger seat and was badly injured. Tungamirai said that, as he lifted Tongogara out of the wrecked car, he heaved a huge sigh and died in his arms.

Two days later, the US Embassy in Zambia reported: 'Almost no one in Lusaka accepts Mugabe's assurance that Tongogara died accidentally. When the ambassador told the Soviet ambassador the news, the surprised Soviet immediately charged "inside job".' The CIA noted that Tongogara was a potential political rival to Mugabe because of his, 'ambition, popularity and decisive style.'

Ian Smith, who knew from Lancaster House that Tongogara was under threat, discussed his death with Rhodesia's police commissioner and head of special branch. 'Both assured me that Tongogara had been assassinated,' he said.

ZANU released an undertaker's statement saying Tongogara's injuries were consistent with a road accident, but no formal post mortem or pictures were released. However, a former Rhodesian detective said he saw photographs of Tongogara's body and that three punctures in his upper torso were 'consistent with gunshot wounds'.

Few people believe ZANU's account of Tongogara's death. Josiah Tungamirai went on to become a major general in the newly formed Zimbabwe National Army, then took command of the Air Force and joined the Politburo. However, he later began to deviate from the party line. While Mugabe advocated forcibly seizing white farms, Tungamirai bought one on a 'willing-buyer, willing-seller' basis. In 1995, he and Edson Zvobgo were seriously injured in a car accident. To calm a nationwide frenzy of speculation, both were forced to issue strong statements that no foul play was involved. After Tungamirai died in

South Africa in 2005, his wife claimed that he had been poisoned.

In February 1980 the elections were held in an atmosphere marked by mistrust from the security forces and intimidation from all sides. There were reports that full ballot boxes had been found dumped on country roads. Despite international misgivings, the Shona majority ensured Mugabe's victory. ZANU-PF won 57 out of the 80 black seats in the new parliament and Mugabe became first prime minister of the new Republic of Zimbabwe on 4 March 1980.

At first Mugabe sought to build a coalition with ZAPU, whose support came from the Ndebele-speaking south. He gave ZAPU's leader, Joshua Nkomo, a series of cabinet positions and incorporated ZAPU's military wing, the Zimbabwe People's Revolutionary Army (ZIPRA), into the new national army.

From the beginning ZANLA and ZIPRA had trouble integrating into the new Zimbabwean army. Both sides had hidden weapons and former ZANLA elements attacked civilian areas in Mutoko, Mount Darwin and Gutu. To his secure rule, Mugabe had announced the need for a militia to 'combat malcontents', though there was little civil unrest in Zimbabwe at the time.

In October 1980, Mugabe signed an agreement with North Korean President Kim Il Sung to have the North Korean military train a brigade for the Zimbabwean army. He told the dissidents that they should 'watch out' as the brigade would be called the *Gukurahundi* – Shona for 'the early rain, which washes away the chaff before the spring rains.'

The following month, at a rally in Bulawayo, Defence Minister Enos Nkala warned ZAPU that ZANU would deliver a few blows against them. The result was an uprising in the western suburb of Ntumbane uprising, where ZANLA and ZIPRA fought a two-day pitched battle. In February

1981, the fighting recommenced. This time, it spread to the northern suburb of Glenville and on to Connemara in the Midlands. From all over Matabeleland, ZIPRA troops flocked to join the battle. White-led ex-Rhodesian Army and Air Force units were despatched to crush them. At least 300 were killed. Their bodies were stored in refrigerated railway wagons in the sidings at Bulawayo.

The government appointed the former Chief Justice of Zimbabwe Enoch Dumbutshena to hold an Inquiry into the uprising. He was often a vocal critic of Mugabe but so far, his report and its findings have never been released.

Many ZIPRA soldiers left the army after the Ntumbane uprisings. Joshua Nkomo complained that members of ZANLA were given preference when it came to promotion. Many feared their colleagues were disappearing mysteriously.

When arms caches were found in February 1982, ZANU-PF now openly accused ZAPU of plotting a civil war. ZAPU leaders were sacked from cabinet or arrested, while Nkomo was accused of plotting a coup d'état. In a public statement Mugabe said: 'ZAPU and its leader, Dr Joshua Nkomo, are like a cobra in a house. The only way to deal effectively with a snake is to strike and destroy its head.'

The following spring Mugabe's government announced: 'ZAPU leader, Joshua Nkomo, fled in self-imposed exile to London after illegally crossing the Botswana frontier disguised as a woman on 7 March 1983, claiming that his life was in danger, and that he was going to look for "solutions" to Zimbabwean problems abroad.'

Nkomo stated: '...nothing in my life had prepared me for persecution at the hands of a government led by black Africans.'

Deputy commander of the Zimbabwe National Army Lookout Masuku, ZIPRA's head of intelligence Dumiso Dabengwa and four others were charged with treason, but acquitted. They were released, though Masuku and

Dabengwa were held without trial for another four years under emergency regulations. Thousands more ZIPRA men deserted the army, fearing that, with their leaders in jail, there was no one to protect them.

By September 1982, the training of the new Fifth Brigade was complete. Their number was drawn from the 3,500 ZANLA troops once commanded by Josiah Tongogara. There were a few ZIPRA troops among them at the start, but they were weeded out before the end of the training. A number of foreigners in the unit, probably Tanzanians, were also removed. The first Commander of Fifth Brigade was Mugabe's cousin Colonel Perence Shiri, who called himself the 'Black Jesus'.

Fifth Brigade was not integrated to the normal army command structures. It answered directly to the Prime Minister's office. Their codes, radios and equipment were not compatible with those of other army units and their uniforms were also different. The most distinguishing feature was their red berets, although there were many reports of Fifth Brigade soldiers operating in civilian clothes in the field. Once in the field Fifth Brigade seemed a law unto themselves.

With Nkomo and other ZAPU leaders out of the way, Mugabe unleashed the Fifth Brigade on Nkomo's Matabeleland homeland in Operation *Gukurahundi*, in an attempt to destroy ZAPU and create a one-party state. Within weeks of being deployed, the Fifth Brigade had murdered more than 2,000 civilians, beaten thousands more and destroyed hundreds of homesteads. Most of the dead were shot in public executions, often after being forced to dig their own graves in front of their family, friends and fellow villagers. The largest number of dead in a single killing involved the deliberate shooting of 62 young men and women on the banks of the Cewale River, Lupane, on 5 March 1983. Seven survived with gunshot wounds, the other 55 died.

The Fifth Brigade also killed large groups of people by burning them alive in their huts. Instances occurred in Lupane and Tsholotsho. Elsewhere, the Fifth Brigade would round up dozens, or perhaps hundreds, of civilians at a water hole or a school, where they would be forced to sing songs in Shona, praising ZANU-PF while being beaten with sticks. After that there would be public executions during which ZAPU officials and ZIPRA soldiers would be killed, but often the victims were defenceless civilians. These were supporters of dissidents, Mugabe claimed, though he admitted mistakes were made.

'We eradicate them,' he revealed in April 1983. 'We don't differentiate when we fight because we can't tell who is a dissident and who is not.'

Operation *Gukurahundi*, it is estimated, claimed the lives of between 10,000 to 30,000 civilians in Matabeleland and the Midlands. By the time the Fifth Brigade was disbanded in 1986, another 400,000 Ndebele were left on the brink of starvation. This was when Mugabe began using food aid as political weapon.

In an attempt to save his people, on 22 December 1987 Nkomo signed a Unity Accord with Mugabe, which effectively dissolved ZAPU and created a one-party state. On 18 April 1988, Mugabe announced an amnesty for all dissidents and Nkomo called on his men to lay down their arms. This was all part of a deal that abolished the post of prime minister and allowed Mugabe to become executive president, accruing more powers along the way. Nkomo came back into government as vice-president. As if being president was not enough, Mugabe then made himself the Chancellor of the University of Zimbabwe after Parliament passed the University of Zimbabwe Amendment Bill in November 1990. Those who opposed him were ruthlessly suppressed. The printing presses of a newspaper critical of his regime were bombed and its journalists seized and tortured. Young opponents of the regime were dragged off to camps, where men were beaten and women raped. Citing human rights violations in Zimbabwe, other universities have revoked the honorary degrees they have bestowed on Mugabe.

On becoming president, Mugabe shrugged aside Canaan Banana, a founder of the African National Council and a leading member of ZANU, who became Zimbabwe's first president in 1980. Two years later, he signed a law that forbade people from making jokes about his name. Once he had fallen from office, Banana fell foul of Mugabe's campaign against homosexuality which, Mugabe claimed, did not happen in Zimbabwe before colonisation.

In August 1995 Mugabe told an audience at the Zimbabwe International Book Fair that homosexuality '...degrades human dignity. It's unnatural and there is no question ever of allowing these people to behave worse than dogs and pigs. If dogs and pigs do not do it, why must human beings? We have our own culture, and we must re-dedicate ourselves to our traditional values that make us human beings... What we are being persuaded to accept is sub-animal behaviour and we will never allow it here. If you see people parading themselves as lesbians and gays, arrest them and hand them over to the police!'

The following month, Zimbabwe's parliament introduced legislation banning homosexual acts. Canaan Banana was arrested and convicted of 11 counts of sodomy and indecent assault. His subsequent trial proved an embarrassment for Mugabe, when his accusers admitted that Mugabe knew all along about Banana's misbehaviour and had done nothing to curtail it. Banana denied all charges, claiming they were a pretext to end his political career. He was sentenced to ten years imprisonment, but fled the country, fearing Mugabe would kill him.

Ndabaningi Sithole also feared for his life and went into self-imposed exile in the US in 1983. He returned to Zimbabwe in 1992 and was elected a Member of Parliament for Chipinge, stronghold of his minority Ndau tribe in south-eastern Zimbabwe in 1995. In 1997 he was tried and convicted of conspiring to assassinate Mugabe. An appeal was filed, but never heard. He was bailed on the grounds of his deteriorating health and died in the US in 2000. The farm near Harare that he bought in 1992 was confiscated.

In 1997, the new British government under Tony Blair stopped funding the 'willing-buyer, willing-seller' land reform programme agreed at Lancaster House on the grounds that the £44million set aside had delivered the land formerly owned by whites into the hands of the ruling élite rather than landless peasants. As a result, Mugabe sent 'war veterans', led by Chenjerai 'Hitler' Hunzvi, to seize white farms. Mugabe's family owns three farms, all forcibly seized from their previous owners. The economy, already damaged by government mismanagement, was further disrupted by the consequent collapse of agriculture. So, in 1998, Mugabe took Zimbabwe into the war in the Congo in an attempt to plunder the country's rich mineral reserves.

In 2005 Mugabe began Operation *Murambatsvina*, meaning 'Drive out the Filth' – or Operation Restore Order, as the government translated it. His men began to demolish what the government termed 'illegal shelters', which it had previously encouraged the urban poor to build. Some 20,000 street vendors were arrested, their pitches destroyed and their goods confiscated. These were then put on sale in 'auctions'. Thousands more escaped arrest, but lost their livelihoods. Licensed businesses were closed down on the grounds that they were illegal. Sculpture parks along the main roads, which had been there for decades and featured in guide books, were destroyed. Roadside vendors, who complained about the destruction of their works, were confronted with riot squads. In one township Irish missionaries were forced to dismantle a clinic and a crèche for children orphaned by the Aids epidemic, while the police demolished shacks inhabited by impoverished orphans.

This happened not just in Harare and Bulawayo. In Victoria Falls, the government press reported that 3,368 houses were knocked down, in some cases these were not casual dwellings but proper houses built of concrete blocks with corrugated iron roofs. Four miles of vending stands that had been used to sell carvings to tourists for three decades were torched. This is estimated to have displaced more than 20,000 people in a tiny town with fewer than 100,000 residents. While in Beitbridge in Matabeleland, more than 100 dwellings were knocked down, a substantial proportion of the small town. Again, vending stands were destroyed.

Homeless families were forced to sleep under trees or on the pavements, with no protection from the winter weather or thieves. They had nowhere to wash, and nowhere to cook food or store it properly. Tiny babies, the sick, the elderly and people on their deathbeds were left out at the mercy of the elements. Bus stations were filled to overflowing with families sitting hopelessly next to furniture and building materials salvaged from the destruction. They waited in vain for buses prepared to carry the loads to rural areas. Those with trucks struggled to find scarce diesel, which now cost up to Z$50,000 a litre, though the official price was Z$4,000 a litre. Those with fuel charged extortionate rates to move desperate families short distances (it cost Z$200,000 to move one wardrobe by bus). Desperate families without the money sold off their possession at a tenth of the transportation cost in the hope of raising the fares for their wives and children to travel to stay with relatives in the countryside. Those who made the trip arrived in remote, starving rural areas without a job, without food, without furniture and without a house in winter, only to be at the mercy of the local ZANU-PF leadership.

Mugabe's government had no contingency plans whatsoever to move people, or to build new houses for them even though it was winter. The deliberate destruction of homes – in a nation already plagued with unemployment, hunger and economic collapse – came about for purely political reasons. Operation *Murambatsvina* was, Mugabe said in June 2005, 'a long-cherished desire.' Quite simply, he was enraged that these people would not vote for him. The inhabitants of Zimbabwe's shantytowns and small businessmen had supported the opposition party, the Movement for Democratic Change. Most of the 41 parliamentary seats that the MDC had won in previous elections were in urban constituencies. Mugabe's aim was to displace MDC supporters from urban centres into rural areas, where they would be forced to tow the line by the local ZANU-PF leadership, who controlled access to food, housing and other communal resources.

Soon after Operation *Murambatsvina* vendors' licences were reissued, but only to those with a valid ZANU-PF membership card. In areas razed to the ground, lots were allocated to members of the army and police, while ZANU-PF supporters took over vacated businesses.

A UN report stated Mugabe's actions had resulted in the loss of home or livelihood for more than 700,000 Zimbabweans and negatively affected 2.4million more. Subsequently the MDC claimed that its supporters were denied access to the vote by 'Hitler' Hunzi and his 'war veterans': protests were met with brutal suppression. Foreign observers regularly report that elections in Zimbabwe are rigged. Even Mugabe's long-time colleague Edson Zvobgo criticised sweeping media laws curtailing the freedom of the press, calling them, 'the most serious assault on our constitutional liberties since independence.' Mugabe even banned the 2005 film *The Interpreter* – a thriller set in the UN building in New York – claiming it was CIA propaganda designed to incite hostility against him.

On 11 March 2007 opposition leader Morgan Tsvangirai was arrested and beaten up after attending a prayer meeting in the Harare suburb of Highfields. Another member of the MDC was killed and other protesters injured. Mugabe said simply: 'Tsvangirai deserved his beating-up by police because he was not allowed to attend a banned rally.'

Mugabe's Police Commissioner Augustine Chihuri described the opposition as a 'crawling mass of maggots bent on destroying the economy.'

While the shantytowns were destroyed, Mugabe was overseeing the construction of his own palace, built in the style of an imperial pagoda, not a mile from one of the bulldozed townships. His notoriously profligate second wife Grace was making one of her regular shopping trips to Paris before the EU travel ban put a stop to them.

Since the seizure of the white-owned farms, agricultural production has plummeted. A third of the population of South Africa depends on food aid from the World Food Programme to avoid starvation. Supplies are denied those who do not support the government. Mugabe blamed the food shortages on drought, while Zimbabwe's state-owned press accused former British Prime Minister Tony Blair of using chemical weapons to create droughts and famines in Africa (Blair had only just come to power when there were food riots in Zimbabwe in 1998).

AIDS is pandemic and women's life expectancy has fallen from 65 under British colonial rule to 34 – the lowest anywhere in the world. The World Health Organisation believes that even that figure could be an overestimate and the real age may be as low as 30. Men's life expectancy has also declined to 37.

According to the charity Solidarity Peace Trust trauma is also killing people before their time: 'The stress and misery mean people are keeling over and dying. The health system has totally collapsed. Now access to education is going the same way and girls are the first to miss out.'

Despite the fact that Mugabe was once a teacher, he has done nothing to prop up the education system.

'We had the best education in Africa,' said Archbishop of Zimbabwe Pius Ncube, head of Zimbabwe's one million Catholics. 'Now our schools are closing.'

In 2007, the situation was so bad that the Archbishop Ncube urged Britain to invade Zimbabwe to topple Mugabe as he presented a 'massive risk to life.' The Archbishop said that, while people struggle to get by on less than £1 a week, Mugabe had spent £1m on surveillance equipment to monitor phone calls and e-mails: 'How can you expect people to rise up when even our church services are attended by State Intelligence people? People in our mission hospitals are dying of malnutrition. Most people are earning less than their bus fares. There's no water or power. Is the world just going to let everything collapse in on us?'

In 1980, the average annual income in Zimbabwe was US$950 and a Zimbabwean dollar worth more than an American one. By 2003, the average income was less than US$400, and the Zimbabwean economy was in free fall. According to Robert Guest, the Africa editor for *The Economist*, Mugabe is responsible for this. 'He has ruled Zimbabwe for nearly three decades and has led it, in that time, from impressive success to the most dramatic peacetime collapse of any country since Weimar Germany,' he wrote.

To make ends meet, teachers have resorted to prostitution. In June 2007, schoolmistress Stella Sithole earned Z$2.1million – the equivalent of £3.50 – a month. That was not enough to pay her bus fare to school. When she quit teaching class to turn tricks, she found no shortage of takers in Harare. Her clients were government ministers, ZANU-PF officials, top police and army officers, and High

Court judges, all of whom benefit from Mugabe's despotic rule. Many have been awarded property that was violently seized from white farmers, but their real wealth comes from access to foreign exchange at less than 1,000th of the rate on the streets.

In June 2007, the official exchange rate was 250, while the rate on the street was 300,000.

'Imagine the money you can make,' a merchant banker told *The Times*. 'Say you buy US$100 at the official rate – that costs you Z$25,000. Then you sell that US$100 on the streets and get Z$30m. With that Z$30m, at the official rate you can buy more than US$100,000 – all for your initial outlay of about 8 cents.'

On top of that, officials get fuel vouchers. A litre of fuel for the privileged costs just Z$400 while everyone else must pay Z$185,000.

'If you're one of Mugabe's cronies, you can live in fantastic wealth,' he continued.

Others struggle to survive on less that £1 a week and more than four million have left the country. That does not bother Mugabe's government – those who have left were more likely to have voted for the MDC than ZANU-PF.

'We would be better off with only six million people, with our own people who support the liberation struggle,' said Didymus Mutasa, Zimbabwe's Minister of State for National Security, Lands, Lands Reform and Resettlement. 'We don't want all these extra people.'

And things are getting worse. According to Steve H. Hanks, Professor of Applied Economics at Johns Hopkins University in Baltimore, inflation reached a staggering 80 billion per cent a month in December 2008. That's an annual rate of 6.5 quindecillion novemdecillion per cent a year – or 65 followed by 107 zeros. In other words, inflation was running at 98 per cent a day. Prices doubled every 24.7 hours and shops simply stopped accepting Zimbabwean dollars. Only government officials or others with access to foreign currency can buy even the basic necessities of life. However, Zimbabwe's police and soldiers are paid in local currency, but under banking rules no one is allowed to withdraw more than Z\$500,000 – 18p – a day. When soldiers in Harare in November 2008 failed to get even that, they rioted.

With the collapse of the sewage system and no fresh water, an epidemic of cholera began to spread. The disease is easily treated, but medicines are only given to ZANU-PF members and hospitals are closed as medical staff have not been paid. Mugabe blamed Gordon Brown, George Bush and Nicolas Sarkozy, saying they wanted to use cholera as an excuse for military intervention, but he denied the existence of cholera, though the World Health Organisation estimated some 18,000 people had been infected by December 2008. That number was expected to treble as the rainy season approached.

At the time of writing, there seems no hope for Zimbabwe. In March 2008, the country held its presidential and parliamentary elections. Generally it was acknowledged that the MDC had achieved a significant majority in Parliament. According to the official results, Morgan Tsvangirai also beat Mugabe by 120,000 votes in the presidential election, but Mugabe refused to concede. Instead he insisted on a run-off in June. Just five days before the ballot, Tsvangirai was forced to pull out because of the increasing levels of violence. According to the MDC, some 200 had been killed and at least 25,000 forced to flee their homes. A power-sharing deal was signed in September 2008 and in February 2009 opposition leader Morgan Tsvangirai was sworn in as prime minister. However, we have yet to see any real change.

In February 2009, Robert Mugabe spent £350,000 on a party celebrating his 85th birthday in lavish style. Mugabe and guests gorged themselves on 8,000 lobsters, 4,000 portions of caviar and 100 kilograms of prawns – all washed down with 2,000 bottles of champagne. Meanwhile his people starved.

Mugabe's critics accuse him of continuing his 'reign of terror' against all who dare to oppose him. Unrepentant, he is even happy to compare himself to Adolf Hitler. At the funeral of a cabinet minister in 2003, he boasted: 'I am still the Hitler of the time. This Hitler has only one objective: justice for his people, sovereignty for his people, recognition of the independence of his people and their rights over their resources. If that is Hitler, then let me be a Hitler tenfold.'

He even has the moustache.

CHAPTER THREE

COLONEL MENGISTU HAILE MARIAM

There are still some who praise Robert Mugabe as an African patriot who has stood up to the forces of colonialism and allowed black people to regain the land and riches stolen from them by whites. However, for 17 years now he has given refuge to an evil dictator who, along with the tens of thousands of others that he killed, was responsible for the death of a man who had been a symbol of African independence since the 1930s. Living in comfort in Zimbabwe is the convicted mass-murderer Colonel Mengistu Haile Mariam, the man who murdered Ethiopia's last emperor, Haile Selassie.

Born in 1937, in Ethiopia's southwesterly Kaffa province, Mengistu seems to have been convinced from an early age that he was destined for greatness. Rumours have circulated that he is a direct descendant on his mother's side from the aristocrat and soldier Dejazmach Kebede Tesemma and his scandalous liaison with the maid of the Empress Zauditu, who ruled Ethopia from 1916 to 1930.

The title 'Dejazmach' means 'commander' or 'general of the gate' – a military rank meaning its holder is the commander of the central body of a traditional Ethiopian army formation. In addition, Dejazmach was used as the title of a provincial governor-general, who was also the commander-in-chief of the province's armed forces, roughly the equivalent of a European count. Kebede Tesemma was known for his involvement in a series of court intrigues. As chief of Zauditu's household in the 1920s, he became a confidant of the Ras Tafari Makonnen, who served as regent and became heir apparent to Zaudita as it was considered unseemly for a woman to rule.

Kebede was an 'Azaj' or palace minister when he met Mengistu's grandmother, Totit. She was an umbrella bearer to Zauditu. Their affair flouted all court protocol and when it resulted in the birth of Mengistu's mother, Kebede's uncle took the blame and prostrated himself before the Empress. Nevertheless, Totit was banished from court and later became an Orthodox nun while her child was brought up in Kebede's household.

Although Zauditu was a conservative, Ras Tafari Makonnen was a progressive, who undermined the power of the feudal landlords, engineered Ethiopia's entry into the League of Nations and outlawed slavery. He even visited London, Paris and Rome, the first Ethiopian ruler ever to leave the country. There were several rebellions against Ras Tafari's progressive policies, but each served to strengthen his position. Zauditu was forced to name him *negus* – or king – in 1928. Two years later, Zauditu's husband Ras Gugsa Wole rebelled against Tafari's rule and was killed in battle. She herself died two days later. There is a theory that she was killed by her Swiss-born doctor at the behest of Kebede Tesemma, acting in Tafari's interest. However, she also suffered from diabetes and had experienced a flu-like illness for several days.

On 1 April 1930 Tafari declared himself emperor and was crowned Haile Selassie – which means 'Strength of the Trinity' (also his baptismal name) – on 2 November. Following this, he drew up a new constitution delegating some of his power to an indirectly elected two-chamber parliament. He built roads, schools and hospitals, and improved the administration, communications and public services. At the same time, the newly instituted market economy boomed, with 25,000 tons of coffee exported annually. This success convinced Italy's fascist dictator Benito Mussolini that he must act quickly if he was to fulfil his dream of an African empire. In October 1935, he invaded Ethiopia.

After a seven-month war, when the Italians used air power and poison gas, Haile Selassie's ill-equipped army was defeated and the Emperor went into exile on 2 May 1936. However, when Italy joined World War II on Germany's side, the British recognised Haile Selassie as the legitimate ruler of Ethiopia and sent him to Khartoum, where the British-led Ethiopian army was being assembled. On 20 January 1941 they invaded, and by 5 May Selassie was back in power in Addis Ababa.

Mengistu was born during the Italian occupation. His father was a former slave from the Konso people, who worked for an aristocratic sub-provincial governor and landowner Afenegus Eshete Geda. He was the half-brother of Dejazmach Kebede's wife, Woizero Yitateku Kidane, and it is thought that it was through this connection that Mengistu's parents had met each other.

As a child Mengistu suffered offensive remarks about his dark appearance, which he inherited from his father. This gave him a chip on his shoulder and he grew to despise all light-skinned Ethiopians. When he took power, he is reported to have told a meeting at Addis Ababa: 'In this country, some aristocratic families automatically categorise persons with dark skin, thick lips and kinky hair as "Barias"' – Amaric for slave – 'let it be clear to everybody that I shall soon make these ignoramuses stoop and grind corn.' Of course, the man who most conspicuously represented light-skinned Ethiopians was Haile Selassie.

Little is known of Megistu's upbringing. He joined the army and underwent officer training at the Oletta Military Academy, reopened by Haile Selassie in 1960. After receiving additional training in the US, he rose to the rank of major.

Although Selassie had been a moderniser in his youth, he grew more conservative with age, allowing very little power to slip from his grasp. This prompted the revolt of part of his army in December 1960. Rebels seized Addis Ababa and were only dislodged after stiff fighting.

Political stagnation continued, however, and by the early 1970s the economy was in trouble. As unemployment soared, people began to openly defy the government. Students and teachers demonstrated on the streets and taxi drivers went on strike. Like everyone else, the army was affected by the shortage of food, fuel and decent drinking water. Disaffection in the south led to the arrest of a number of generals and commanding officers, eventually making way for Mengistu and other junior officers. Meanwhile in the face of further street demonstrations, the aristocratic government under Aklilu Hapte Wold resigned. It was replaced by a liberal administration under Oxford-educated Endelkachew Makonnen, who carried the same surname as Haile Selassie.

In 1974 famine struck the northern provinces of Tigre and Wollo. Hundreds of thousands of Ethiopians starved and entire villages were wiped out. The Endelkachew government could not cope with such a crisis. At the same time soldiers who had served as members of the United Nations Peacekeeping Force in the Congo complained that they had not been paid. Now Endelkachew had lost the support of the army, the country was essentially without a government.

The army took control and an ad-hoc committee was formed under Colonel Alamzawd Tasamma, commander of the airborne brigade. But the true power behind the throne was his assistant – Major Atnafu Abate of the Fourth Division – who was, at the time, a third-year student at Haile Selassie University. He began to imprison government officials on various pretexts and when members of parliament raised their objections, he arrested them too, along with other army officers who dared to oppose him.

Colonel Alamzawd – thought to have been a relative of Endelkachew – was effectively sidelined. Major Atnafu took it upon himself to call on all military units to send a delegate to the headquarters of the Fourth Division where, on 28 June 1974, the Co-ordinating Committee of the Armed Forces, Police and Territorial Army formally convened. This would become the notorious Derg – 'committee' or 'council' in Ge'ez – and would run Ethiopia for the next 13 years.

The representative of the Third Division from Harar was Major – soon to be Colonel – Haile Mariam Mengistu. The meeting was chaired by Atnafu with no agenda, the names of government officials read out and a show of hands decided whether or not they would be imprisoned. Mengistu then made his move, raising his hand to speak. When given the floor, he asked why his fellow delegates were there. Were they there simply to imprison people? Or did they have broader goals? When no answer came he strode to a blackboard and wrote the two words: 'Ityopya Teqdam' – 'Ethiopia First'. This should be their watchword.

Mengistu first published the slogan two years before. In an article in the national daily Addis Zemen, he spelt out the eight goals of 'Ityopya Teqdam'. Now he asked for two more suggestions to make a modern-day Ten Commandments. These were forthcoming and he sat down to wild applause. His bodyguard Sergeant Demeke Banjaw then suggested that he should take over as chairman of the committee. Mengistu was elected to acclaim and Atnafu resentfully relegated to the role of vice chairman. His position was consolidated by a serious of hearty dinners that melded the Derg into a cohesive body but Mengistu knew that he was in a vulnerable position for the committee sat in the headquarters of Atnafu's Fourth Division. Consequently he was afraid to leave the compound. To keep an eye on Atnafu, he shared his bedroom.

Members of the Derg were sent to force concessions out of Haile Selassie while making pledges of loyalty. On 22 July Endelkachew Makonnen and his entire cabinet were under arrest. In late August, the army paraded through Addis Ababa with the slogan '*Ityopya Teqdam*' emblazoned across their vehicles. The Ministry of the Pen, the Crown Council and other institutions embodying imperial power were dismantled, while the Emperor and the Royal Family's business interests – the St George Brewery, the Ambassa (Lion) Bus Transport Company and the Haile Selassie I Welfare Foundation – very publicly confiscated. The Derg effectively portrayed Haile Selassie, once seen as the caring father of his peoples, as a greedy tyrant.

This image was reinforced on the night of 12 September – Ethiopia's New Year's Day – when Jonathan Dimbleby's 1973 TV documentary on the famine was broadcast, skilfully inter-cut with footage of lavish imperial feasts. Screens were erected outdoors for those with no TV in their own homes and the whole country was shocked. The following morning representatives of the Derg went to the palace and read out a public statement proclaiming Haile Selassie's deposition. The Emperor was subsequently bundled into a Volkswagen Beetle and taken to the Fourth Division headquarters. Along with his daughter and other members of the Royal Family, he was given dingy three-bedroom quarters. Now the dynasty that could trace its roots back to King Solomon and the Queen of Sheba was effectively at an end.

Although tanks and armed units had been moved into the streets, only around 15 of the 120-man committee were involved in the coup. Others heard about it from the radio broadcasts. They protested, but to no avail: collective decision-making was at an end.

Members of the popular movement – the teachers and students who had originally taken to the streets – began to call for the establishment of a People's Government. Masquerading as the guardian of the revolution, the Derg renamed itself the Provisional Military Administrative Council. The original Derg comprised junior officers, NCOs and privates – senior officers were deemed too close to the regime. However, the Derg soon realised that they needed a senior military man on board to give them a veneer of respectability. They chose the charismatic commander of the Third Division, Lieutenant-General Aman Mikael Andom, who became chairman and head of state. Known as the 'Desert Lion', he had held back the Somali army on Ethiopia's eastern border in 1964. An Eritrean by birth, he was well suited to solving one of Ethiopia's most pressing problems – the attempted secession of Eritrea, which was the province that gave Ethiopia its only access to the coast.

While General Aman was away in Eritrea, the 'Ethiopia first' creed went into force. Leaders of organisations opposing it were arrested. When their followers protested, they were brutally suppressed, along with dissent military units including the Corps of Engineers, the Air Force and the Imperial Guard. Clearly, the coup would be anything but bloodless.

When General Aman returned, he proposed a federal solution for the problem of Eritrea. Mengistu and his cohorts greeted the proposal with silence. Realising his days were numbered, Aman took to sleeping with a gun beside his bed. Fearing for his life, he failed to turn up for official functions. This enraged Mengistu, who called a meeting on 23 November 1974, during which he claimed that Aman had tried to usurp the power of the Derg. He accused him of plotting a coup and played taped conversations and messages in which he had tried to appeal to the Third Division for help. Mengistu fumed and whipped up the feelings of the committee until they called for Aman's blood, but that was not enough for him; he also demanded that anyone associated with Aman would have to go. Their number included government dignitaries, members of the former regime and any army officer against whom Mengistu harboured a grudge.

Other members of the Derg warned that the actions of Aman must not be used as an excuse to execute others. Courts should be established to try the accused and they should not just be condemned, as before, on a show of hands – now lives were at stake. As the government of Ethiopia, they argued, the Derg would attract international condemnation if it did not at least make a show of respecting human rights.

Mengistu attacked those who opposed him, arguing they did not need courts and the Derg was supreme, with the right to give or take away life. Additionally human rights were of no concern as they were violated daily, in both the Communist world and the West. As he sat down, a burst of gunfire was heard from the direction of General Aman's house near the old airport. He had pre-empted the committee and sent four tanks and four armoured personnel carriers carrying a company of soldiers to Aman's house to arrest him. Apparently, the General had returned fire with a pistol. It was said that when the arresting party entered the house, they found General Aman lying dead on his bed in full-dress uniform bearing his decorations with a .45 Colt by his side.

That night, 59 prisoners of the regime – including previous prime ministers Aklilu Hapte Wold and Endelkachew Makonnen – were taken from the former wine-cellar where they had been held and transported to Addis Ababa Central Prison. At around 3am they were executed by firing squad. The next day their deaths were announced to a shocked nation.

Some of the victims were drawn from the Derg itself, which served to keep the others in line. A few days later at a meeting Mengistu insisted the Derg was collectively responsible for the deaths. He also maintained they should pick another chairman who was not a member of the committee itself to show they did not want power for themselves. This time it was to be Lieutenant-General Tafari Benti's turn.

Under Mengistu's guidance it was then decided that 'Ethiopian socialism' should be their aim. Just as in China's cultural revolution, students and teachers were sent to the countryside. The official excuse was that they were to undertake a programme in literacy. In actual fact, it was a convenient way to get rid of political rivals in the popular movement. Many would die at the hands of the Derg, whose members were sent out to rural posts. Most were unqualified for their roles and used their positions to line their pockets and settle political scores. At the same time, shedding members this way concentrated the power of the Derg into fewer and fewer hands.

At the rally to bid farewell to the first batch of teachers and students, it was announced that banks, insurance companies and factories would be nationalised. Members of the crowd shouted: 'Menge, Menge!' Placards praised the Derg and Mengistu by name. For the first time he publicly basked in the trappings of power.

Land was nationalised and the landlords, largely Amharas, were lynched. Merely speaking Amharic invited summary death. Survivors of the rural massacres flocked to the cities. Unemployment rocketed overnight, leading to an explosion in mugging, theft, prostitution and other crimes.

However, one person to whom the nationalisation of land did not apply was Mengistu's grandmother, who was still alive when he seized power. She continued to own the land just 30 miles from Addis Ababa, granted to her by Zauditu for services prior to her expulsion from the palace in 1928. According to popular legend, the elderly nun did not thank her grandson for this favour and used to curse him for deposing the Emperor, who was head of the Orthodox Church.

With the countryside thrown into chaos, agricultural production slumped and prices climbed. The government tried to stem this by introducing price controls but because the prices they fixed were lower than the cost price, this only made the situation worse. Merchants stopped selling foodstuffs because they were losing money. In 1976, when two merchants were found with just two sacks each of sorghum hidden in their houses, they were publicly executed for anti-revolutionary and anti-people activities. Later, half-a-dozen merchants were executed for 'economic sabotage'. They had been hoarding pepper.

People were only allowed to own one small house of a specified size. Extra houses or rooms were nationalised and the rent – half that paid by the tenant before – was given to the government. No new housing was built and now the government could no longer afford the upkeep on those they owned. Addis Ababa's already grave problem of homelessness and overcrowding grew worse.

By early 1975 Haile Selassie I University and all senior secondary schools closed. Some 60,000 students and teachers were now in rural areas participating in the government's 'Development Through Co-operation' campaign. Its purposes were to promote land reform and improve agricultural production, health and local administration and to teach peasants about the new political and social order.

The Provisional Military Administrative Council then moved headquarters to the Emperor's Menelik's Palace. The 83-year-old Haile Selassie went too and was now imprisoned in quarters in his own palace. He seems to have been quite robust for his age: eyewitnesses have testified that he showed no signs of senility and knew exactly what he was doing. On 25 August 1975 Mengistu told members of the Derg that the Emperor was seriously ill from a prostate infection, but his doctor was out of town and could not be contacted. The following day the evening news announced that the Emperor had died because of the absence of his physician. No one believed the story. Rumours circulated that Mengistu had had him strangled, though it is now thought that he was suffocated with a pillow and his body buried under a lavatory, where his remains were found in 1992.

In July 1976 there was a new purge. Air Force Major Sisay Habte, a leading member of Derg, was hauled in front of a military tribunal, charged with conspiring against the revolution and executed. Brigadier-General Getachew Nadaw, commander of the Second Division, and two members of the Derg – Lieutenant Bawqatu Kasa and Lieutenant Selashi Bavyana – were accused of being his accomplices. In a remarkably similar fashion to the death of General Aman, the Brigadier-General died in a shoot-out at his home. The two lieutenants fled to their native province of Gojjam but were later caught and killed. Another member of the Derg – Major Kiros Alamayahu, who had been leading the development agency – was arrested and died in jail.

This convinced other members of the Derg that they must act quickly for their own survival. They restructured the committee, removing power from the vice chairman – still the position officially held by Mengistu – and handing it over to a Standing Committee. Behind the reforms were the newly powerful secretary-general of the Derg, Captain Almayahu Hayle, and head of the Economic Committee, Captain Mogas Walda-Mikael. However, in the reshuffle, they left in place the head of Derg's security branch,

Colonel Daniel Asfaw. Formerly Mengistu's classmate at the Oletta Military School, he was also his chief hatchet man.

On 3 February 1977 Captain Almayahu and Captain Mogas attended a meeting of the Derg's Standing Committee with the chairman General Tafari Benti and Lieutenant-Colonel Asrat Dasta. The records are not clear about what happened next. They were either killed in a shoot-out, ordered to commit suicide by Mengistu or summarily shot. In any case all four were now dead. Mengistu might have counted this as a complete triumph, had it not been for the death of his executioner Daniel Asfaw and Sanay Likke, leader of Mengistu's Marxist-Leninist movement Revolutionary Flame, who had been shot dead by Asfaw's deputy, Captain Yohannes Meserker, a supporter of Alamayahu's group.

Now Mengistu emerged from behind the scenes to become chairman of Derg, commander-in-chief and head of state; now-vacant positions on the Derg's Standing Committee were filled by his supporters. Soon afterwards the execution of Atnafu Abate, long a thorn in Mengistu's side, followed along with the killing of another round of aristocrats and former officials that included the Patriarch of the Ethiopian Orthodox Church, Abuna Theophilos. The Church was then disestablished, its landholdings confiscated. Mengistu himself has acknowledged that the Derg ordered these deaths but he refuses to accept personal responsibility and claims the executions were a collective decision. In interviews jailed members of the Derg admitted they were made at his behest.

Although essentially a military dictator, Mengistu Haile Mariam allied himself with Cuba, the Warsaw Pact and the Soviet Union, who provided aid. Members of his Revolutionary Flame went to Havana, Moscow and East Germany for ideological training. However, Revolutionary Flame was not the only communist organisation in Ethiopia. It shared the Politburo with the Ethiopian

People's Revolutionary Party (EPRP) and the All-Ethiopia Socialist Movement – whose acronym in Amharic was MEISON. The EPRP pressed for an immediate move to a 'people's democracy', while MEISON were insistent on a 'controlled democracy' – that is, it believed the Derg should be allowed to restructure the country before it returned to barracks. Both were deluding themselves.

The EPRP was the first to break away. Labelling Mengistu a fascist, it began a campaign of assassination against members of Revolutionary Flame and MEISON. Public buildings were bombed. Mengistu described this as the 'White Terror' and responded by launching his own 'Red Terror' in dramatic fashion. During a speech before a huge crowd in Addis Ababa he produced two bottles of what appeared to be blood and smashed them to the ground, shouting, 'Death to counter-revolutionaries! Death to the EPRP!' This was intended to show what the revolution would do to its enemies.

Mengistu asserted all 'progressives' – that is, Derg supporters – were given 'freedom of action' in helping to root out the revolution's enemies (the EPRP). Peasants, workers, public officials and even students thought to be loyal to the Mengistu regime were provided with arms for the task. The campaign was highly organised, with neighbourhood watch committees called 'Kebeles' set up to meet and discuss individual suspects in their area that should be eliminated. Once a decision was reached, each member would sign a document ratifying it. Copies were sent to different levels of the administration and the party apparatus. The campaign left a mountain of evidence documenting its crimes, showing that extra-judicial murder met with the approval of the Derg, the party and Mengistu himself.

Over the next two years, thousands of young men and women turned up dead in the streets of the capital and other cities, systematically murdered by militia attached to the Kebeles. Once they had finished killing EPRP suspects, they turned on members of MEISON. According to Human Rights Watch, families were required to reimburse the administration for the price of bullets used to kill their loved ones when they reclaimed the bodies for burial. Many could not afford to do so and the severed heads of victims were sold in the market.

But the Kebeles did not just restrict themselves to those suspected of opposing the Derg – anyone would do. In May 1977 the Swedish general secretary of the Save the Children Fund reported, '...a thousand children have been killed, and their bodies are left in the streets and are being eaten by wild hyenas... You can see the heaped-up bodies of murdered children, most of them aged 11 to 13, lying in the gutter, as you drive out of Addis Ababa.'

It would seem the Kebeles simply killed anyone they wanted to – with official sanction; they were also free to torture and mutilate anyone they chose. According to former economics minister Yehwalashet Girma, genital mutilation was common. Some were tortured and mutilated because the Kebeles did not like the way they looked or dressed; teenage girls were kept as sex slaves and repeatedly raped.

Higher up in the administration there were killers, too. By this time, Legesse Asfaw had taken over as Mengistu's chief executioner and would kill anyone to whom he took a dislike, even to the extent of gunning down government ministers in broad daylight. His cruelties meant he became known as the 'Devil'. Asfaw also allegedly ordered the bombing of civilians, in 1988, in the market place of Hawzen in Tigray.

Major Berhanu Bayeh of the police was in charge of a torture chamber in the Menelik's Palace. There, tennis balls were forced into mouths so victims were unable to cry out. Hung by their ankles, their feet were beaten with wire brushes and they were given electric shocks. In overcrowded and stinking conditions, they were forced to eat their own excrement and drink their urine. During the torture questions were asked for the record but no real answers were expected. Many simply disappeared. Mengistu himself is alleged to have murdered opponents by garrotting or shooting them, his explanation being that he led by example. Hundreds of thousands are thought to have died. Human Rights Watch describes the Red Terror as 'one of the most systematic uses of mass murder by a state ever witnessed in Africa.'

Even when the EPRP and MEISON had been eliminated, the killing did not stop. As recently as the late 1980s it was not uncommon to see students, suspected government critics or rebel sympathisers hanging from lampposts each morning.

Mengistu also faced organised opposition. Monarchists were on the verge of capturing the old capital of Gondar in the northwest, when factional fighting divided their forces. Then the Somali army attacked in the Ogaden region and was on the verge of capturing Harrar and Diredawa, when Somalia's former allies, Cuba and the Soviet Union, launched an airlift of arms and advisors to come to Ethiopia's rescue. With an estimated $18-billion-worth of Soviet arms Mengistu turned back the Somali invasion and made deep inroads against the Eritrean secessionists and the Tigray People's Liberation Force. By the end of the 1970s, Mengistu had the second largest army in sub-Saharan Africa, along with a formidable navy and air force.

Famine hit areas in northern Ethiopia partially held by rebels of the Tigray and Eritrean People's Liberation Fronts in 1984. Keeping the news from the rest of the world, Mengistu used the disaster as an excuse to forcibly relocate hundreds of thousands of villagers from northern Ethiopia to areas in the south. The move was designed to empty rebel-held areas of potential supporters but further dislocation only intensified the famine. By early 1985 some

7.7million suffered drought and food shortages. Of that number 2.5million were at immediate risk of starvation.

In early 1986, seeking further aid from Moscow, Mengistu introduced a new constitution modelled on that of the Soviet Union and established his new Marxist-Leninist Worker's Party of Ethiopia as the country's ruling party. The following year, the country was renamed the People's Democratic Republic of Ethiopia with Mengistu – now a civilian – as president. Surviving members of the Derg also retired from the military and joined the Central Committee of the WPE Political Bureau.

In 1987 another drought threatened a further five million in Eritrea and Tigray. News of the famine had by then got out and the international community rode to the rescue. However, Mengistu's regime prevented shipments of food from reaching rebel-held areas. Due to the combined effects of famine and internal disruption, Ethiopia's economy was now in a state of collapse. According to Human Rights Watch, Mengistu's 'counter-insurgency strategy caused the famine to strike one year earlier than would otherwise have been the case and forced people to migrate to relief shelters and refugee camps. The economic war against the peasants caused the famine to spread to other areas of the country. If the famine had struck only in 1984/5, and only affected the "core" areas of Tigray and north Wollo (3.1million affected people), and caused only one quarter of the number to migrate to camps, the death toll would have been 175,000 (on the optimistic assumptions) and 273,000 (on the pessimistic assumptions). Thus between 225,000 and 317,000 deaths – rather more than half of those caused by the famine – can be blamed on the government's human rights violations.'

By May 1991 the Ethiopian People's Revolutionary Democratic Front, a coalition of regional and ethnic rebel groups led by the Tigray People's Liberation Front and backed by Sudan and the US, advanced on Addis Ababa. In a deal brokered by the US to prevent further bloodshed, Mengistu fled the country with a great deal of money and his Rolls-Royce, leaving behind almost the entire membership of the original Derg and the WPE leadership, who were promptly arrested. Mengistu was granted asylum in Zimbabwe, where he made himself comfortable as an official guest of his friend Robert Mugabe. He blamed his downfall on Mikhail Gorbachev and the collapse of the Soviet Union, which cut off aid to Ethiopia.

In 1994 he was charged with genocide, imprisonment, illegal homicide and illegal confiscation of property but Mugabe refused to extradite him to stand trial. Instead he was tried in an Ethiopian court, *in absentia*, for his role in the killing of nearly 2,000 during the Red Terror. His charge sheet and evidence list was 8,000 pages long. Evidence against him included signed execution orders, videos of torture sessions and personal testimonies.

On 12 December 2006, Mengistu was found guilty as charged and sentenced to life in prison in January 2007, along with 105 other Derg members, only 35 of whom appeared in court. It is thought that hundreds of thousands of university students, intellectuals and politicians were killed during his rule. Amnesty International estimates a total of half a million were killed during the Red Terror of 1977 and 1978. Added to that are the deaths of those denied food aid during the famine and the victims of his forced relocations. In all, he may have been responsible for the deaths of as many as 1,500,000, making him the seventh largest mass murderer of modern times.

In an interview with the Star, a South African newspaper, Mengistu dismissed the Red Terror as merely a 'fight between two different social groups', one of which was trying to overthrow his government.

'We had to organise people into urban defence units and rural defence committees and peasants associations to defend the country,' he said. 'The so-called genocide was this war in defence of the revolution.'

He also denied killing Haile Selassie and insisted the revolution had been necessary to replace the 'very backward, archaic and feudalist system' under the Emperor. His socialist revolution had helped millions of poor peasants struggling under imperial rule, he maintained.

Mengistu also denied having ordered the death of Haile Selassie, saying: 'He was 80 years old and a very weak man. We tried our best to save him but we could not keep him.'

In his view, the Ethiopian government who had put him on trial comprised 'narrow nationalists and counter-revolutionaries' with 'no legal or moral ground to judge the Ethiopian revolution.'

Mengistu Haile Mariam's catalogue of evil did not end with flight from Ethopia, though. According to the newsagency ZimOnline, he was the brains behind Operation *Murambatsvina*, Mugabe's vicious slum-clearance campaign that left nearly one million homeless in 2005.

Citing authoritative sources within Zimbabwe's feared Central Intelligence Organisation, ZimOnline stated that Mengistu is now acting as President Robert Mugabe's security adviser and warned that the swelling slum population in Zimbabwe would create a fertile breeding ground for mass uprising. With the Zimbabwean economy in free fall, Mengistu advised Mugabe that the only way to pre-empt a mass revolt or any other form of mass action was for Zimbabwe to depopulate its cities with brutal clean-up exercises.

According to the intelligence official, the former Ethiopian dictator believed that because of the deteriorating economic situation, spontaneous riots worse than the food riots erupting in Harare and elsewhere in 1998 could erupt at any time. Urgent pre-emptive action was necessary, he warned Mugabe.

'His idea was that reducing the urban population

through such an operation would greatly diminish the chances of an uprising,' the intelligence official was quoted as saying.

State Security Minister Didymus Mutasa denied Mengistu to be the author of the slum-clearances: 'That is totally untrue. Mengistu had absolutely nothing to do with the operation and I think it is unfair to make that kind of allegation against him. Mengistu is a guest in our country; he is here in exile and is simply resting. He does not interfere at all with the affairs of our country.'

According to ZimOnline, Mengistu first suggested the slum clearance to Mugabe in February 2005 at one of the regular meetings he holds with the Zimbabwean President and other security chiefs. There followed several months of meticulous planning. Operation *Murambatsvina* began that May, a few weeks after Mugage's ruling ZANU-PF party trounced the opposition party Movement for Democratic Change in a disputed parliamentary election.

The planning meetings held at CIO headquarters in Harare were chaired by Mengistu himself and he subsequently showed Operation *Murambatsvina*'s 'high command' video clips of Zimbabwe's 1998 food riots as well as mass uprisings in the Ukraine, Yugoslavia and Ethiopia. Later he drew up the final plan, which he then submitted to Mugabe, who endorsed it.

According to this, Operation *Murambatsvina* would to be implemented in phases, with police and army vehicles on hand to dump urban residents left homeless in rural areas. Many would not recover from the destruction of their homes.

Meanwhile, Mengistu lived in the lap of luxury in the plush Gunhill suburb of Harare with a 24-hour security guard provided by the CIO and the police VIP protection unit at the Zimbabwean taxpayers' expense. Their protection is needed. In 1995, he survived an attempt on his life when Eritreans Solomon Ghebre Haile Michael and

Abraham Goletom Joseph tried to assassinate him in an ambush outside his home. Both were arrested and sentenced to ten and five years' imprisonment respectively. On appeal, when it was revealed their families had been tortured during Mengistu's reign in Ethiopia, this was reduced to two years each. The allegations of torture were not disputed in court.

The Mugabe government has since allocated Mengistu two large farms and he owns a separate home in Harare's Bluffhill district. He has at least six cars, including a Mercedes Benz, a Toyota Prado, a Toyota Avensis, a BMW and a twin-cab truck. In addition, he is part of a special scheme providing ZANU-PF officials with fuel from the National Oil Company of Zimbabwe. He gets cheap petrol for his own personal use, as well as for the farm. His vehicles are also serviced free of charge.

When the MDC almost won the 2000 parliamentary elections and the 2002 presidential elections, Mengistu was rattled. If ZANU-PF fell from power, he feared that he would be extradited to Ethiopia, where he would spend the rest of his life in jail. Though he made plans to relocate to North Korea or China, he knew that he would not enjoy the same comforts as in Zimbabwe.

'For that reason, he has put his services at Mugabe's disposal to ensure ZANU-PF rules forever,' said another highly placed security official quoted by ZimOnline. As if the people of Zimbabwe had not suffered enough.

CHAPTER FOUR

RADOVAN KARADZIC

For almost 13 years, former leader of the Bosnian Serbs Radovan Karadzic was one of the world's most wanted men. Accused of leading the slaughter of thousands of Bosnian Muslims and Croats, he was indicted for war crimes by the International Criminal Tribunal for the former Yugoslavia (ICTY) in The Hague. According to the United Nations, forces under his command killed at least 7,500 Muslim men and boys from Srebrenica in July 1995 as part of a campaign to terrorise and demoralise the Bosnian Muslim and Bosnian Croat population. He is also charged with the indiscriminate shelling of Sarajevo, and the use of 284 UN peacekeepers as human shields in May and June 1995.

Then there is the murder and rape of thousands of innocent civilians in the Republic of Bosnia and Herzegovina between April 1992 and July 1995, the destruction of sacred places, torture of captured civilians and wanton destruction of private property. At the time of writing, Radovan Karadzic faces trial for one count of genocide; three counts of crimes against humanity including persecution on political, racial and religious grounds and the sniping campaign against the civilian population of Sarajevo; five counts of grave breaches of the Geneva Conventions including the unlawful confinement of civilians in detention facilities and the appropriation and plunder of property; and seven counts of violation of the laws and customs of war including the unlawful confinement of civilians and shelling civilian gatherings. While he was on the run, the US government offered $5million for information leading to his arrest and convict. Another $5million is yet to be collected for Ratko Mladic, Karadzic's army chief of staff.

Karadzic has denied the charges against him and refuses to recognise the legitimacy of the UN tribunal.

'If The Hague was a real juridical body I would be ready to go there to testify or do so on television, but it is a political body that has been created to blame the Serbs,' he told *The Times* in February 1996.

Appearing before the tribunal in late August 2008, Karadzic failed to respond to the 11 counts against him. Again he refused to recognise the legitimacy of the court, calling it a 'bastardised judicial system' and an instrument of NATO, whose sole intention is to 'liquidate' him. The court entered pleas of not guilty on his behalf.

Radovan Karadzic was born on 19 June 1945 in ?avnik, Montenegro – reportedly in a stable – to a family from the Drobnjaci Serb clan. His father, Vuk Karadzic, had been a member of the Chetniks – the Serbian guerrilla force who fought against the German invaders and Croatian collaborators during World War II, then turned against Tito's Communist partisans. When Tito came to power in Yugoslavia in 1945, Radovan's father was arrested and remained in jail for much of his childhood.

The young Radovan was naturally close to his mother Jovanka. As a child he was a hard worker, who used to help her in both the home and field. She has said that he was a serious boy, who helped his school friends with their homework and was respectful towards the elderly.

In 1960 he moved to Sarajevo, in Bosnia and Herzegovina, to study Medicine at Sarajevo University's School of Medicine, graduating as a physician and a psychiatrist. It was there that he met his wife Ljiljana. In 1974 Karadzic went to New York for a year's postgraduate training at Columbia University. Returning to Yugoslavia, he worked as a psychologist in the Kosevo Hospital. There, he wrote and published poetry and books for children, including *There Are Miracles, There Are No Miracles*. Then in 1985 he was sentenced to three years imprisonment for embezzlement and fraud. Already well connected, he never served any time.

Karadzic then fell under the influence of the writer and Serb nationalist Dobrica ?osic, who encouraged him to go into politics. After working briefly for the Green Party, he helped set up the *Srpska Demokratska Stranka* – the Serbian Democratic Party – in Bosnia and Herzegovina in 1990. Formed as a response to the rise of nationalist and Croat parties in Bosnia, its aim was to gather the Republic's Serbian community together, secede from Bosnia and join a Greater Serbia. Under Karadzic, the SDS organised the creation of 'Serbian autonomous provinces' inside Bosnia and the establishment of an assembly to represent them.

In June 1991 Croatia and Slovenia voted to secede the old Socialist Federal Republic of Yugoslavia, followed by Macedonia. As Bosnia and Herzegovina prepared to follow suit and break away from the Yugoslav government in the Serbian capital Belgrade, Karadzic offered a stark warning.

'This, what you are doing, is not good,' he told the Bosnian Parliament on 14 October 1991. 'This is the path that you want to take Bosnia and Herzegovina on, the same highway of hell and death that Slovenia and Croatia went on. Don't think that you won't take Bosnia and

Herzegovina into hell, and the Muslim people maybe into extinction. Because the Muslim people cannot defend themselves if there is war here.'

A separate Bosnian Serb Assembly was established on 24 October 1991 to represent the interests of the Serbs in Bosnia and Herzegovina, who made up around 31 per cent of the population. The following month, the Bosnian Serbs held a referendum, which resulted in an overwhelming majority in favour of remaining in the Yugoslav federation with Serbia and Montenegro. So, on 9 January 1992, the Bosnian Serb Assembly proclaimed the Republic of the Serb People of Bosnia and Herzegovina. On 28 February, a new constitution was adopted, declaring the Serb Republic's territory included Serb autonomous provinces and other Serbian ethnic settlements in Bosnia and Herzegovina. This territory was declared part of the federal Yugoslav state still administered by the authorities in Belgrade.

But Karadzic was leading the people of Bosnia and Herzegovina down the highway to hell and death: it was only over the next two days – 29 February and 1 March 1992 – that the Bosnians and Herzegovinans went to the polls to vote in a referendum on whether they should also secede from Yugoslavia. At Karadzic's behest, the Serbs boycotted the referendum, while Bosnian Muslims – or Bosniacs, who made up 44 per cent of the population – and the Croats (17 per cent) turned out. Some 64 per cent of the eligible voters went to the polls, with 98 per cent of them voting in favour of independence. On 6 April 1992, Bosnia was recognised as an independent state by the UN and the European Community. The following day, the Republic of the Serb People of Bosnia and Herzegovina was simply titled the Serb Republic or *Republica Srpska*.

Karadzic declared himself first president of the new republic, whose administration was based for the immediate future in Pale. It was not without its backers. As a proponent of a Great Serbia, Karadzic was supported by the president of Serbia and fellow war criminal Slobovan Milosevic. And as the Serbs were Orthodox Christians, they were also supported by Russia and Greece.

Inevitably, the result of the establishment of *Republica Srpska* within Bosnian territory led to war. Most Bosniacs and many Croats claimed the fighting was caused by Serbian and Croatian aggression, while the Serbs considered it a civil war. According to the International Court of Justice, Serbia gave military and financial support to the Serb Republic and its army – which was under Karadzic's command – while Croatia offered military support to Croat forces of self-proclaimed breakaway Croatian Community of Herzeg-Bosnia.

Karadzic's *Republica Srpska* claimed the Bosnian capital of Sarajevo its own. In the months leading up to the Bosnian War, the Yugoslavia National Army – under the control of the government in Belgrade – began to deploy in the hills surrounding the city of Bosnia, bringing artillery and other equipment later used in the siege. In April 1992, the Bosnian government demanded that the Yugoslav government should withdraw its forces. Milosevic's camp agreed to remove only those men who were not of Bosnian nationality, but this proved to be an insignificant number. The rest, supposedly Bosnian Serbs to a man, were transferred to the army of the Serb Republic.

On 2 May 1992, the city was blockaded by the Bosnian Serb forces, led by Ratko Mladic. Roads leading into Sarajevo were closed; water and electricity were cut off and shipments of food and medicine ceased. Although more heavily armed the Serbian forces were outnumbered by Bosnian defenders. Attacks by even armoured columns were stoutly resisted, so the besieging forces withdrew to some 200 fortified positions in the surrounding hills from where they began to bombard the city.

Throughout the rest of 1992 and the first half of 1993,

heavy fighting continued and a number of atrocities were committed, including the massacres at Foca and Prijedor. Serbian forces shelled continuously and snipers roamed the city. Some streets became 'sniper alleys' and signs saying *Pazite, Snajper!* – 'Beware, Sniper!' – began to appear. The Serbs seized some neighbourhoods, but Bosnian government forces managed to hold onto Sarajevo Airport until United Nations' airlifts began in late June 1992.

There was an international arms embargo, which favoured the well-equipped Serb besiegers. However, the Sarajevo Tunnel, completed in mid-1993, allowed enterprising black-marketeers to smuggle arms through Serb lines. While small arms, rocket-propelled grenades, anti-aircraft missiles and anti-tank missiles could reach the defenders, however, they were still denied larger weapons. By April 1995, just five tanks and 20 artillery pieces were defending the city, nowhere near enough to stage a breakout.

During the siege an average of 329 shells landed in the city every day. At the height of the bombardment, on 22 July 1993, 3,777 shells a day hit Sarajevo. By September 1993, virtually every building had been damaged and some 35,000 were completely destroyed. Among the buildings targeted were hospitals, media facilities, industrial assets and UN compounds. The National Library burnt to the ground.

Karadzic was unrepentant. In an interview in 1993, he made a terrible boast: 'Sarajevans will not be counting the dead. They will be counting the living!'

Mortar fire took a terrible toll on civilians. On 1 June 1993, 15 were killed and 80 injured at a football game. Eleven days later, 12 people queuing for water were killed. The worst civilian death toll occurred at the first Markale marketplace massacre on 5 February 1994, when 68 civilians were killed and 200 wounded. As a result, the UN demanded that Serb forces withdraw their heavy weapons or face air strikes. They pulled back, dramatically reducing the shelling of the city, but it did not cease. After the Serbs ignored further ultimatums, NATO jets attacked Bosnian Serb ammunition depots and other strategic military targets. On 26 May 1995, 284 UN peacekeepers were seized by Ratko Mladic and taken to strategic points to be used as human shields. They were shown in chains on Serbian TV. Justifying the hostage taking, Radovan Karadzic's spokesman Jovan Zametica said: 'The United Nations in this particular situation have decided to hire a murderer: it is called the NATO alliance. It is a hired killer. If NATO wishes to continue with its air strikes then it will have to kill the UN troops here on the ground, because we have positioned UN troops and observers around potential targets that NATO might decide to go for. The international community therefore will have to pay a very heavy price. And it will not stop at that. The Serbs are determined to make a point to the whole world.'

By 18 June 1995, after further pressure from NATO and the UN, the hostages were released.

From the outset of the war, Serb forces attacked the non-Serb civilian population in the area of eastern Bosnia claimed by the Serb Republic. Once towns and villages were securely in the hands of Serb forces, Bosniac apartments and houses were systematically ransacked or burnt down. Civilians were rounded up, sometimes beaten or killed in the process. Men and women were separated and imprisoned in concentration camps. There were reports of the systematic 'cleansing' of the towns of Prijedor, Banja Luka, Bijeljina, Vlasenica and Trebinje.

One key area was Central Podrinje, the region around Srebrenica. Its population was predominantly Bosniac, but if it was excluded from the Serb Republic, the crescent-shaped *Republica Srpska* would be cut in two. Consequently, Karadzic's forces began 'ethnic cleansing' of the area and other Bosniac enclaves in Eastern Bosnia. In Bratunac,

Bosniacs were killed or forced to flee to Srebrenica. According to Bosnian government figures, 1,156 died. Thousands more were killed in nearby Cerska, Foca, Snagovo and Zvornik.

Srebrenica was seized in early 1992 and its Bosniac population expelled or killed. In May 1992, Bosnian government forces recaptured the town. By January 1993, they had linked up with Bosniac-held Cerska to the northwest and Zepa in the southwest, expanding the Srebrenica enclave to 350 square miles, although it was never linked to the main area of Bosnian government-controlled land to the west.

In an attempt to break out, Bosnian forces attacked the Serb base in Kravica. Much of the village was destroyed. However, the ICTY, the United Nations court of law dealing with the war crimes, did not condemn the Bosnians as being responsible for this because Serb forces had used artillery against the villages surrounding Srebrenica and the village of Bjelovac had even been attacked by Serbian warplanes.

Over the next few months, Serb forces used their superior fire power to capture the Cerska and Konjevi? Polje, threatening the link between Zepa and Srebrenica. The size of the Srebrenica enclave was quickly reduced to 60 square miles. Bosniacs from outlying areas fled to Srebrenica, swelling its population to some 60,000.

In March 1993, General Philippe Morillon, the French commander of the United Nations Protection Force (UNPROFOR), visited Srebrenica. By then the overcrowded town was under siege. Advancing Serb forces had cut off running water, food and medicine were in short supply and the only electricity came from makeshift generators.

Over the next two months, the UN High Commissioner for Refugees (UNHCR) evacuated several thousand Bosniacs from Srebrenica, though the Bosnian government protested this was aiding the Serbs' ethnic cleansing of a predominantly Bosniac area. Despite this, the Serbs were intent on capturing Srebrenica and on 13 April 1993, a spokesman told the UNHCR that they would attack the town unless the Bosniacs surrendered. On 16 April 1993, the United Nations Security Council passed a resolution declaring Srebrenica and its surroundings a 'safe area'. Two days later, Dutch UNPROFOR troops moved in.

Srebrenica was instead an armed camp, with a ragtag Mountain Division of ill-equipped Bosnians surrounded by the Serb army's Drina Corps, equipped with tanks, armoured vehicles, mortars and artillery. Serb forces prevented UNPROFOR equipment and ammunition from getting through. By early 1995, with the civilian population on the brink of starvation, the UN forces themselves began to run low on food, medicine, fuel and ammunition. Dutch soldiers on leave from Srebrenica were not allowed back and their number dropped from 600 to 400 men, then in March and April, UNPROFOR noticed a build-up of Serb forces.

In March 1995, Radovan Karadzic was under pressure from the international community to make peace. Instead he issued 'Directive 7'. This instructed the army of the Serb Republic to 'complete the physical separation of Srebrenica from Zepa as soon as possible, preventing even communication between individuals in the two enclaves. By planned and well thought out combat operations, create an unbearable situation of total insecurity with no hope of further survival or life for the inhabitants of Srebrenica.'

Clearly, this directive was ordering genocide.

As the noose tightened, the situation inside Srebrenica deteriorated further. In May 1995, the Bosnian military commanders were ordered to leave by helicopter. An appeal was made for a humanitarian corridor to the enclave to be opened. This fell on deaf ears and on 7 July, the mayor of Srebrenica reported that eight residents had died of starvation.

The following day, a Dutch armoured vehicle came under fire and withdrew. Further Serb incursions met with little resistance, or any significant reaction from the international community so, on 9 July, Karadzic ordered the Drina Corps to take Srebrenica.

The next morning they attacked. Hopelessly outnumbered, the Dutch troops fired warning shots over their heads. They fired mortars, but not directly at the Serb attackers. Their commander called for air support. The following day, NATO planes bombed Serb tanks advancing towards the town, but further air strikes were aborted due to poor visibility. Any future plans to defend were abandoned when the Serb army threaten to kill Dutch troops.

It was clear what would happen next. Ratko Mladic told Radovan Karadzic and his deputy Momcilo Krajisnik, later convicted for crimes against humanity and sentenced to 27 years in prison, that their plans to kick the Bosniacs out of Srebrenica could not be carried out without committing genocide.

'People are not little stones, or keys in someone's pocket, that can be moved from one place to another just like that,' warned Mladic. 'Therefore, we cannot precisely arrange for only Serbs to stay in one part of the country while removing others painlessly. I do not know how Mr Krajisnik and Mr Karadzic will explain that to the world.'

By the evening of 11 July 1995, thousands of Bosniac refugees from Srebrenica were crammed into the Dutch compound just outside the town at Potocari. Another 20,000 huddled in the surrounding fields and factories. The vast majority were women, children, elderly or disabled. However, at least 300 men were inside the compound and between 600 and 900 outside.

Conditions were deplorable. There was little food or water, and the July heat was unbearable. In the ensuing panic, those who fell were trampled. There was little the Dutch troops could do, but try to calm them.

The next day, the refugees witnessed Serb soldiers setting fire to surrounding houses and haystacks. In the afternoon, they mixed in the refugees, picking out victims for rape and summary execution. Some witnesses saw piles of up to 100 bodies. One witnessed a child killed with a knife, its head cut off. Three young brothers – two teenagers and a child – were taken away. Their mother found them with their throats slit. Girls were raped, sometimes within sight of the Dutch troops, who were powerless. Some women were so afraid that they committed suicide by hanging themselves.

Buses arrived to take the refugees north towards Bosniac-held territory. As they boarded, men of military age were stopped and taken to a building in Potocari known as the 'White House'. Sometimes older and younger men were taken, too. It was clear to the Dutch what was happening: troops saw Serb soldiers take a man behind the 'White House'. They heard a shot and the two Serbs reappeared, alone. Another saw an unarmed Bosniac man despatched with a single shot to the head. Throughout the afternoon of 13 July, gunshots went off at a rate of 20 to 40 an hour. When a UN Military Observer heard that men were being taken behind the 'White House' and not coming back, he ventured forth to find out what was going on. As he approached, he heard gunshots but he was stopped by Serb soldiers before he could investigate further.

Worse allegations were made. There was talk of executions carried out at night under arc lights, bodies bulldozed into mass graves. Some, it was said, were buried alive. The streets were littered with corpses. Left to their own devices, Serb forces indulged in sadistic tortures, cutting off ears, noses and lips before finally killing their victims. Many committed suicide rather than undergo this mutilation. It was even said that parents were forced to watch as Serb soldiers murdered their children.

Only women and children were getting off the buses

at Kladanj in Bosnia. Although some 25,000 women from Srebrenica reached safety in Tuzla, others were not so fortunate. One witness said he saw a bus full of women being driven away from Bosnian government-held territory.

Some men took to the woods. One small group of between 700 and 800 tried to escape into Serbia northeast-wards over Mount Kvarac and through Bratunac, or to the southeast across the River Drina to Bajina Basta. Another group of some 300–800 headed for Zepa to the southwest. It is not known what happened to them, or how many survived.

Others joined up with the remnants of the Bosnian Mountain Division to form a column that would attempt a breakout to the northwest towards Tuzla in Bosnian-held territory, a distance of around 45 miles over hilly territory in the heat of summer. Between 10,000 and 15,000 men set off at around midnight on 11 July 1995, around a third being soldiers from the Mountain Division, though not all of them were armed.

The break out took the Serb Army by surprise: the Drina Corps were given orders to devote all available manpower to finding the column and taking prisoners. They were told that the men in the column were 'hardened and violent criminals who will stop at nothing to prevent being taken prisoner and to enable their escape into Bosnian territory'.

The next day, the column was crossing an asphalt road near Kamenica when the Serb artillery opened up. Only about a third made it across the road. Hundreds more men were killed and the column split in two parts. Day and night, heavy shelling continued against the part of the column that remained. Men from the rear of the column who survived this ordeal described it as a 'man-hunt'.

By the evening of 12 July 1995, the Bosnian Serb forces were capturing large numbers of the men at the rear.

Ambushes were set up in some places; in others, the Bosnian Serbs shouted into the forest, urging the men to surrender and promising that the Geneva Conventions would be complied with. Otherwise, the Serb forces fired into the woods with anti-aircraft guns and other weapons, or used stolen UN equipment to trick the Bosniacs into believing the UN or the Red Cross were present to monitor their capture. When they were captured, however, the Muslim men were stripped of their personal belongings and, in many cases, summarily executed.

One witness saw the Serbs forcing a Bosniac man to call other Bosniacs down from the mountains. Some 200–300 men appeared, lined up in seven ranks, each some 40 metres in length, with their hands behind their heads. They were then mown down by machine guns. Among those who disappeared in the maelstrom were four children, aged between 8 and 14. The Serbs sent one of the Muslims who tried to surrender back to the column with a cross carved in his forehead, his ears cut off and one of his eyes gouged out.

Most of the men started out with enough rations for only two days. By the third day, they turned to eating snails, grass and leaves. The summer heat caused dehydration and there were few sources of drinking water up in the hills. Everyone suffered a lack of sleep and some began to demonstrate the symptoms of severe mental distress, turning on others and killing them outright, or committing suicide.

The front part of the column escaping the massacre on the asphalt road forded the River Jadar and regrouped on the morning of 13 July. The following day, they were approaching Mount Velja Glava when they found it to be occupied by Serbs. Skirting the mountain, they eventually ran into an ambush near Snagovo. The Serb forces were equipped with anti-aircraft guns, artillery and tanks, but the column managed to break through despite heavy losses. On the way they captured a Serb officer – which gave them a bargaining counter – and a walkie-talkie, which they used to contact their Corps headquarters.

Reaching Krizevici on 15 July, they tried to negotiate safe passage through the Serb lines, but soon found that the Serbs were merely using talks to stall the column while they called up reinforcements. Meanwhile the remainder of the column – now comprising about 2,500 people – was held up by 500 Serb soldiers and policemen.

The ridge at Baljkovica just beyond Krizevici marked the Serb front line and the Army of the *Republica Srpska* formed two lines to prevent the column reaching Bosnian-held territory. Fortunately, a heavy hailstorm on the evening of 15 July forced the Serbs to take cover. Nevertheless, when the column reached the ridge, at about 3am on 16 July, heavy fighting ensued. By the early afternoon, they managed to break through, however.

When the remnants of the column arrived at Tuzla, they were described as 'an army of ghosts'. Exhausted and emaciated, the survivors were clad in rags or just their underwear, their bleeding feet wrapped in rags or plastic. Some were carried on makeshift stretchers. There were children with them, many visibly terrified from their ordeal. Some men had cracked under the immense stress – one soldier began to fire on his own unit and had to be shot to prevent further bloodshed. A medical station doled out tranquillisers.

Only some 3,000–4,000 of the marchers who had left Srebrenica four days earlier arrived safely in Tuzla on 16 July. Most were military personnel – the remaining Bosniacs were killed, captured or trapped behind Serb lines. The epic journey claimed an unknown number of lives and countless bodies remained unburied in the woods. Once the armed part of the column fought its way through the lines, Serb forces closed the corridor and resumed hunting down parts of the column still in areas under their control.

On 16 July 1995, around 2,000 refugees were still hiding in the woods in the area of Pobudje, with many more scattered elsewhere. Months later some of them managed to find their way into Bosnian-held territory, following a line of corpses.

Those in the part of the column unsuccessful in passing the asphalt road Kamenica who did not wish to give themselves up decided to turn back towards Zepa. They attempted to navigate by following overhead power cables and survived by stealing potatoes and other vegetables from the fields around the Serbian villages at night until local Serbs began to mount patrols. Along the way, they often found corpses, by then in a state of decomposition. A few hundred managed to reach Zepa just before the Serbs occupied the enclave on 25 July 1995.

After a second Markale massacre in Sarajevo on 28 August 1995, when 37 were killed and 90 wounded, NATO stepped up its campaign of air strikes. They flew 3,515 sorties against 338 targets to protect safe areas in Sarajevo, Tuzla and Bihac. Eventually their actions forced warring parties to the negotiating table. In November 1995, Bosnian President Alija Izetbegovic, Croatian President Franjo Tudman and Serbian President Slobodan Milosevic – representing the Bosnian Serbs as Radovan Karadzic was already a wanted man – met at Wright-Patterson Air Force Base, near Dayton, Ohio, along with delegates from the US, the UK, the EU and the Russian Federation. A peace agreement was drawn up and signed in Paris on 14 December 1995.

The Bosnian War claimed between 100,000 and 110,000 lives, with around 1.8million displaced. Sixty-five per cent of the dead were Bosniacs, 25 per cent Serbs and 8 per cent Croats. At least 83 per cent of civilian victims were Bosniacs. It is thought the figure would have been higher had many of the families of the Srebrenica victims not claimed their loved ones were soldiers in order to claim government benefits. A CIA report of March 1995 before the massacre at Srebrenica concluded that 90 per cent of the crimes committed during the Bosnian War were carried out by Serbs as part of their policy of 'ethnic cleansing' and 'leading Serbian politicians almost certainly played a role'.

'The systematic nature of the Serbian actions strongly suggests that Pale and perhaps Belgrade exercised a carefully veiled role in the purposeful destruction and dispersal of non-Serb populations,' the report stated.

It also contained specific evidence that Bosnian Serb leaders, including Radovan Karadzic, knew of the concentration camps where many Muslims and Croats evicted from their homes in 1992 had been held. Karadzic consistently denied responsibility for the killing and imprisonment of Muslims in the 70 per cent of Bosnia held by Serbs in 1995. He claimed the departure of nearly three-quarters of a million Muslims from this area was due to the 'chaos and fear' resulting from an uncontrollable war rather than anything his soldiers might have done.

Even so, Karadzic and Mladic went into hiding. An amended indictment, issued on 31 May 2000, charged Karadzic with two counts of genocide, five counts of crimes against humanity covering extermination, murder, persecutions on political, racial and religious grounds, persecutions and inhumane acts including forcible transfer; three counts of violation of the laws or customs of war, covering murder, unlawfully inflicting terror upon civilians and the taking of hostages; and one count of grave breaches of the Geneva Conventions concerning wilful killing, though the indictment has since been amended.

In his defence Karadzic's supporters say he is no less guilty than any other political leader in wartime. Among Bosnian Serbs, his ability to evade capture has made him a hero. In 2001, hundreds of supporters demonstrated in support of him in his home town.

While Karadzic's mother urged her son not to give himself

up, the UN, EU and NATO put pressure on Balkan governments to apprehend him. Although the Bosnian Serb forces
had long been blamed for the massacre at Srebrenica, it was
only in June 2004 that officials of the *Republika Srpska*
acknowledged their security forces had planned and carried
out the mass killing – and this only after the Srebrenica
Commission set up by the international community's High
Representative Paddy Ashdown made its preliminary report.
The Serb commission's final report acknowledged the mass
murder of men and boys was planned: it found more than
7,800 were killed after compiling 34 lists of victims. This was
the biggest mass murder in Europe since World War II.
Although a number of women and children were killed,
along with a large number of older men, a concerted effort
was made to capture and kill all Bosniac men of military age,
whether they sought refuge in Potocari or joined the
retreating Bosniac column. All this was planned and co-
ordinated at a high level, the commission found.

Several thousand Bosniacs were herded together at
assembly points in the field near Sandici and on the Nova
Kasaba football pitch, where they were searched and put
into smaller groups. Others were held in the agricultural
warehouses in Kravica, a school in Konjevi? Polje, the
village of Lolici and the village school of Luke. By the late
afternoon of 13 July, some 6,000 had given themselves up
on the road. Many were seen by the women and children
taken by bus to Kladanj: their presence was also captured
on aerial photographs.

An hour after the evacuation of the women and children
was completed, the buses returned to the areas where the
men were held. During the afternoon, Mladic visited the
700 men at Sandici and told them that they would come to
no harm. They were to be treated as prisoners of war and
exchanged for other prisoners. He also reassured them that
their wives and children had reached Tuzla safely. When
the buses arrived, the men were ordered to hand over any

valuables and to throw their remaining possessions onto a large heap. Some were taken to Bratunac; others were marched to the warehouses in Kravica.

The men in the football ground at Nova Kasaba were also forced to hand over their belongings. Again, Mladic turned up. This time he announced that the Bosnian authorities in Tuzla did not want the men. Inside, they were loaded onto buses and trucks and taken to Bratunac or the other locations. Another 1,000 Bosniac men, who had been separated from the women and children at Potocari, were taken to Bratunac to join the men from the column. Almost to a man, they were executed.

While some Bosniac men were killed – singly or in small groups – by the soldiers who captured them and others killed where they were temporarily detained, most were killed in well-organised mass executions which began on 13 July 1995. There was a chilling routine to these mass murders: after being held for several hours in an empty school or warehouse, the men were taken by bus or truck to another site for execution. The unarmed prisoners were often blindfolded; their shoes were taken and their wrists bound behind their backs. The killing fields were usually in isolated places. Once there, the men were taken off the truck or bus in small groups, lined up and shot. Those who survived the first burst of gunfire were shot individually, though sometimes afterwards they were left to suffer for some time. Their bodies were then buried in mass graves.

Finding the graves, exhuming the bodies and finally identifying the victims was a slow process. By 2002, some 5,000 bodies had been exhumed but only 200 successfully identified. Nevertheless, genocide prosecutions were already going ahead in The Hague and the details of what had happened in and around Srebrenica in July 1995 began to unfold in court. The ICTY discovered a small-scale execution had taken place some time before midday on 13

July, on the banks of the river Jadar. Seventeen men delivered by bus had been lined up and shot. One man, though hit by a bullet in the hip, managed to jump into the river and make his escape.

That afternoon the first large-scale execution had taken place in the Cerska valley, west of Konjevi? Polje. A witness, hidden in trees, saw two or three trucks and an armoured vehicle followed by an earth-moving machine drive towards Cerska. He then heard gunshots, which went on for half an hour. Afterwards he witnessed the armoured vehicle coming back up the road. A UN translator saw bodies, some of them still alive, being tossed into a ditch along the side of the road. Other witnesses saw a pool of blood on the road to Cerska that day. Aerial photos and excavations later revealed a mass grave there.

Cartridges found at the scene indicated the executioners fired from one side of the road while the victims were lined up along the other. One hundred and fifty bodies lay covered in earth. A post mortem revealed they had been killed by rifle fire. All were male, aged between 14 and 50. Many had their hands tied behind their backs. All but three were wearing civilian clothes. Nine were later identified as people on the list of missing persons from Srebrenica; all were Bosnian Muslims.

Later that afternoon, between 1,000 and 1,500 men from the fields near Sandici arrived at a warehouse owned by the Agricultural Cooperative in Kravica. An aerial photograph taken at 2pm shows two buses standing in front of the sheds. Others had travelled the one kilometre from Sandici on foot. A witness saw some 200 men, stripped to the waist and with their hands in the air, being forced to run in the direction of Kravica.

At around 6pm, when all the men were in the warehouse, Serb soldiers threw in hand grenades and opened fire with various weapons, including rocket-propelled grenades. According to a Dutch report on the massacre, more killing took place in and around Kravica and Sandici, while the main body of prisoners were taken to the warehouse. Some 200 or 300 men had been formed up in ranks near Sandici and mown down with machine guns. At Kravica, it seems the local population joined in with the killings. Some victims were mutilated and killed with knives. The bodies were taken to Bratunac or simply dumped in the river that runs alongside the road.

Three men survived the mass murder in the warehouse at Kravica. One said: 'All of a sudden there was a lot of shooting in the warehouse, and we didn't know where it was coming from. There were rifles, grenades, bursts of gunfire and it was... it got so dark in the warehouse that we couldn't see anything. People started to scream, to shout, crying for help. And then there would be a lull, and then all of a sudden it would start again. And they kept shooting like that until nightfall in the warehouse.'

Armed guards shot at the men who tried to climb out of the windows to escape the massacre. When the shooting stopped, the shed was full of bodies. Another survivor, who was only slightly wounded, recalled: 'I was not even able to touch the floor... After the shooting, I felt a strange kind of heat, warmth, which was actually coming from the blood that covered the concrete floor, and I was stepping on the dead people who were lying around. But there were even people who were still alive, who were only wounded, and as soon as I would step on one, I would hear him cry, moan, because I was trying to move as fast as I could. I could tell that people had been completely disembodied, and I could feel bones of the people that had been hit by those bursts of gunfire or shells, I could feel their ribs crushing. And then I would get up again and continue.'

On climbing out of a window, he was seen by a guard who shot at him. He lay still, pretending to be dead, and somehow managed to escape the following morning.

The first witness spent the night under a heap of bodies. Next morning, he watched as the soldiers examined the corpses for signs of life. The few survivors were forced to sing Serbian songs and were then shot. Once the final victim had been killed, an excavator was driven in to shunt the bodies out of the shed. Once removed, the asphalt outside was hosed down with water.

In September 1996 it was still possible, though, to find hair, blood, human tissue and traces of explosives on the walls to be used in evidence. Some remnants of bones were discovered near one of the outer walls.

Ammunition cartridges found at the scene established a link between the executions in Kravica to a mass grave known as 'Glogova 2', where the remains of 139 people were found. No blindfolds or restraints were unearthed. The secondary grave, 'Zeleni Jadar 5', was also thought to contain the remains of victims from the massacre at the Kravica warehouse. Some 145 bodies, a number of them charred, were found there. Pieces of brick and window frame found in the 'Glogova 1' grave containing another 191 bodies also established a link with the killings at Kravica.

The buses carrying the women and children from Potocari to Kladanj were stopped at the village of Tisca, where they were searched. Twenty-three Bosniac men and boys found on board were removed. They were taken to a school, where their wrists were bound with telephone wire. This was plainly a well organised operation as there was a soldier on a field telephone at the school, who appeared to be receiving and transmitting orders. Sometime around midnight, the men were loaded onto a truck, their hands still tied behind their backs. At one point the truck stopped, but a soldier said: 'Not here – take them up there, where they took people before.' When the truck stopped again, Serb soldiers came round to the back of the truck and started shooting at the prisoners. One managed to untie his hands, leapt from the truck and, dodging bullets, fled into the woods. Eventually he reached safety.

A large group of the prisoners were held overnight in Bratunac. On the morning of 14 July, they were bussed in a convoy of 30 vehicles to the Grabavci School in Orahovac. There, they were packed into a school gym already half-filled with prisoners arriving since the early morning. Within a few hours, the building was completely full. Survivors estimated to be between 2,000–2,500 men were there, although the ICTY Prosecution believe the number was closer to 1,000. Some were very young and others quite elderly, though 700–800 were of military age. Every now and then, the guards would fire into the roof to quieten the prisoners down. Some prisoners were taken outside and killed. Eventually Mladic arrived and told the men: 'Well, your government does not want you and I have to take care of you.'

After being held in the gym for several hours, the men were led out in small groups. Each was blindfolded and given a drink of water. They were told that they were going to a camp in Bijeljina. In fact, they were being taken to an execution site just one kilometre away. There, they were lined up and shot from behind. Those who survived the first round were shot again. Two adjacent fields were used. Once one was full of bodies, the executioners moved to the other. Earth-moving equipment dug the graves while the executions were going on. One witness – who managed to survive the shootings by pretending to be dead – said that Mladic himself drove up in a red car and watched some of the executions.

Another recalled, 'When we reached the location, I jumped down from the truck and pulled the blindfold from my eyes. I saw that the field was full of people who had been shot dead. They had brought us here to kill us too. We were formed up in two ranks with our backs to the Chetniks. To our left was a yellow bulldozer. I stood close to the people that had already been shot before us. I grasped my amulet and fell to the ground among the other bodies just before they began to shoot. There was screaming and shouting all around me. I heard the command, "Fire!" and then again: "Fire!" The young lads were crying out for their parents, the fathers for their sons but there was no help.

'I lay motionless between the bodies and heard the Chetniks ask: "Is anyone wounded? We'll take him to the hospital." If anyone replied, they would go over to him and finish him off. I remained silent. The man who had fallen on top of me was still alive. They came closer and finished him off. He convulsed and kicked my shoe off. They stopped shooting. I heard laughing and talking. Another truck arrived and then the bulldozer started up. It began to move the bodies into a heap and to crush them. It came very close to me as though it was going to crush me too. Then it would have been better to have been killed with a bullet. Suddenly the bulldozer stopped and a tall, stocky man got out and lit a cigarette. I could see everything because the light of the reflectors was on him. He turned and walked over to the group of Chetniks who were now in the middle of shooting another group of prisoners. I thought: this is the right moment. I pushed away the man who lay on top of me, found my shoe and began to crawl towards the woods, pulling myself over dead bodies all the way.'

These executions began in the afternoon of 14 July 1995 and were completed shortly before midnight. The process of burying the victims was then stopped and resumed the next morning.

Forensic evidence supports crucial aspects of the survivors' testimony. Both aerial and satellite photographs show that the ground in Orahovac was disturbed between 5 and 27 July 1995 and again between 7 and 27 September 1995. Two primary mass graves were uncovered in the area and named 'Lazete 1' and 'Lazete 2' by investigators.

The Lazete 1 gravesite was exhumed by the ICTY prosecutors between 13 July and 3 August 2000. All of the 130 individuals uncovered, for whom sex could be determined, were male; 138 blindfolds were found in the grave. Material identifying 23 people listed as missing from Srebrenica was found during the exhumations. Lazete 2 contained the bodies of 243 victims. They were male and the vast majority died of gunshot injuries. Also 147 blindfolds were found.

Forensic analysis of soil and pollen samples, blindfolds, ligatures and shell cases showed bodies from the Lazete 1 and 2 graves had been dug up and re-buried at secondary graves named Hodzici Road 3, 4 and 5, which aerial photography revealed to have been dug between 7 September and 2 October 1995. At least 184 bodies were found there. The vast majority had been killed by rifle fire.

On the 14 July and 15 July, another large group of some 1,500–2,000 prisoners were taken from Bratunac to the school in Petkovici. As at the other detention sites, the conditions at Petkovici School were deplorable. It was extremely hot and crowded. The men had no food or water and some prisoners became so thirsty they drank their own urine. Periodically, soldiers came in and beat the prisoners or called them out to be killed. A few prisoners discussed trying to escape but the others said it was better to remain – surely the Red Cross was monitoring the situation and they would not all be killed?

Eventually, the men were called outside in small groups. They were ordered to strip to the waist and remove their shoes. Then they had their hands tied behind their backs. During the night of 14 July, the men were taken by truck to a stony area near the dam at Petkovici. On the way, a survivor peeked out from under his blindfold and saw Mladic, who was also on his way to the execution site. When the prisoners arrived they could see immediately what was going on. A large number of bodies were strewn on the ground, their hands still tied behind their backs.

Groups of 5–10 men were taken out of the trucks, lined up and shot. Some begged for water before being killed, but their pleas were ignored. One survivor said: 'I was really sorry that I would die thirsty, and I was trying to hide among the people for as long as I could, like everybody else. I just wanted to live for another second or two. And when it was my turn, I jumped out with what I believe were four other people. I could feel the gravel beneath my feet. It hurt… I was walking with my head bent down and I wasn't feeling anything… And then I thought that I would die very fast, that I would not suffer. And I just thought that my mother would never know where I had ended up. This is what I was thinking as I was getting out of the truck.'

He was shot, but only wounded and lay still, expecting another round of gunfire to end his life – but it did not come. When Serb soldiers had finished with a round of killing, they laughed and made jokes: 'Look at this guy, he looks like a cabbage.' Then they walked around killing the wounded. The witness said he almost called out for the soldiers to put him out of his misery.

'I was still very thirsty,' he remembered. 'But it was sort of between life and death. I didn't know whether I wanted to live or to die anymore. I decided not to call out for them to shoot and kill me, but I was sort of praying to God that they'd come and kill me.'

After the soldiers left, he found another survivor and between them, they managed to untie each other's hands. They then crawled over the heap of bodies towards the woods to hide. When dawn arrived, they looked down on the execution site to see what they estimated to be 1,500–2,000 bodies. Heavy earth-movers were already bulldozing bodies into mass graves.

Aerial photos confirmed the earth near the Petkovici dam had been disturbed between 5 and 27 July, and again between 7 and 27 September 1995. When the grave there was opened in April 1998, investigators found 'grossly disarticulated body parts' and concluded other bodies had been removed using a mechanical excavator. The remains of no more than 43 remained. Only 15 could be identified as male; the sex of the rest remained undetermined. Six body parts showed definite gunshot wounds, with a further 17 revealing probable or possible gunshot wounds. One ligature was located on the surface and a piece of cloth possibly used as a blindfold found loose in the grave.

Forensic analysis showed other bodies had been removed and re-buried in a secondary grave known as 'Liplje 2'. Traces of mechanical teeth marks and wheel tracks show the grave was dug by a wheeled front loader with a toothed bucket. A minimum of 191 bodies were located in this grave – 122 were determined to be male, the remainder undetermined. Where cause of death could be determined, it was from gunshot wounds. Twenty-three ligatures were uncovered, though nothing that could be identified as a blindfold was found.

On 14 July 1995, more prisoners from Bratunac were taken by bus further north to a school in the village of Pilica, 12 miles north of Zvornik. Some 1,000–1,200 men were held in the school gymnasium with no food or water for two days and nights. Several died from the heat and dehydration.

The officer-in-command, Lieutenant-Colonel Vinko Pandurevic, complained of the onerous burden placed on his shoulders. He was required to find room for large numbers of prisoners in his area, guard them and dispose of the dead, and he threatened to release the prisoners if no one else could be found to take responsibility for them. Even after the executions, Pandurevic declared it incomprehensible that someone should have sent '3,000 men' to be confined in the schools when he was also expected to deal with the fleeing column. From the number he gave, it has been concluded that he was also responsible for other mass murders in the area.

On 16 July, the men were called out of the Pilica School and loaded onto buses with their hands tied behind their backs. They were then driven to the Branjevo Military Farm, which supplied pigs to the Serb Army. There, they were lined up in groups of ten and shot.

Convicted war criminal Drazen Erdemovic, who admitted killing at least 70 Bosniacs at the Branjevo Military Farm, said in his testimony: 'The men in front of us were ordered to turn their backs. When those men turned their backs to us, we shot at them. We were given orders to shoot.'

He said that only one of the victims was in military uniform. Another had put up some resistance and had attempted to escape, but the remainder showed full compliance. He also admitted that members of his unit displayed terrible cruelty. If they recognised one of the prisoners, he would be humiliated and beaten before being killed. They used machine guns, which tended to cause wounds rather than being immediately fatal, deliberately to prolong their victim's suffering. One survivor recalled: 'When they opened fire, I threw myself on the ground... And one man fell on my head. I think that he was killed on the spot. And I could feel the hot blood pouring over me... I could hear one man crying for help. He was begging them to kill him. And they simply said: "Let him suffer. We'll kill him later."'

Between 1,000 and 1,200 men were killed that day at the Branjevo Military Farm. The murders began at 10am and were finished by 3pm. More killings took place the next day. Aerial photographs of the area taken on 17 July show a large number of bodies lying in the field near the farm, as well as the tracks of an excavator. Three men escaped, but were recaptured by the Bosnian Serb police on 25 July. This time, however, they were treated as prisoners of war and survived to testify to the ICTY.

Once Erdemovic's unit had finished killing at the Branjevo Military Farm on 16 July, they were told that a group of 500 Bosniac prisoners from Srebrenica were trying to break out of the nearby Dom Kultura club. Erdemovic and his unit refused to do any more killing, however. They were then told to attend a meeting with a lieutenant-colonel at a café in Pilica. As they waited, they heard shots and grenades exploding. This lasted around fifteen to twenty minutes, then a soldier from Bratunac arrived and reported that 'everything was over.'

There were no survivors to explain exactly what happened in the Dom Kultura club. Over a year later, it was still possible to find physical evidence of the atrocity. Traces of blood, hair and body tissue were found in the building, and cartridges and shells littered throughout its two storeys. It could also be established that explosives and machine guns had been used. Human remains and personal possessions were found under the stage and blood had dripped through the floorboards. Unusually these mass executions had not taken place at some remote spot, but in the centre of town on the main road from Zvornik to Bijeljina.

More killings took place at Kozluk between 14 and 17 July 1995. Some 500 or so prisoners were forced to sing Serbian songs on the trucks as they were transported to the execution site. The bodies were dumped in a quarry that has been used as a landfill site alongside the River Drina. This was accessible only by driving through the barracks occupied by the Drina Wolves, a regular police unit of *Republika Srpska*. One army excavator spent eight hours in Kozluk on 16 July, and an army truck made two journeys between Orahovac and Kozluk that day. A bulldozer was also active in Kozluk on 18 and 19 July. The grave had been partially cleared between 7 and 27

September 1995, but investigators found 340 bodies there. In 292 cases, the victim had clearly been killed by rifle fire: in 83 cases, they had been killed by a single shot to the head; in 76 by one shot through the torso; in 72 by multiple gunfire wounds; five were wounds to the legs; and one killed by gunshot wounds to the arm. The estimated age of the victims ranged between 8 and 85. A number of bodies showed signs of pre-existing disability or chronic disease, ranging from arthritis to amputations. The sick as well as the healthy had been murdered. Many had clearly been tied and bound, using strips of clothing or nylon thread. Fifty-five blindfolds and 168 ligatures were discovered.

Along the ?ancari Road are 12 known mass graves. One of them, '?ancari Road 3', was a secondary grave linked to Kozluk. In addition to the usual analyses of soil, material and shell cases, fragments of green glass bottles and bottle labels from the Vitinka bottling factory near the Kozluk site were found in both graves. The remains of 158 victims were found at ?ancari Road 3. Thirty-five bodies were still more or less intact and indicated that most had been killed by gunfire. All were male. Eight blindfolds and 37 ligatures were found.

Another ?ancari Road site, '?ancari Road 1', was the secondary site of the Branjevo Military Farm mass grave. At least 174 bodies were found there but only 43 complete sets of remains. In cases where the cause of death could be established, it was the result of rifle fire. Of the 313 various body parts found, 145 displayed gunshot wounds of a severity likely to prove fatal.

More killings took place along the Bratunac-Konjevi? Polje road. Serb soldiers summarily executed hundreds of Bosniacs, including women and children, near Konjevi? Polje on 13 July. Men trying to escape along the Bratunac-Konjevi? Polje road were informed that the Geneva Convention would be observed if they turned themselves in. In Bratunac, they were told Serb soldiers would escort them to Zagreb for an exchange of prisoners. United Nations uniforms and vehicles taken from the Dutch reassured them. Some 150 or 200 Bosniacs were captured there on 17 and 18 July; about half of them were summarily executed.

After the closure of the corridor at Baljkovica, several groups of stragglers tried to escape into Bosnian territory. A number captured by Bosnian Serb forces in the area of Nezuk and Baljkovica were killed on the spot. Around Nezuk, some 20 small groups surrendered to Serb troops, who lined them up and they were then summarily executed. On 19 July, a group of around 11 men were killed in Nezuk itself. Nearby, another 13 men, all Bosnian soldiers, were executed that day. One Bosnian soldier on his way to Tuzla witnessed several executions carried out by police on 19 July. He survived because 30 Bosnian soldiers were needed for an exchange of prisoners following the capture of a Serb officer at Baljkovica.

On 20 July to 21 July, near the village of Meces, Serb soldiers used megaphones to urge Bosniac refugees from Srebrenica to surrender, assuring them of their safety. When some 350 men did so, the Serbs took around 150 of them, made them dig their own graves and then shot them. The following day an excavator was used to dig a large pit. Around 260 captured Bosniac men were forced to stand around it and told not to move or they would be shot. Those who did move were shot. The rest were pushed into the hole and buried alive.

Small groups of Bosniacs hid in the woods and survived by eating mushrooms, leaves and snails. Then on 23 July, the Bosnian Serbs began a sweep through the area, killing anyone they found. Meanwhile, the Serb army began clearing the bodies from around Srebrenica, Kamenica, Snagovo and Zepa. Municipal services were called in to help. In Srebrenica itself, the refuse left by the refugees that littered the streets was collected and burnt, while the town itself was disinfected and deloused.

From 1 August to 1 November 1995, there was an organised effort to remove the bodies from primary mass gravesites and re-bury them. The ICTY found that this re-burial effort was evidence of the organised nature of the massacres and the noncombatant status of the victims – if the victims died in normal combat operations, there would be no need to make such elaborate provisions to hide their remains.

By 2006, 42 mass graves had been discovered in and around Srebrenica; investigator specialists believed 22 more to be in existence. By then, 2,070 victims had been identified while body parts that filled more than 7,000 bags awaited identification.

In 1996, the Dutch Institute for War Documentation began an investigation into the massacre at Srebrenica. Published in 2002, its report details the mass murder of some 8,000. The government of *Republika Srpska* immediately issued a report claiming the Srebrenica massacre had never happened. Only 2,000 had died, it said. All had been soldiers from the Bosnian Army and many had died of 'exhaustion'. Nevertheless, on 30 September 2003 former US President Bill Clinton officially opened the Genocide Memorial at Srebrenica. The following year, the ICTY's presiding judge Theodor Meron made a speech there, saying: 'By seeking to eliminate a part of the Bosnian Muslims, the Bosnian Serb forces committed genocide. They targeted for extinction the 40,000 Bosnian Muslims living in Srebrenica, a group which was emblematic of the Bosnian Muslims in general. They stripped all the male Muslim prisoners, military and civilian, elderly and young, of their personal belongings and identification, and deliberately and methodically killed them solely on the basis of their identity.'

Then in 2004, Paddy Ashdown, High Representative for

Bosnia and Herzegovina, forced the government of *Republika Srpska* to form a committee to investigate the events. Its report, released that October, confirmed the names of 8,731 missing and dead persons from Srebrenica – 7,793 who disappeared or were killed between 10 July and 19 July 1995 and a further 938 afterwards. Serb nationalists disputed this, claiming that Ashdown pressured the committee to dismiss the earlier report exonerating the Serbs. Despite this, the new President of *Republika Srpska* Dragan ?avic made a televised address admitting that Serb forces killed several thousand civilians at Srebenica in violation of international law and on 10 November 2004 the government of *Republika Srpska* issued an official apology. The following year they called on Radovan Karadzic to hand himself in.

If further evidence was needed, it came in the form of a video tape introduced at the trial of Slobodan Milosevic, in The Hague on 2 June 2005. After receiving the blessing of an Orthodox priest, soldiers were shown tying up six captives, dressed in civilian clothing, and physically abusing them. Victims were later identified as two men in their early twenties and four minors, as young as 16. The tape then shows four of them being executed and then lying dead in the field (the cameraman could then be heard to complain that the camera's battery was almost exhausted). Still it had the power to record the soldiers ordering the remaining captives to take the dead bodies into a nearby barn. Once they had done this, they were also killed. The former soldiers on the video were quickly identified and arrested.

The killers were not without their sympathisers, though. On 6 July 2005, just days before a ceremony to mark the tenth anniversary of the massacre, the police found two powerful bombs at the memorial site that would have caused widespread loss of life and injury, had they exploded.

The following day, NATO troops arrested Karadzic's son, Aleksandar, on the grounds that he was 'suspected of giving support to a war crimes suspect indicted by the International Criminal Tribunal for the Former Yugoslavia'. He was released after 10 days. Then, on 28 July 2005, Karadzic's wife Ljiljana called for him to surrender for the sake of their family, who were under 'constant pressure from all sides'.

On 25 January 2007, Bosnian newspaper *Oslobodjenje* reported that Karadzic was hiding in Russia. An unnamed official of the State Investigation and Protection Agency was quoted as saying: 'We got this information by wiretapping a telephone conversation abroad.'

The Russian Embassy in Sarajevo denied the allegation and the Federal Migration Service in Moscow stated that it had no information to indicate that Karadzic was hiding in Russia. Nevertheless, the passports of his wife, son, daughter and son-in-law were seized at the request of the ICTY. They were suspected of helping him evade capture.

On 18 July 2008, Radovan Karadzic was arrested in Belgrade, where he had been living openly under a false identity. Having grown a large white beard and his hair long, he posed as a practitioner of alternative medicine under the name Dragan Dabic. A regular contributor to a health magazine, he even gave public lectures. Living alone in a modern tower block, he told his girlfriend that he had found grandsons who lived in America. He drank red wine and sang songs accompanied by the gusle – a one-stringed Serbian instrument – in a local bar sporting pictures of him and his fellow fugitive Ratko Mladic. A neighbour said that he was a very polite man, who always said hello: 'The only thing which was weird was that he was wearing black all the time and with that hair, and he seemed to me like he was in a sect or something.'

Describing himself a 'Spiritual Explorer' and an expert in 'Human Quantum Energy', Karadzic walked freely round the city and spoke publicly comparing meditation to the silent techniques practised by Orthodox monks.

'The person I got to know was a person that everybody would like to be their friend,' said Goran Kojic, editor of the Belgrade magazine *Healthy Life*. 'He was a highly cultured man, he was very tolerant, he had a sense of humour, he was very positive, he was very intellectual – so he was a great person.' In fact, members of Kojic's family had died in the siege of Sarajevo.

'I was shocked to hear who he really is,' said Gordana Blagojevic, the owner of a shop, where Karadzic bought yogurt and wholegrain bread, sometimes accompanied by his girlfriend.

Karadzic was sent to The Hague, where he was held in the same cell as his former mentor Slobodan Milosevic. In a written submission he told the court that US Dayton negotiator Richard Holbrooke had told him that he would not be prosecuted for war crimes if he disappeared from the scene. Holbrooke denied this. In August 2008, he refused to plead to all 11 charges against him. The court entered non-guilty pleas for him.

Despite the charges against him, for some Serbs Karadzic remains a war hero and his creation *Republica Srpska* still exists. However, there can be little doubt that he is responsible for the deaths of over 11,000 people at Sarajevo, 8,000 in Srebrenica and thousands more in the 'ethnic cleansing' of Bosnia. He brought back to Europe a standard of barbarity not seen since Hitler's death.

CHAPTER FIVE

CHARLES TAYLOR

In The Hague, Radovan Karadzic joined former Liberian warlord Charles Taylor, who was being tried on 11 counts of war crimes and crimes against humanity. These included terrorism, murder, rape, sexual slavery, mutilation and recruiting child soldiers. The charges only related to his part in Sierra Leone's brutal civil war, not to barbarity in his home country or the other neighbouring countries he sought to destabilise. A spokesman for Human Rights Watch called him, 'one of the single greatest causes of spreading wars in West Africa.'

Charles McArthur Taylor was born on 28 January 1948 in Arthington, Liberia, 16 miles north of the capital, Monrovia. He was the third of 15 children. His mother was a member of the Gola tribe of indigenous Africans, while his father was an Americo-Liberian. They were descendants of freed American slaves returned to West Africa in the early nineteenth century. As founders of Liberia as a country in the modern sense, they regarded themselves as élite and although they made up just five per cent of the population, they held power consistently until a coup by Master Sergeant Samuel Doe in 1980.

Taylor's father was a schoolteacher of modest means. At first, his son wanted to follow in his footsteps. Like many Americo-Liberians, Taylor studied in the US. In 1972, he arrived at Bentley College in Waltham, Massachusetts, graduating with a degree in Economics in 1977. While there, he became a leader of Liberian dissidents. He mounted a demonstration against Liberian President William Tolbert when he visited the States in 1979 and was briefly arrested after threatening to take over the Liberian diplomatic mission in New York. An Americo-Liberian, Tolbert was resented by the indigenous Africans. Later, Taylor took the name 'Ghankay' – 'The Warrior' – and claimed his mother's Gola heritage in a bid to appeal to Liberians of direct African descent.

In April 1980, when Tolbert was overthrown and killed by Master Sergeant – later General – Samuel Doe, Taylor joined his government, landing a plum job running Liberia's General Services Agency, which gave him control of much of the country's budget. But he fled back to the US in 1983, after being accused of embezzling $900,000. Intended for machine parts, it had turned up in a bank account in New York. Already he had earned the nickname 'Superglue' as money seemed to stick to his hands.

In 1984 he was arrested in the US and held in the Plymouth County House of Correction in Massachusetts under a Liberian warrant. Facing extradition back to Liberia, he escaped from jail with another four inmates by sawing through the bars on a window and climbing to the ground using a knotted sheet. Others claim there was some collusion in his departure by the American authorities who were becoming disillusioned with the corrupt and repressive regime of Samuel Doe, who seemed to be pocketing much of their aid. According to Taylor's lawyer, former US Attorney-General Ramsey Clark, no charges were ever filed against him as a result of the jailbreak.

Taylor headed for Mexico, then to Ghana at the

invitation of Dr H. Boima Fahnbulleh, another of Doe's former ministers. A week after arriving in Accra, he was arrested on the grounds that he had got out of the US so easily that he must be a spy for the CIA. After three months he was released and granted political asylum. He befriended the Ambassador of Burkina Faso, who arranged an audience with the country's 37-year-old President Thomas Sankara, who was seen as something of a hero by West African revolutionaries.

After being jailed again briefly in Ghana, Taylor headed for Burkina Faso, where he joined a group of Liberian exiles, including Prince Yormie Johnson, who became his lieutenant. They received military training assistance from the Burkinabe government. However, they received an approach from Blaise Compaore, commander of Burkino Faso's élite parachute regiment who was linked by marriage to President of the Ivory Coast, Felix Houphouet-Boigny. Compaore had his own ambitions. He hired the Liberians to assassinate Thomas Sankara, once his close friend, and install him as president.

Once Compaore had seized power, he showed his gratitude by introducing Taylor to Colonel Gadaffi, who was eager to build a pan-African revolutionary force. Having recently survived the 1986 American air strike on his palace in Tripoli that had killed his 15-month-old adopted daughter, Hanna, Gadaffi was particularly keen to overthrow Samuel Doe in Liberia, by now the centre of US intelligence gathering in the area. However, Taylor's high-level contacts bred jealousy among other Liberia dissidents.

In training camps in Libya, Taylor met other African malcontents, including Foday Sankoh – later to launch the Revolutionary United Front in Sierra Leone. They formed an alliance against the pro-Western regimes in West Africa. Travelling on a Burkino Faso passport, Taylor travelled around West Africa rallying support. However, he received a less than sympathetic hearing in Freetown, where he was briefly jailed. He offered the notoriously venal President Joseph Momoh cash in return for permission for his Liberia guerrillas to operate out of neighbouring Sierra Leone. In a move that would have dire consequences for the country, Momoh promptly went to Doe, who offered more money to prevent Taylor from using Sierre Leone as a base.

With the backing of Blaise Compaore in Burkino Faso and Felix Houphouet-Boigny in the Ivory Coast, Taylor established the National Patriotic Front of Liberia (NPFL), a guerrilla army consisting of Gio and Mano tribesmen from northern Liberia, who had been persecuted under Doe's regime.

On 24 December 1989, Taylor crossed the border from the Ivory Coast into Liberia's northern Nimba County with around 100 men. As they pushed out of Nimba County towards Monrovia, they undertook a full-scale ethnic purge. Seizing the port of Buchanan on 19 May 1990, they killed hundreds of Krahn and Mandingo who had taken refuge there. Five hundred were slaughtered in the Mandingo town of Bakedu, where the Imam was reportedly beheaded, his severed head placed on a copy of the Koran. Later the NPFL was accused of burning 1,000 mosques and Islamic schools. Journalists also discovered heaps of unburied corpses on waste ground at the end of Spriggs Payne airfield outside Monrovia.

From the beginning, the NPFL recruited child soldiers, many of them orphaned by the war. They proved fearless fighters and intensely loyal to 'pappy' Charles Taylor. Bizarrely, they took to wearing women's clothing, fright wigs and various voodoo regalia, believing this would protect them from being killed. AK47-toting killers would be seen in wedding dresses, evening gowns and frilly blouses. Some donned shower caps and feather boas, and carried dainty purses. Girls were also recruited; they painted their faces white.

Taylor's   child   soldiers   were   also   fortified   by amphetamines, marijuana and palm wine. One of the most notorious commanders in the war was Joshua Milton Blahyi, whose *nom de guerre* was 'General Butt Naked'. He went into battle wearing only laced-up boots and his weapon, and admitted to meeting Satan and sacrificing children.

'Before leading my troops into battle,' he revealed, 'we would get drunk and drugged-up, sacrifice a local teenager, drink their blood, then strip down to our shoes and go into battle wearing colourful wigs and carrying dainty purses we'd looted from civilians. We'd slaughter anyone we saw, chop their heads off and use them as soccer balls. We were nude, fearless, drunk and homicidal. We killed hundreds of people – so many I lost count.'

Taylor's forces were commanded by Elmer Johnson, a close friend since they studied together in Massachusetts: Johnson had served in both the Liberian Army and the US Marines, participating in the invasion of Grenada in 1983. He lost an eye during an early coup attempt against Doe and had teamed up with Taylor again in Libya. Though he trained his men rigorously to instil discipline, Johnson was popular with the rank and file, so much so that Taylor grew fearful that his friend might have ambitions of his own. However, on 4 June 1980 Johnson was killed in an ambush. The Liberian Army claimed responsibility but there were rumours that he had been murdered on Taylor's orders.

Around that time another ally, Moses Duopu – who Taylor had known since his student activist days in the US and to whom he was related by marriage – was killed. There was no conclusive proof but again it was thought Taylor was responsible.

In July 1990 the popular politician Jackson Doe – who was seen as the rightful winner of the 1985 election that Samuel Doe had rigged – came over to the NPFL lines to widespread jubilation. Taylor had him slaughtered with a bayonet, some say beheaded. He then drank his blood. Between June and

August 1990, some 80 people – anyone who might mount a challenge to Taylor – were murdered behind NPFL lines. This was not well known at the time as the world's news cameras were focused on the public killings.

To help evacuate foreign nationals, a force of some 2,000 US Marines were anchored off the coast. Many hoped they would intervene to prevent further bloodshed, but on 2 August 1990 Iraq invaded Kuwait and all America's forces were needed to fight the first Gulf War. Instead, ECOMOG – the Economic Community of West African States Ceasefire Monitoring Group – stepped in with a force largely composed of Nigerian soldiers. Taylor had already been taking Nigerian nationals hostage because President General Ibrahim Babangida was an ally of Samuel Doe. Now he began to seize nationals of other ECOMOG countries and threatened to kill ten of them for every single NPFL man killed by ECOMOG. President Babangida, he said, was 'a black Hitler.'

Despite his ruthless purge, Taylor still had rivals within his own ranks. A split developed in the NPFL between Taylor's men and Prince Johnson's élite Black Scorpions. Johnson, a former military policeman trained in South Carolina, had been with Taylor since their time in Burkina Faso. With the rebel forces besieging Monrovia, he accused Taylor of killing both his mother and other members of his family.

After clashes between rival forces, Prince Johnson broke away to form his own Independent National Patriotic Front. He then seized the initiative. In Monrovia, his men captured, tortured and killed Samuel Doe. In a video that went on sale, Johnson is seen sipping a Budweiser and being fanned by a female attendant while Doe's ear is cut off. In some versions, he is also shown eating the ear. Through the act of killing Samuel Doe, Prince Johnson assumed the right to become natural successor.

In the months that followed, Taylor and Johnson fought

for Monrovia. Johnson had most of the trained Liberian fighters under his control, but Taylor threw his fanatic boy soldiers against them.

The Economic Community of West Africa attempted to broker a peace. Negotiations in Banjul, Gambia, were set up in the Interim Government of National Unity under Dr Amos Sawyer. Prince Johnson was persuaded to accepted asylum in Nigeria, but Taylor refused to attend the conference, preferring to continue the civil war. He took on peacekeepers sent by Gambia, Ghana, Guinea, Nigeria and Sierra Leone to bolster ECOMOG, while observers sent by the United National Observer Mission in Liberia were held hostage.

While the Interim Government established itself in Monrovia, Taylor's men surrounded the city, setting up checkpoints manned by gun-toting children and decorated with human skulls. At these checkpoints you could be shot or maimed simply because the guard spotted a gold ring or a pair of shoes that they wanted. Often the killings were purely for ethnic reasons. Fighters from the countryside would be particularly hard on Monrovians from their own tribe. Esther Paygar, a police captain from Nimba County, was spared because she was from the 'right' ethnic background, but it was then discovered that the father of her three children was Krahn. She was forced to watch while they were beheaded.

During this time, many personal scores were settled. Children killed teachers who had failed them. Those who showed signs of prosperity – expensive clothes or a fat belly – were also murdered. The US embassy estimated that at one checkpoint, known as 'No Return', no fewer than 2,000 were killed during 1990, their bodies left to rot in the surrounding bush.

There were numerous acts of random violence. Eyewitness James Samuels, who escaped through Sierra Leone, reported that after seeing an NPFL fighter named

Young Killer murder a couple on a whim, he saw another rebel dressed in a skirt, stockings and a woman's wig walking along a line of refugees, begging in mock supplication to let him kill them. He pulled people randomly out of line and shot them, then announced that he liked the number 20. Counting backwards down the line, he pulled out the twentieth refugee and shot them. Samuels also recalled how he saw another young rebel empty a sack of severed penises on the ground in front of his commander. It transpired there were 52 of them and the commander joked that, from now on, the youngster should be known as 'Fifty-two Reporter'.

The drugs used to make the child soldiers fearless also kept them dependent on their commanders. Generals were seen smoking joints the size of hot-dogs, while their young fighters, high on 'bubble' as they called amphetamines, modelled themselves on Rambo and gangster rappers. One child soldier, calling himself MC Ram Dee, entertained comrades with a rap that ran:

I am a rebel
I fought off the trouble
I took the bubble
I said double trouble
I'm a man who's not stable...

In an interview these children frequently said that they loved their 'pappy', Charles Taylor, and did as he ordered without question because they believed he loved them too.

With Taylor in control of the countryside outside Monrovia, logging companies and mining outfits were forced to deal with him. He negotiated personally and levied a tax in US dollars on each transaction. The US ambassador estimated he had $75million a year passing through his hands though his income soared to $100million, if the money he made from exporting marijuana from northern Liberia was added in. Fishermen were told that every fish in the sea belonged to Taylor.

While the Interim Government in Monrovia grappled with the national debt they had inherited, Taylor was free to spend his cash on arms from the countries of the former Warsaw Pact and his men were allowed to supplement their income by looting the towns under their control. Taylor continued his attempts to take Monrovia and the resulting atrocities filled more mass graves. Twelve peace accords were negotiated and broken.

After a change of regime in Nigeria, however, a thirteenth peace accord was negotiated and on 31 August 1995, Taylor drove into Monrovia. He was dressed in white, 'making every effort to appear as a Messiah,' it was said, 'like Christ arriving in Jerusalem on Palm Sunday'. Not that this put an end to the fighting. Taylor's bodyguards were involved in a fist fight with those of another faction when both their leaders tried to use the lift in the Executive Mansion at the same time. Then, on 31 October 1996, an attempt was made on Taylor's life. ECOMOG soldiers found him hiding in one of the presidential bathrooms.

Taylor tricked another faction leader Roosevelt Johnson into resisting ECOMOG and then, with arms supplied by Nigeria, he launched his attack. In just days, more than 2,000 were killed in Monrovia. The US was forced to pressurise the Nigerian government to quell the fighting. Meanwhile, Taylor quietly tightened his grip on the rest of the country.

An uneasy peace ensued and the civil war officially ended with the elections in 1997, when Taylor ran on the slogan: 'I killed your ma, I killed your pa, you will vote for me'. Seventy-five per cent of war-weary electorate did just that, fearing if he did not win then the fighting would continue – and with good reason. Between 1989 and 1997, it is estimated that 150,000 Liberians were murdered, that is 1 out of every 17. Countless others were mutilated and 25,000 women and girls were raped. Entire villages were cleared. Hundreds of thousands fled to neighbouring countries and the entire region was destabilised.

While fighting his own civil war, Taylor supported Foday Sankoh and his Revolutionary United Front in Sierra Leone. In March 1991, he sent some of his toughest units with the RUF across the border into Sierra Leone to take revenge on President Momoh, who had slighted Taylor when he was trying to launch the war and had provided a base for ECOMOG forces. They attacked villages in the diamond-rich district around Koindu. By proxy, the war in Sierra Leone became an extension of the Liberian conflict, with the RUF acting for the NPFL and the Sierra Leone army for ECOMOG. In return for blood diamonds, Taylor smuggled weapons to Sankoh. The RUF became notorious for mass rape and hacking off the hands, feet, ears and noses of thousands of civilians during the 10-year civil war. Sankoh also authorised Operation 'Pay Yourself' which encouraged his troops to loot and he did not hesitate to kill allies questioning his brutal tactics.

When Sankoh found himself under arrest in Nigeria, Taylor supported his deputy Sam Bockarie, who fought alongside him in Liberia. Nicknamed 'Mosquito' for his ability to attack enemies when they were off-guard, Bockarie was advised by him throughout the fighting. At the end of the civil war in Sierra Leone, Bockarie fled to Liberia. It is thought that Taylor then used him to assassinate Ivory Coast rebel leader Felix Doh on 25 April 2003. Taylor came under international pressure to hand Bockarie over to the Special Court for Sierra Leone, which had indicted both Sankoh and Bockarie for war crimes and crimes against humanity. Eventually Bockarie was killed in a shoot-out with the Liberian authorities sent to arrest him, although it is thought that he was killed deliberately to prevent him testifying against Taylor – also indicted by the

Special Court. Sankoh had already been arrested, but died in custody while awaiting trial.

Following the election of Taylor, the fighting did not cease in Liberia. In 1999, Liberians United for Reconciliation and Democracy – thought to be with the backing of neighbouring Guinea – rebelled against his rule in northern Liberia. Taylor's response was brutal. Those suspected of supporting the LURD were then beaten, tortured or summarily executed. In some cases, they were confined to houses that the soldiers set on fire, so the victims were burnt to death. Often young women and girls were raped and forced to become 'wives' to the soldiers. Young men used as forced labour were made to carry looted goods and captured weapons; villages were systematically razed to the ground. Children were conscripted and sent to the front without proper training.

According to Human Rights Watch, in April 2001 Taylor's troops raided a small clinic in Sasahun and executed six adults, including one patient who was recovering from an appendix operation. Three months later, they rounded up hundreds of civilians and burned at least 15 of them to death in Kamatehun, near the border with Guinea.

In September 2001, scores of ethnic Gbandi civilians captured in the bush by Taylor's troops were taken to Kamatehun, where troops forcibly confined some 30 of them in four houses and burned them to death. Troops killed another 15 civilians by cutting their throats. Later that month, three youths accused of supporting the LURD were detained and killed by government soldiers in Masambalahun, eight miles to the south. The following month soldiers forced civilians caught hiding to carry boxes of ammunition to Vahun – on the border with Sierra Leone – and then lined up and shot six of them. Another six were confined to a house and burned to death.

In December 2001, soldiers who had driven LURD forces from Kolahun fired indiscriminately into houses in the town, killing civilians. They also gang-raped six women, including a 12-year-old girl and a woman who was pregnant. On leaving the town, they forced civilians to carry the goods they had looted to Foya, two-and-a-half hours' walk away. That same month, between Yenahun and Kamatehun, government soldiers raped a number of women and executed a family who tried to leave.

In January 2002, at Sawmill, Taylor's soldiers shot a 30-year-old woman point-blank in the forehead, killing her. Her four-year-old son was wounded when she opened the door to her house. In February 2002, officers from the Anti-Terrorism Unit detained and tortured three men accused of being rebels in Klay. It cannot be doubted Charles Taylor was responsible: his son Charles Taylor Jr was head of the ATU. Known to victims as the 'Demon Forces', it was largely manned by Taylor loyalists from The Gambia and Burkina Faso specialising in theft, looting and murder, often at random. Then again, on 19 June 2002, an ATU officer and presidential guards opened fire on a taxicab in Monrovia, killing a six-year-old and critically injuring his mother and the driver.

In September Lieutenant Isaac Gono, a driver attached to Charles Taylor Jr's command, was beaten to death by colleagues in a disciplinary measure for denting a vehicle. Four ATU men and former Deputy Minister of Labour Bedell Fahn were arrested for torturing two Nigerian men to death in October 2001. Fahn was sentenced to ten months in prison, but soon released. Two ATU members were acquitted.

One of Taylor's first acts as president had been to fill the ranks of the security and police forces with his own men, purging anyone who dared to oppose him during the war. The newly created security forces, including the ATU and Special Security Service, reported directly to him and were free to commit abuses with impunity. At the ATU base at Gbatala, victims were held in water-filled holes in the ground, burned with molten plastic, beaten and sexually abused, and forced to drink urine and eat cigarette butts. Meanwhile, within the Liberian National Police the élite Special Operations Division created by Taylor and made up of his former guerrillas became known as responsible for arbitrary arrests, mistreatment and extortion.

Government soldiers and militia have been responsible for widespread looting, in towns and villages occupied by them and at checkpoints on the roads. Local residents are often forced to carry looted belongings and captured weapons long distances. As civilians flee areas of conflict, they are repeatedly made to pay government soldiers to pass through checkpoints to safety or cross the border into Sierra Leone. Meanwhile, journalists, human rights lawyers and representatives of international human rights organisations are arrested and held without charge.

When the United Nations also accused him of being a gunrunner and a diamond smuggler, having designated himself a Baptist lay preacher Taylor turned up at a mass prayer meeting dressed from head to foot in white. After addressing the meeting, he prostrated himself on the ground to pray for forgiveness, while simultaneously denying the charges.

As always, there was an ethnic dimension to the renewed civil war. The Taylor government indiscriminately accused ethnic Mandingos, Krahns and Gbandis of supporting rebel incursion. This allowed the LURD to recruit them. Then, in 2003 a second group of rebels, the Movement for Democracy in Liberia, backed the government of the Ivory Coast and went into action in the south. During rebel attacks on Monrovia in June–August 2003, government forces committed widespread rape and sexual violence, particularly around the Bushrod Island area to the north of Monrovia. Again, they relied heavily on child soldiers. By the end of the summer, Taylor's government controlled around a third of the country, Liberia's economy was in disarray, its infrastructure in ruins. Hundreds of thousands had died in the fighting and from now-endemic disease; much of the population was homeless and starving. Pressure was put on Taylor to stand down, but he refused to do so without the assurance that he would not be handed over to the Special Court for Sierra Leone to stand trial.

Eventually Nigeria offered asylum: the country would shield him from the Special Court provided he stayed out of politics. On 11 August 2003, in a ceremony conducted in front of South African President Thabo Mbeki, Ghanaian President John Kufuor and Mozambican President Joaquim Chissano, Taylor handed over power to his deputy Moses Blah and flew to Calabar, where the Nigerian government provided luxurious seaside mansions for him and his entourage. Thinking he was now safe, he continued to meddle in Liberian politics and remained unrepentant about his crimes. When the BBC's Robin White suggested during an interview that some people thought he was little better than a murderer, he replied: 'Jesus Christ was accused of being a murderer in his time.'

In 2003, the US Congress passed a bill that included an offer of a reward of $2million dollars for his capture. The US then presented a draft resolution to the UN Security Council seeking to freeze Taylor's assets and those of his family, while Interpol issued a 'red notice', giving countries the international right to arrest him. He appeared on Interpol's Most Wanted list, with a note warning that he could be dangerous.

Within weeks of taking office in January 2006, Ellen Johnson-Sirleaf, the new democratically elected President of Liberia and one-time support of Taylor, was pressured by the US to make an official request to Nigeria asking for his extradition. Forewarned, Taylor disappeared from his home in Calabar. A few days later, he was captured while trying to flee across the border into the Cameroon with two large boxes stuffed with cash.

The Nigerians flew him to Liberia. However, Mrs Johnson-Sirleaf did not want him in the country, fearing he would stir up trouble. During the election his party members had been seen on the streets shouting: '*Our pappy, dat dey carry, dey go bring back*' – 'Our leader, who they took away, will be brought back'. She handed him over to the UN, who flew him by helicopter to Freetown in Sierra Leone. There, he was charged on an amended indictment with 11 counts of war crimes and crimes against humanity. Appearing before the court on 3 April 2006, he pleaded not guilty. However, there were fears that his trial might reignite conflict in the area. Some Sierra Leoneans feared that, even from his cell, Taylor could mobilise a guerrilla army capable of attacking the court in Freetown from the surrounding hills. Once the UK agreed to give him space in a British prison if found guilty he was sent to The Hague to face trial.

Taylor is now charged with terrorising the civilian population in violation of the Geneva Conventions by burning civilian property; unlawful killing and violence to life, health and physical or mental wellbeing; rape, sexual slavery and other forms of sexual violence; outrages upon personal dignity in violation of the Geneva Conventions; the use of child soldiers; enslavement and pillage. Charges of inflicting collective punishments, extermination, murder, intentionally directing attacks against personnel involved in a humanitarian assistance or peacekeeping mission and hostage taking were dropped.

All the charges relate to crimes committed in Sierra Leone under the direction of Taylor or by those under the control of, or subordinate to him. For the crimes committed in Liberia, it seems he will go unpunished. Liberia now has a Truth and Reconciliation Committee sitting. However, his son has faced trial for crimes committed in Liberia: arraigned in Federal court in the US on eight counts of torture. Born in Boston, Charles Taylor

Jr is a US citizen and became the first person ever to be indicted under 1994 Federal anti-torture statutes. In October 2008, he was convicted of using electric shocks, scalding water, a hot iron, lit cigarettes, stinging ants, molten plastic and bayonets to torture victims between 1999 and 2003. Like father, like son.

CHAPTER SIX

IAN BRADY

There has long been debate as to who was really to blame for the 1960s Moors Murderers, where a couple's bizarre and deviant sexual relationship drove them to torture and murder defenceless children for pleasure in a case that appalled the world. Some have even painted blonde bombshell Myra Hindley as a femme fatale, who lured the rat-like Ian Brady into their excesses.

The problem with that theory is that Ian Brady was already deeply warped when Myra Hindley first met him. A 21-year-old stock clerk at Millwards chemical company in Manchester, his mind was full of sadistic fantasies. He had a collection of Nazi memorabilia and recordings of Nazi rallies; in his lunch hour, he read Hitler's *Mein Kampf* and studied German grammar. Brady believed then, as now, in the righteousness of the Nazi cause and regrets only that he could not have joined in with its sadistic excesses.

Ian Brady was born Ian Duncan Stewart on 2 January 1938 at the Rottenrow Maternity Hospital. He grew up in the tough Gorbals district of Glasgow. His parents were not married. His mother, Margaret 'Peggy' Stewart, was a tearoom waitress in a hotel. She claimed his father was a journalist who died a few months before their son was born, although he has never been identified. Peggy would sign herself as Mrs Stewart – at the time being an unmarried mother carried a strong social stigma.

With no husband to support her, she found it necessary to continue working as a waitress, if only part-time, to support herself and her newborn son. Often she was unable to afford a babysitter, so when she went out to work she would have to leave the baby home alone.

It soon became apparent that Peggy could not cope on her own and she began to advertise for permanent babysitters who might take the child into their home, providing the care and attention she was unable to give. John and Mary Sloane answered her advertisement. With four children of their own, they were reassuringly caring and trustworthy. Ian was just four months old when his mother handed him over to the Sloanes, along with his child allowance. At first, she would visit every Sunday with gifts for the growing boy. It was only later that he learnt she was his mother. For the moment, Mary Sloane was 'Ma'. Slowly, Peggy's visits became less frequent and they stopped altogether when her son was 12. By then, she had married an Irish labourer named Patrick Brady and had moved to Manchester with him.

Despite the Sloanes' best efforts to provide a loving environment, Ian felt he did not belong. Withdrawn and difficult, he had frequent temper tantrums, which often ended with him banging his head on the floor. At primary school he was similarly alienated. His fellow pupils saw him as secretive and an outsider; unlike the other boys, he did not play sport and was considered something of a cissy. His teachers regarded him as a bright child but complained that he never really applied himself.

When Ian was nine years old, he seems to have had an odd epiphany. The Sloanes had taken him on a picnic to the moors around Loch Lomond, the first time he had ever left the Gorbals. After lunch, his adoptive parents fell asleep on the grass. When they woke, Ian was 500 yards away, standing on the top of a steep slope. They whistled and called out to him, but could not attract his attention. For an hour, he stood there motionless, silhouetted against the vastness of the sky. Eventually, the two Sloane boys were sent to climb the hill and fetch him. He told them that the family should go home without him: he wanted to be alone.

On the way home on the bus Ian was unusually talkative and outgoing for the first time in his life. Alone on that hillside, he had felt himself at the centre of a limitless terrain, a kingdom that was his own; it filled him with a sense of strength and power. Although it was true that the moors gave him a sense of mystical power and his name would be forever associated with them, for most of his life he was to remain locked away from the open spaces and the sky.

At the age of 11, he was bright enough to pass the entrance exams to Shawlands Academy, a school for those with above-average intelligence. Once enrolled, he made no efforts to fulfil his evident potential, however. He was lazy, virtually gave up on schoolwork and began to misbehave. Eventually he left school early, with no formal qualifications. The only thing that seemed to interest him was the Nazis – he read books about them and they were virtually his sole topic of conversation. When he played war game with his friends, he always insisted on being a German.

Between the ages of 13 and 16, Ian was arrested three times for burglary and housebreaking. On the first two occasions he was given probation. The third time, he faced a custodial sentence, but the judge suspended this on the condition that he move to Manchester and live with his mother and her husband. At this point, he had not seen Peggy for four years and had never met his stepfather.

At the end of 1954, the 16-year-old moved to Moss Side. He knew no one there. With his strong Glaswegian accent, he found himself an outsider again. Although he did not get on with his stepfather, he took his name – Brady – and took the job that Patrick found for his stepson as a porter at the local market. Increasingly withdrawn, he found solace in books, particularly the works of the Marquis de Sade and Friedrich Nietzsche, giving particular attention to Nietzsche's theories of *Übermensch* and 'The Will to Power'. Like the Nazis, he believed this justified a philosophy that permitted cruelty and torture, where superior creatures had the right to control, even destroy, weaker ones. He was also drawn to Dostoyevsky's *Crime and Punishment*, where a young intellectual named Raskolnikov brutally murders an old pawnbroker woman on the grounds that some people, such as Julius Caesar and Napoleon, are above the everyday morality of good and evil.

Brady also indulged his sadistic fantasies by collecting books about torture, sadomasochism, domination and servitude, and he took a job as a butcher's assistant, where he cut up meat. This helped finance his gambling and heavy drinking, which led to a conviction and fine for being drunk in public. But his wages were never enough. A little over a year after he moved to Manchester, Brady returned to a life of crime. He was working in a brewery when his employers discovered that he had been stealing lead seals. Convicted for aiding and abetting, he was sentenced to two years in borstal, an institution for young offenders. As there were no places available for three months, he was sent to Strangeways Prison in Manchester at the age of 17. Of course this experience quickly toughened him up.

When Brady was finally moved on to Hatfield borstal in Yorkshire, he took advantage of the looser regime to run a book and brew his own alcohol. After a drunken scuffle with a warder, he was sent to Hull Prison. There, he actively

The second plane hits the Twin Towers in New York on the most infamous date in recent history: September 11, 2001. Although al-Qaeda leader Osama bin Laden (*inset*) has never been formally indicted for the attacks, both the American and British governments quickly established that he was responsible.

© *PA Photos*

Above left: After fighting a successful campaign against white-minority rule and taking the reigns of power of an independent Zimbabwe, Robert Mugabe was hailed by many as a true African hero. But, over the years, he has developed into a brutal dictator who has betrayed his own people and led his country to the brink of disaster.

Above right: A defaced election poster with a portrait of President Robert Mugabe on a street in Harare, April 2008.

Below left: Former Ethiopian president Mengistu Haile Marian directed the 'Red Terror' against supposed enemies of his regime. In December 2006 he was found guilty, in absentia, of genocide and could therefore face the death penalty – but Mengistu has been living in exile in Zimbabwe since 1992, under the protection of Robert Mugabe.

Below right: Ethiopian women, on Martyrs' Day in May 2007, hold photos of their loved ones who were victims of the Derg regime, led by Mengistu.

© PA Photos

Above: Bosnian Serb Leader Radovan Karadzic, photographed (*above left*) in April 1996, shortly before going into hiding to avoid charges of crimes against humanity. For over ten years he avoided capture living under a false identity (*above right*) and making a living peddling alternative medicine. He was finally arrested in July 2008.

Below: Former Liberian President, Charles Taylor, attending a religious gathering in July 2003. He is currently being held in The Hague and, at his first appearance in court, in 2006, he pleaded not guilty to a 650-count indictment. © *PA Photos*

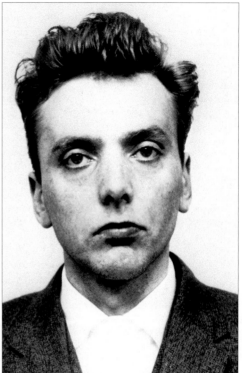

Above: The infamous mugshots of Myra Hindley and Ian Brady, the Moors Murderers.

Below: Heavily swathed in plastic sheeting, human remains are carried from a screened grave on Saddleworth Moor, October 1965. The body was eventually identified as that of 12-year-old John Kilbride, who had been abducted and murdered by Brady and Hindley almost two years previously.

© PA Photos

Above: Cult leader Charles Manson has now spent nearly 40 years in prison for his central role in the killing spree of 1969, inspired by his twisted interpretation of the songs from The Beatles' *White Album*. In March 2009, Corcoran State Prison released a recent photograph of the 74-year-old.

Below: The body of actress Sharon Tate, the wife of director Roman Polanski, is taken from their home in Bel Air, California, 9 August 1969. She and four others were found murdered by Charles Manson and his 'family'.

© PA Photos

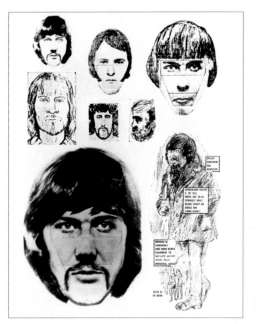

Above left: Identikit and photo-fit pictures of the Yorkshire Ripper.

Above right: The real Ripper, Peter Sutcliffe, who in 1981 was convicted of murdering 13 women. This picture was taken at his sister's wedding in 1980.

Below: The gruesome discovery of the Ripper's third victim, Irene Richardson, in Roundhay Park, Leeds, in February 1977. She had been bludgeoned to death with a hammer and, after killing her, Sutcliffe had mutilated her corpse with a knife.

© PA Photos

Above left: Civil servant Dennis Andrew Nilsen, who is known to have killed at least 15 boys and young men.

Above right: The entrance to Nilsen's second floor flat at 23, Cranley Gardens in Muswell Hill, London. Three men were murdered and dismembered at this address.

Below left: Police were called to 23 Cranley Gardens in February 1983 after a drain clearing company discovered a suspicious, sludgy, grey matter in the sewers outside the house. It was human flesh.

Below right: Nilsen enters a police van after appearing at Highgate Magistrates Court, London.
© *PA Photos*

Above left: Josef Fritzl, the Austrian man who was sentenced to life in a psychiatric prison for holding his daughter captive for 24 years and fathering her seven children.

Above right: A photo taken by a forensic team of the view into one of the secret, windowless rooms underneath Fritzl's house in Amstetten, Austria.

Below: Fritzl hides his face as he enters court, prior to the second day of his trial, 17 March 2009.

© PA Photos

sought to learn more of the criminal way of life in the hope of making a great deal of money. He also took a course in book-keeping.

After his release in November 1957, his family noticed he was even more silent and brooding than before. He was on the dole for several months before taking up work as a labourer at the Boddingtons Brewery between April and October 1958. Although still intent on a life of crime, he decided for the time being to put his book-keeping skills to legitimate use. In February 1959, he began work as a stock clerk at Millwards Merchandising. Almost two years later, in January 1961, a new shorthand typist arrived. Her name was Myra Hindley.

Myra had problems of her own. She was 19 when they met and was known as a loner and a daydreamer. Born in the Crumpsall district of Manchester on 23 July 1942, she was the first child of Bob and Hettie Hindley. Her father served in a parachute regiment during World War II, so he was away during the first three years of her life. Hettie lived with her mother, Ellen Maybury, who looked after Myra while Hettie went out to work as a machinist.

When Bob Hindley returned from the war, they found a house not far from Hettie's mother. Bob had trouble readjusting to civilian life. He worked as a labourer but spent a lot of his time in the local pub. Myra was reportedly beaten by her drunken father and he was allegedly violent towards Hettie. When their second child, Maureen, was born in August 1946, her parents decided to send Myra back to live with her grandmother, Ellen Maybury. This further alienated her from her father. The Hindleys divorced in 1965, around the time of Myra's arrest, and her mother subsequently remarried.

Myra attended Peacock Street Primary School from the age of five. She was considered sensible and mature, but her attendance was poor as her grandmother was lonely and kept the little girl at home on the slightest excuse.

Although Hindley had an IQ of 107, she failed her eleven-plus exam and was sent to the Ryder Brow Secondary Modern, where she was in the top stream. However, poor attendance continued to dog her academic career. She showed some flair for poetry and creative writing. It was noted that she was tough, aggressive and rather masculine, enjoying contact sports and judo. Athletic and a strong swimmer, she was not considered particularly feminine. She was teased about the shape of her nose and nicknamed 'Square Arse'.

Considered a responsible girl, Myra was much in demand as a babysitter in her teens. She was capable and demonstrated a genuine love of children. When she was 15, she befriended 13-year-old Michael Higgins. A shy and delicate boy, she took him under her wing. She was devastated when he drowned in a nearby reservoir where the local kids used to swim; also racked with guilt. He had asked her to come with him that day, but she had been busy and believed that she could have saved him, had she been there.

Hindley was inconsolable. Her moods fluctuated between black depression and hysteria. Her family grew concerned. She collected money from neighbours for a wreath. Michael had been a Catholic and she visited his church each night to light a candle for his soul, eventually converting to Catholicism herself. Her grief took a further toll on her school work and she left before sitting her O-levels.

After leaving school in 1957, her first job was as a junior clerk at Lawrence Scott and Electrometers, an electrical engineering firm in Gorton. She was much like other teenage girls at the time: she would go to cafés and dances, danced to rock'n'roll and flirted with the local boys. Eager to look older, she wore dark make-up and puffed on the occasional cigarette.

On her seventeenth birthday, she got engaged to Ronnie Sinclair, who worked as a tea-blender at the local Co-op store. Given the constraints of the times, it seemed that her life was laid out for her: she would marry and they would buy a small house, settle down and have kids. It soon became clear that she craved a more exciting life and broke off the engagement.

Myra filled out application forms to join both the Army and the Navy, but she never sent them in. The opportunity came up to work as a nanny in America, but she never followed it through. She went down to London in search of a job, but when she found nothing suitable, she returned to Manchester.

On 16 January 1961, she started work at Millwards. As soon as she saw Ian Brady, Hindley said she felt an 'immediate and fatal attraction'. While others found him sullen and morose, she thought him taciturn and aloof. These characteristics she regarded as 'enigmatic, worldly and a sign of intelligence'. Most of the men she knew she considered immature, dull, naive, and unambitious, but Brady was well-dressed and rode a motorbike. Everything about him fascinated her.

'Ian wore a black shirt today and looked smashing... I love him,' she wrote in her diary.

For nearly a year Brady took no notice of her.

'The pig! He didn't even look at me today,' she wrote more than once.

At the Christmas office party on 22 December 1961, Brady's tongue was loosened by a few drinks and he finally asked her out. 'Eureka!' she wrote in her diary. 'Today we have our first date. We are going to the cinema.' The film? *Judgment at Nuremberg*.

Soon Hindley surrendered her virginity to Brady. She was madly in love and wrote schoolgirlishly: 'I hope Ian and I love each other all our lives and get married and are happy ever after.'

But their relationship was far more sophisticated than that. Hindley became Brady's love slave. He introduced her to sadomasochism and lent her books on Nazi atrocities; he also took pornographic photographs of her and filmed them having sex. Some of the pictures showed the weals of a whip across her buttocks. He said he was going to sell the pictures. Instead they kept them in a scrapbook.

Brady played her Nazi marching songs and encouraged her to read some of his favourite books – *Mein Kampf, Crime and Punishment*, books on Nazi atrocities and the works of the Marquis de Sade. Besotted, Hindley complied with anything he asked of her. At his behest, she bleached her hair blonde, wore long, high-heeled boots and leather miniskirts. He called her 'Myra Hess' – or 'Hessie' – after Hitler's deputy Rudolf Hess and the sadistic concentration camp guard Irma Grese.

Family and friends soon noticed the change in her. At work she became surly, overbearing and aggressive. Her sister Maureen later testified that, after meeting Brady, Myra no longer lived the normal life of a teenage girl, going to dances with girlfriends. Instead she became secretive. She gave up babysitting, claiming that she hated babies. And when Brady told her there was no God, she stopped going to church. Within six months, Brady moved in with Hindley at her grandmother's house. By then Hindley's grandmother was a frail woman who spent most of her time in bed, giving them the run of the place.

With Hindley as a submissive acolyte, Brady's ideas became more outrageous. When he told her that rape and murder were not wrong, in fact murder was the 'supreme pleasure', she did not question his views. Early in 1963, Brady wanted to put his lover's obedience to the test. He began planning a bank robbery and told her that he needed her to be his getaway driver. Immediately she began driving lessons, bought two guns and joined the Cheadle Rifle club to practise. He never went ahead with the crime, but Hindley had shown herself willing.

Now he knew she would do whatever he asked, whatever the consequences.

Brady was ready to indulge his most perverse fantasies. He was about to step over the mark, like Raskolnikov in *Crime and Punishment*, to find out whether he was, like Caesar and Napoleon, above everyday morality. Then, he thought, he could lead the life that others could only dream about. What he himself dreamed about was the rape, torture and murder of children – children that the compliant Hindley would not balk at providing.

Their first victim was one of Hindley's neighbours, 16-year-old Pauline Reade. On the night of 12 July 1963, Pauline was on her way to a dance at the Railway Workers' Social Club. Originally, she had planned to go with her three girlfriends, Pat, Barbara and Linda, but when their parents learned that alcohol was being served, they forbade them. Determined not to miss out, Pauline decided to go alone.

Wearing her prettiest pink party dress, she left home at eight o'clock. Pat and her friend Dorothy had seen her leave home. Curious to see whether their friend would really have the nerve to go to the dance alone, they followed her. When they had almost reached the club, the two girls decided to take a short cut so they could get there before her. When they arrived, there was no sign of her. They waited, but she never turned up.

On the way, Pauline had accepted a lift from Hindley, who asked her to help her find a missing glove in exchange for a record. They drove up to Saddleworth Moor. Brady followed on his motorbike. Reaching the Moor, Hindley stopped and they got out. Pauline was innocently searching undergrowth when Brady pounced on her. He fractured her skull with a spade and then raped her before slitting her throat with a knife. The cut was so deep that her spinal cord was severed and she was practically decapitated. They buried her body in a grave three-feet deep.

When Pauline had still not arrived home by midnight, her parents went out to look for her, spending the rest of the night on a fruitless search. In the morning, they called the police. They too failed to find any trace of the missing girl. She had simply vanished without trace. Her body was not discovered until 1 July 1987.

Four months later, Hindley hired a car and another child disappeared. On 23 November 1963, 12-year-old John Kilbride and his friend John Ryan spent that Saturday afternoon in the cinema. When the film finished at five o'clock, they went to the market in Ashton-under-Lyne to see if they could earn a few shillings helping the traders pack up their stalls. The last time John Ryan saw his friend he was standing beside a salvage bin near the carpet dealer's stall while Ryan went to catch the bus home.

Like most kids, John Kilbride had been warned not to go with strange men, but back in the 1960s, no one thought to warn children of strange women. When he was approached by Hindley, Kilbride agreed to go with her to help carry some boxes to her car. Brady was sitting in the back. Tragically, the young boy got in. When they reached the Moors, Hindley stopped the car. Brady got out and took the child with him. While Hindley waited, Brady subjected the 12-year-old to a sexual assault and then tried to slit his throat with a six-inch serrated blade. When this failed to kill him, he strangled him with a ligature – a piece of string or possibly a shoelace – and buried his body in a shallow grave.

When John did not return home for dinner, his parents called the police, who began a major search. With thousands of volunteers, the police combed the surrounding area for clues. They found nothing. Once again, a child had gone missing without a trace.

When Hindley returned the hire car it was covered in the distinctive peaty mud of Saddleworth Moor but no one was any the wiser. Brady and Hindley laughed when they read about the massive police search for the missing boy. John Kilbride's family were naturally distraught: all they knew was that their son had not come home. They would only discover what had happened to him when his body was found on the moor on 21 October 1965. It was clothed, but his jeans and underpants were pulled down.

In May 1964, Hindley bought a vehicle of her own: a white Mini van. The following month, another child went missing. Every Tuesday evening Keith Bennett would go to his grandmother's home in Gorton for the night. Tuesday, 16 June 1964 was no different. As Winnie's house was only a mile away, he was old enough to walk there by himself. His mother watched him over the crossing and onto Stockport Road, then left him to go to the bingo hall in the opposite direction. It was just four days after his twelfth birthday.

When Keith did not turn up at his grandmother's house, she assumed his mother had decided not to send him. Keith Bennett's disappearance was not discovered until the next morning when Winnie arrived at her daughter's home without the boy. The police were called. Another fruitless search was conducted. A third child had vanished.

Near the Stockport Road in Longsight, Hindley had spotted a fair-haired boy and offered him a lift. He accepted. She drove to Saddleworth Moor, where she asked him to help her search for a lost glove. Brady lured Keith Bennett into a gully, where he sexually assaulted the child. Then he strangled him with a piece of string and buried his body. Hindley stood at the lip of the ravine and watched the rape and murder. Despite a renewed search that began in 1986, Keith Bennett's body has never been found. Later, Ian Brady offered to show police where the child was buried if he was allowed to die. To date, he has not done so.

Another six months passed before Brady and Hindley struck again. During that time, Brady, Hindley and her grandmother had moved to 16 Wardle Brook Avenue, on the council estate in Hattersley. On the afternoon of Boxing Day 1964, 10-year-old Lesley Ann Downey went to the local fair in Hulme Hall Lane just ten minutes walk from her home with her two brothers and some of their friends. It was not long before they had spent all their pocket money. When the kids left for home, Lesley Ann stayed behind. A classmate saw her standing alone next to one of the rides, shortly after 5.30pm.

Hindley abducted her from the fairground and took her back to Wardle Brook Avenue. There, the girl was undressed and forced to pose for pornographic photographs. Brady took nine obscene pictures of the little girl, showing her naked with a gag in her mouth. In four of the photos, she had her hands bound – in one, she was kneeling in an attitude of prayer.

Brady and Hindley also recorded themselves tormenting the child, who could be heard crying, retching, screaming and begging to be allowed to go home safe to her mother. The tape went on for 16 minutes. Afterwards, the little girl was raped and strangled with a piece of string. During their trial in April 1966, Brady made a telling slip of the tongue while being cross-examined. He told the prosecuting counsel that, after the tape was made, 'we all got dressed', suggesting Hindley was actively involved in the sexual abuse of the child, if not the murder. The next morning, Brady and Hindley drove to Saddleworth Moor where they buried Lesley Ann's naked body in a shallow grave. They could not be bothered to dress her and left her clothes at her feet.

When Lesley Ann Downey did not return home for dinner, her mother and her fiancé Alan began searching for her. They called the police who began combing the nearby countryside. Missing-person posters went up and thousands were questioned, but once again there was no sign of the missing child. It would be another ten months before Lesley Ann's parents discovered the terrible truth about their daughter.

Brady and Hindley knew exactly what had happened to the missing children – and revelled in it. With the guns Hindley had bought, they went up on the Moors for shooting practice. While there, they would visit the graves of their victims and photograph each other kneeling on them. They kept the pictures at Brady's office at Millwards. Later, Hindley confessed she had destroyed the photographs she kept there once Brady was arrested.

Even the extended abuse and murder of Lesley Ann Downey did not satisfy the depraved Brady. He wanted to extend his evil empire and decided to recruit Myra's 16-year-old brother-in-law David Smith into the murderous cabal. He had married her younger sister Maureen the year before. The Hindley family had not approved of the union as Smith was known around Gorton as a thug and already had convictions for violent offences in the juvenile courts.

Brady began to systematically corrupt Smith, believing he could lure anyone into his world of brutality and murder. He bragged to Smith about the murders already committed, saying he had the photographs to prove them. They were drinking at the time and Smith thought Brady was joking. He showed the youth his guns and talked to him about robbing a bank; he lent him books about the Marquis de Sade and got him to copy out quotations. 'Murder is a hobby and a supreme pleasure' and 'People are like maggots, small, blind, worthless fish-bait', Smith wrote in an exercise book under Brady's guidance.

The brainwashing had been going on for about a year when Brady decided to ensnare Smith into his vicious schemes by making him party to murder. On 6 October 1965, 17-year-old Edward Evans was lured back to 16 Wardle Brook Avenue. Brady later claimed Evans was a homosexual he had picked up at Manchester Central Station and that he had voluntarily gone home with him on the promise of sexual activity. There is no proof that Evans was actually homosexual. Brady may well have been trying to besmirch the young man's character as homosexuality was still illegal in Britain at that time.

That night Hindley invited Smith to the house, saying that Brady wanted to give him some miniature wine bottles. Smith arrived about midnight and was in the kitchen when he suddenly heard a loud scream from the living room.

'Help him, Dave,' Hindley said.

Smith rushed through into the sitting room to find a youth in a chair with Brady astride him. Brady had an axe in his right hand. The youth groaned and Brady smashed the axe down on this head repeatedly, hitting him at least 14 times. The groaning stopped, but the boy continued to gurgle so Brady put an electrical cord around his neck and pulled it tight.

'You fucking dirty bastard!' he said over and over again. When the young man finally stopped making any noise, Brady looked up.

'It's the messiest yet,' he said with some satisfaction. 'Usually it takes only one blow.'

He handed the axe to the dumbstruck Smith. This may simply have been an attempt to incriminate him by getting his fingerprints on the murder weapon. Smith was terrified by what he had seen. Fearing for his life, he helped clean up the bits of bone, blood and brains splattered across the living room. Meanwhile Brady and Hindley wrapped the body in a plastic sheet and trussed it with a rope. The couple made jokes about the murder as they carried the corpse upstairs to the spare bedroom.

Hindley then made a pot of tea and they all sat down.

'You should have seen the look on his face,' said Hindley, flushed with excitement, and she started reminiscing about the previous murders. Once, she said, they had bumped into a policeman while burying one of their victims on Saddleworth Moor.

'Do you believe me now?' asked Brady.

Smith could not believe all this was happening, but he realised that if he showed any sign of disgust, outrage or even disapproval he would be their next victim. It was the early hours of the morning when he finally made his excuses and left, promising to return the next day to help dispose of the body. When he got back to his flat, he was violently ill.

He told his wife everything and she urged him to go to the police. Armed with a knife and a screwdriver, they went out to a phone box at dawn and reported the murder. A police car picked them up and took them to the station, where Smith told his lurid tale to policemen who could hardly believe their ears.

At 8.40am, Superintendent Bob Talbot went round to Hindley's house to check on Smith's story. When he knocked on the door of 16 Wardle Brook Avenue, it was answered by Hindley. Inside, he found Brady lying naked on a divan and writing a note to his employer, saying that he was taking time off work because he had suffered an injury to his ankle. Talbot explained that he was investigating an act of violence reported to have taken place the previous night in the house. The police then proceeded to search the premises. When they got round to the spare bedroom upstairs, they found the door locked. Talbot asked for the key. After Hindley argued with him for several minutes, Brady told her to hand it over. Reluctantly, she did as she was told.

Inside they found Edward Evans' body and the axe just as Smith had described. Brady was arrested immediately, but there was no evidence against Hindley. At the police station, Brady admitted killing Evans. He told police that there had been an argument between himself, David Smith and the victim. A fight ensued, which quickly got out of hand. Smith had kicked Evans several times. There had been an axe on the floor, which Brady said he had picked up and used to hit Evans. According to him, only he and Smith had anything to do with Evans' death. They were alone when they had wrapped up the body and hidden it in the back bedroom. Myra had nothing to do with the murder.

When Hindley was questioned, she confirmed Brady's story, saying she had been frightened and horrified by what had happened. She was not arrested until four days later, after police had found a three-page document in her car describing in detail how she and Brady had planned to carry out the murder.

Confronted with the evidence, Hindley put on a brave face, flaunting her loyalty. She would only say: 'My story is the same as Ian's... Whatever he did, I did.' The only time she showed any emotion was when she was told that her dog Puppet had died.

'You fucking murderers!' she screamed at the police.

The investigation may well have gone no further had Smith not told police of Brady's boast that he had killed others and of Hindley's tale that they had buried other bodies on Saddleworth Moor. A 12-year-old girl named Pat Hodge told police that she had often gone up to the Moors on picnics with Hindley and Brady. Numerous photos of the Moors were discovered at their home.

The police also found a detailed plan that Brady had drawn up for the removal of all clues to Evans' murder. One of the items mentioned was, curiously, Hindley's prayer book. When police examined this, they found a left-luggage ticket from Manchester Central Station stuck down the spine. There, they found two suitcases containing books on sexual perversion, coshes and pictures of Lesley Ann Downey, naked and gagged in Hindley's bedroom. There was also the tape of a little girl's screams. The adult voices on the tape clearly belonged to Ian Brady and Myra Hindley. However, the police needed Leslie Ann Downey's mother's assistance to identify the child's voice. She was forced to listen in horror to her daughter as she begged for mercy during the last moments of her life. Other photographs showed Hindley with her dog Puppet posing beside what appeared to be a grave on Saddleworth Moor. These helped the police locate the bodies of Lesley Ann Downey and John Kilbride.

Despite damning evidence against them, Brady and Hindley denied murdering Lesley Ann Downey. They claimed Smith had brought the child to the house so Brady could take pictures. The tape, they said, merely recorded their attempts to subdue the little girl while they photographed her. Hindley protested she had only used a harsh tone because she was worried that neighbours might hear the girl. Lesley Ann Downey had left their house with Smith, unharmed, they said. Smith must have murdered her later.

The evidence linking Brady and Hindley to the murder of John Kilbride, though slight, was sufficient to charge them. They found the name 'John Kilbride' written in Brady's handwriting in his notebook and a photograph of Hindley on John's grave at the moors. It was also found that the car Hindley had hired on the day of his disappearance had been returned covered in mud and, according to Hindley's sister, Brady and Hindley went shopping in the market at Ashton-under-Lyne, where Kilbride had last been seen on Saturdays.

Despite their best efforts, the police could not find the bodies of the two other missing children or any evidence to link Brady and Hindley to their disappearance. On 27 April 1966, Hindley and Brady appeared at Chester Assizes, charged with the murders of Edward Evans, Lesley Ann Downey and John Kilbride. They pleaded not guilty to all counts.

At the trial the perverted nature of their crimes was revealed. The pathologist disclosed that Edward Evans' fly had been undone and he had found dog hairs around the boy's anus. John Kilbride's body was found with his trousers and underpants around his knees. Hindley, it transpired, got turned on by watching Brady perform sexual acts on his victims. Brady's witness-box slip revealed both he and Hindley had been naked during the photographic sessions with Lesley Ann Downey.

Throughout the trial, Brady and Hindley continued their attempts to blame David Smith for the murders. As a result, they appeared cowardly. At no time did they show any remorse or pity for the victims or their families. Brady was found guilty of the murders of Edward Evans, Lesley Ann Downey and John Kilbride. He was sentenced to three concurrent terms of life imprisonment. Hindley was found guilty of the murders of Downey and Evans and given two concurrent life sentences, plus seven years for harbouring Brady, knowing that he had murdered John Kilbride. Both escaped the death sentence, which had been abolished for murder only weeks before they had been arrested.

The judge, Mr Justice Fenton Atkinson, called Brady and Hindley 'two sadistic killers of the utmost depravity'. He recommended both should spend 'a very long time' in prison before being considered for parole. In his opinion Brady was 'wicked beyond belief' and there was no reasonable possibility of him ever reforming. However, he did not think this was necessarily true of Hindley, 'once she is removed from his influence.'

Brady did not bother to appeal. Hindley did so, but her appeal was rejected when the court of appeal ruled that no miscarriage of justice had occurred. They were also refused permission to see each other, although they were allowed to write. Brady's hold over Hindley continued for the first few years of their imprisonment, but a rift between them grew when they were refused permission to marry. In 1972, Brady's hold was broken when Hindley realised that she would never see him again and she broke off all contact.

A year later, Hindley attempted to escape with the help of Patricia Cairns, a lesbian prison warder who had fallen in love with her. The attempt was unsuccessful and Hindley was transferred from Holloway prison in north London to Cookham Wood, Kent.

Brady has shown no contrition in prison and refuses to be broken. He sees himself as a martyr in his own perverted cause. Hindley, on the other hand, petitioned to be released, but Brady countered her every move by revealing more of her involvement in the crimes. He saw any attempt on her part to go free as disloyalty.

Over two years, Hindley compiled a 20,000-word document in which she portrayed herself as the innocent victim of Brady's manipulative personality, though she continued with her original story that he was the guilty party and Smith was his accomplice. Brady countered this in 1978 by releasing his first public statement, saying that he did not intend to apply for parole as he 'accepted the weight of the crimes both Myra and I were convicted of justifies permanent imprisonment, regardless of expressed personal remorse and verifiable change.'

Further snookering Hindley's chances of being released, Brady told the Parole Board in 1982: 'The weight of our crimes justifies permanent imprisonment. I will not wish to be free in 1985 or even 2005.'

When her application for parole was refused again in 1985 and her case thrown out by the European Court of Justice, Hindley changed tack. Early in 1987, she made what she said was a full confession, admitting both the knowledge of, and involvement in all five murders, including those of Pauline Reade and Keith Bennett, although she still maintained she had not actually committed any of the murders herself. Brady countered this by publishing his own confession shortly afterwards, though he rejected any public show of remorse.

The confessions confirmed Pauline Reade and Keith Bennett had been buried somewhere on the moors though neither Hindley nor Brady could pinpoint exactly where.

However, after an extensive search Pauline's body was finally located on 1 July 1987. She was identified by her pink party dress.

Brady and Hindley's confessions differ significantly. Hindley admitted tricking Pauline into coming to Saddleworth Moor by offering her some records if she would help find a lost glove. Once there, she said, Brady arrived on his motorbike and went with Pauline to continue the search while Hindley herself waited at the car. Brady had raped the girl and cut her throat, then returned to the car to get Hindley to help him bury the body. According to Brady, Hindley played a much more active role, however, physically and sexually assaulting the girl with him.

While Keith Bennett's body has never been found, Hindley admitted luring him into the car after asking him to load some boxes but once at Saddleworth Moor, it was Brady alone who had taken the boy down the ravine, where he raped and then strangled him, burying his body somewhere nearby.

In her account of Lesley Ann Downey's murder, Hindley claimed she had been in the bathroom when Brady raped, then strangled the child. Brady countered this by claiming that it was in fact Hindley who had strangled the terrified 10-year-old with her bare hands.

Even though political campaigner Lord Longford claimed Hindley had seen the error of her ways – she returned to the Catholic faith and was also studying for an Open University degree – Brady's intervention help turn public opinion against her once again. Hindley's application for parole was once more turned down. Home Secretary Michael Howard declared she would never be released, along with 23 other prisoners, including Ian Brady, Peter Sutcliffe and Dennis Nilsen.

In 1997, Hindley was allowed to challenge the Home Secretary's decision in a judicial review by the High Court, where her counsel, Mr Edward Fitzgerald QC, claimed that hers was the only case in which a 'secondary party' to murder had been given a natural life tariff. Again her challenge was unsuccessful.

Meanwhile, Brady wrote to new Home Secretary Jack Straw supporting his position that his former lover should never be released after she had been allowed to plead her case on the BBC's *Panorama*:

> *First accept the determinant. Myra Hindley and I once loved each other. We were a unified force, not two conflicting entities. The relationship was not based on the delusional concept of* folie à deux, *but on a conscious/subconscious emotional and psychological affinity. She regarded periodic homicides as rituals of reciprocal innervation* [sic], *marriage ceremonies theoretically binding us ever closer. As the records show, before we met my criminal activities had been primarily mercenary. Afterwards, a duality of motivation developed. Existential philosophy melded with the spirituality of death and became predominant. We experimented with the concept of total possibility. Instead of the requisite Lady Macbeth, I got Messalina. Apart our futures would have taken radically divergent courses...*

While Lady Macbeth encouraged her husband to murder King Duncan to advance his ambitions, the Roman Emperor Claudius's wife Messalina persuaded him to condemn those who rejected her sexual advances or opposed her will.

> *The reason why the trial judge made a distinction between Myra Hindley and myself: before entering the witness box, I instructed both her counsel and my own to ask me specific questions designed to give the fullest opportunity of providing a cover for Myra. This managed to get her off on one murder charge. I also told her to adopt a distancing*

strategy when she went into the witness box, admitting to minor crimes whilst denying major. When, upon my advice, she appealed against sentence on the grounds that she should have been tried separately, Lord Chief Justice Parker denied the appeal, stating that, far from being disadvantaged by being tried with me, it had been to her great benefit as all my evidence had been in her favour.

For twenty years I continued to ratify the cover I had given her at the trial whilst, in contrast, she systematically began to fabricate upon it to my detriment. Therefore, when I learned from the Panorama programme this week that she was now claiming I had threatened to kill her if she did not participate in the Moors murders, I considered that the lowest lie of all. The fact that she continued to write several lengthy letters a week to me for seven years after we were imprisoned contradicts this cynical allegation. Perhaps her expedient demonomania now implies that I exercised an evil influence over her for seven years from my prison cell three-hundred miles distant? In character she is essentially a chameleon, adopting whatever camouflage will suit and voicing whatever she believes the individual wishes to hear. This subliminal soft-sell lured the innocent and naïve. As for the parole board, I advised her to build on three pillars: educational studies, powerful contacts and religion. She did. I myself have never applied for parole and never shall, which is why I can afford the luxury of veracity and free expression.

He also mentioned when Hindley made an 'apparent offer to undergo hypnosis to aid recollection', he had suggested drug-induced hypnosis using sodium pentothal – the 'truth drug' which corrodes subconscious defence mechanisms – she dropped the idea.

Add to this the published fact that, (a) her seven years of coded letters are in the hands of my solicitors, (b) an

*autobiography I wrote many years ago lies in a vault and
is to be released after my death or until I instruct
otherwise.*

*In the aforementioned Panorama programme, former
Home Office Minister A. Widdicombe stated there are
twenty-three prisoners in the UK who will never be
released. Why has the public heard so little of them? In
this and other special hospitals run by prison warders
there are also patients no-one has heard of, who have been
rotting behind bars for forty and fifty years for relatively
minor offences. That puts the present loud debate over
Myra Hindley in proper perspective, and crystallises the
reason why I have long advocated UK prisoners and
patients in special hospitals should have access to
voluntary euthanasia.*

Hindley continued to blame the strength of her love for
Brady for allowing herself to be pushed into murder. In a
letter, she described him as having 'such a powerful
personality, such an overwhelming charisma, if he'd told
me the moon was made of green cheese or that the sun rose
in the west I would have believed him.'

In March 2000, Brady wrote another letter in response to
a BBC programme in which Hindley had claimed that she
was 'overwhelmed by Brady's powerful personality', saying
that she only took part in the killings 'out of twisted love
for Brady' and because she was 'emotionally immature and
unsophisticated'.

Brady stated: 'Myra is a chameleon who simply reflects
whatever she believes will please the person she is
addressing. She can kill in cold blood or rage. In that
respect we were an inexorable force.'

The letter also accused her of indulging in 'destructive
delusion and absurdity': 'She has stooped to new depths,
alleging I coerced her to serially murder by use of drugs,
rape, blackmail, physical violence and practically every

other crime in the book,' he continued. 'All the concrete evidence against her has been jettisoned in favour of transparent mendacity and evidential amnesia.'

Formerly Hindley claimed she had committed her crimes out of love for him, he said: 'Now she maintains she acted out of hate for me – a completely irrational hypothesis by any standards in the context of serial homicide.'

Whichever way she turned, he showed no mercy.

After receiving the last rites, Myra Hindley died on 15 November 2002. She had spent 37 years in prison. Her solicitor told the press that his client had 'truly repented' for her crimes but was 'acutely aware' that she would not be forgiven for them, saying: 'Myra was deeply aware of the terrible crimes she had committed and of the suffering caused to those who died and to their relatives.'

Brady is anything but repentant. During his 19 years in Parkhurst Prison, he befriended fellow murderer and Nazi aficionado Graham Frederick Young. In 1985, he was diagnosed as mentally disordered and sent to Broadmoor. Later he was transferred to a high-security ward in Ashworth Hospital after staff found a metal bucket handle taped under a sink which could have been fashioned into a crude weapon.

Brady has made repeated attempts to kill himself. His hunger strikes have resulting in force feeding. He has fought in the courts, unsuccessfully, for his right to starve himself to death. Alongside his unpublished auto-biography, he wrote *The Gates of Janus*, which examines the psychology of serial killers. Though he mentions Yorkshire Ripper Peter Sutcliffe – who he met in jail – he makes no mention of his own crimes. He also wrote: 'It was hard not to have empathy for Graham Young.' The book was published and he received £12,000 to 'help support' his mother, which was, naturally, highly controversial.

Before she died, Hindley suggested there may have been

another victim, a young hitchhiker. Brady has never addressed the question. He still torments Keith Bennett's mother with the possibility that he might be able to locate the site of her son's grave.

In January 2006, the BBC reported that a woman tried to send 50 paracetamol to Brady at the prison hospital. The attempt was foiled when the envelope was X-rayed, revealing the pills in two sweet tubes inside a hollowed-out crime novel. This would have been sufficient for a successful suicide attempt.

Brady continues the legal fight to be allowed to starve to death, but the authorities and the public are determined that he will continue to rot in jail. After all, the families of his victims are still suffering.

CHAPTER SEVEN

CHARLES MANSON

It was in California in 1969 that Charles Manson led his hippie-style commune, 'The Family', in a murderous rampage, famously killing among others the actress Sharon Tate, who was eight-months pregnant. Inspired by his misinterpretation of the lyrics of The Beatles' *The White Album*, his aim was to set off a race war that would lead to him becoming world leader.

Charles Manson was born in Cincinnati, Ohio, on 12 November 1934, the bastard son of a drugstore cowboy calling himself Colonel Scott, who left long before the birth. Manson claimed that he was listed in hospital records as 'No Name Maddox', though these have yet to surface. His mother, Kathleen Maddox, was just 18 at the time. She had run away from home in Ashland, Kentucky, to escape her Bible-bashing mother and supported herself with prostitution. By the time her son's birth was registered on 3 December 1934 – three weeks after the event – he had been given the name Charles Milles Maddox. His father was listed as dry-cleaning worker William Manson. Apparently he briefly married Charlie's mother and gave the young boy his surname.

Kathleen Maddox had difficulties with both marriage and motherhood, and regularly abandoned her son. Manson said that she once sold him to a childless waitress for a pitcher of beer, only to be recovered several days later by his uncle. By the time he was six, his mother found she was unable to support herself or her boy even by prostitution, so she left him with his grandmother, while she and her brother Luther robbed a gas station. They were caught and jailed for five years.

Manson stayed with his strict grandparents for a few weeks. Then he was farmed out to his mother's sister Joanne, also very religious, in McMechen, West Virginia. When Kathleen was paroled, she came back for the boy. Manson was ecstatic. They began a shiftless existence together, roaming the Midwest, living in run-down hotels. Kathleen was always on the murky fringes of crime and Manson could never be sure whether they would stay together or he would be farmed out to someone else. Eventually Kathleen met a man who wanted to be with her, but he did not want her young son. Manson's mother made him a Ward of Court and he was sent to the Gibault Home for Boys in Terre Haute, Indiana. Kathleen visited him there and promised he would be back with her 'pretty soon'. Eventually she rejected him and they lost contact. Later, he was sent to the famous orphans' home, Boys' Town in Nebraska, but was kicked out for his surly manner and constant thieving.

Still in his early teens, Manson became a drifter and was soon arrested for stealing food. He was sent to Indiana Boys' School, where he escaped 18 times. In 1951, he was arrested again for the theft of a car and burgling a petrol station in Beaver City, Utah, and served four years in a federal reformatory. Reformatories, he found, were a great improvement on children's homes. While the harsh, often sadistic regimes in orphanages taught him to survive, reformatories were the universities of petty crime. Though he had a high IQ, Manson had had practically no

CHARLES MANSON | 143

formal education. Social workers found him aggressively antisocial. On his own admission, he held a razor to another boy's throat while he sodomised him just days before he was to be paroled.

In November 1954, he was released into the custody of his aunt in McMechen. There, he met miner's daughter Rosalie Jean Willis. They married in January 1955, but soon he was arrested for transporting stolen cars across the state line into California and sentenced to three years in Terminal Island Federal Prison in San Pedro, Los Angeles. Soon afterwards, his wife bore him a son. She then divorced Manson and went out of his life, taking Charlie Jr with her. When he heard that his wife was with another man, Manson tried to escape, stealing a car in the process. Recaptured, he lost any chance of parole.

In jail, he took an intensive course, supplied by other experienced inmates, on how to be a pimp. Released in 1958, Manson set about his new career in Hollywood. His first attempt failed miserably. He fell in love with his main woman, who then dumped him. But he was nothing if not tenacious and was arrested repeatedly under the Mann Act for transporting women across state lines for immoral purposes.

Manson started forging cheques. When he was caught passing a stolen cheque for $38, he absconded to Mexico, but the police caught up with him when he continued pimping there. He was returned to Los Angeles, where he was sentenced to ten years in the federal penitentiary on McNeil Island, Washington State.

Just 5ft 2in, Manson had a hard time in prison and was repeatedly raped by other prisoners, many of them black. This left him with a lifelong chip on his shoulder. To survive in prison, he had already become shifty, cunning and manipulative, but he also began developing techniques that gave him control over others. This set him in good stead when he was released on 21 March 1967.

When he went to jail, it had been the 1950s. The world was conservative, restrained even. By the time he came out, everything had changed. A new generation was turning on, tuning in and dropping out. At 32, he headed for the centre of it all: San Francisco. He had heard what was going on from new inmates coming into the jail, but had scarcely believed it. Now he was in the outside world, he saw it was all true.

'Pretty little girls were running around every place with no panties or bras and asking for love,' he later recalled. 'Grass and hallucinatory drugs were being handed to you on the streets. It was a different world than I had ever been in and one that I believed was too good to be true. It was a convict's dream and after being locked up for seven solid years, I didn't run from it. I joined it and the generation that lived in it.'

It was the 'Summer of Love'.

One of Manson's first experiences on the outside was attending a Grateful Dead concert, where he dropped a tab of acid. People remember him dancing like someone possessed, then suddenly falling into a trance and curling up in the foetal position.

When he arrived in San Francisco he had just $30. He used it to buy a guitar and started to busk. Suddenly, he became something of a star in the hippie Haight-Ashbury district. People also flocked to him on the campus of the University of California at Berkeley. The world was turning against the establishment and 'straight' society. Suddenly, an institutionalised reject like Manson was all the rage. He soon discovered that he could use the manipulative powers learned in jail on the long-haired flower children of southern California. With his hypnotic stare, his unconventional lifestyle and the strange meaningless phrases he babbled, he was the perfect hippie guru, peppering his rhetoric with biblical quotations learnt from his family as a child.

He also joined the Process Church, founded in London by ex-Scientologist Robert Sylvester DeGrimston Moore. In England, DeGrimston tried to recruit the pop glitterati – The Beatles, The Rolling Stones – with some success. Marianne Faithfull posed nude, clutching a rose and apparently dead, for the front cover of one issue of *Process* magazine. DeGrimston also began to turn out books, explaining the Process's creed in more detail. In the first, *As It Is*, published in 1967, he pointed out that Christ had said: 'Love thine enemy.' Christ's enemy was Satan, so his followers should love Satan, who was to be reconciled with Christ on the Day of Judgement. In his second book, *Jehovah on War*, DeGrimston wrote simply: 'Thou shalt kill.'

In 1967, the Process moved to San Francisco, where DeGrimston tried to form a union with Anton LaVey's First Church of Satan. LaVey dismissed DeGrimston and his followers as 'kooks'. Nevertheless, the Process began to build a following among Hell's Angels, drug addicts and minor figures from the world of pop music and the movies. Their headquarters was at 407 Cole Street. Manson lived just two blocks away at number 636. Process members were expected to spend some time in satanic worship. Sex, blood rituals and sacrifices were a good way to maintain a hold over members.

DeGrimston referred to his followers as 'The Family'. There were brothers, sisters and fathers – but no mothers. Manson, who was about to form his own 'Family', contributed an article to the 'Death' issue of *Process* magazine. Though a rambling incoherent piece, it revealed Manson's growing obsession with death. During his time in California, DeGrimston published his third book of theology: *Satan on War*. In it, he wrote: 'Release the fiend that lies dormant within you, for he is strong and ruthless and his power is far beyond the bounds of human frailty.' Those words might have been written for Manson.

Manson's contempt for authority and convention made

him a hero of the counter-culture and he soon developed a penchant for the fashionable middle-class girls who had taken the then chic option and dropped out of mainstream society. The first was Mary Brunner, a university librarian. She was a slim, flat-chested redhead and not very pretty but she was naïve and impressionable, very much his type. He stopped sleeping in the park and moved in with her. Soon he picked up another girl called Darlene and discovered something new: by sleeping with Mary and Darlene on a strict rota basis, he found he could control them both. He had discovered the power of sex. Soon Brunner found that she was sharing her apartment with 18 other women.

The Process Church moved down to Los Angeles, so Mary bought a VW bus and Manson got permission from his parole officer to travel down the coast. On the way, they sampled communal living – and loving – in the hippie communes being established throughout California. Eventually, they reached Los Angeles, where Manson intended to establish himself as a rock superstar.

On Venice Beach, he met another slim redhead, Lynette 'Squeaky' Fromme. She had just had a row with her father and was emotionally vulnerable. Manson brought her back to Mary and had sex with her. The three formed the nucleus of 'The Family'. This was Manson's entourage of hangers-on. They comprised a harem of young girls who were all about ten years younger than him – and a number of docile males, who would do anything he told them to. They numbered as many as 30–35 at one time. Manson controlled them through acid – the hallucinogenic drug LSD – and sex. Every woman who came to The Family was initiated: she would be given a tab of acid, then have a few hours of sex with him. Soon she would join in the skilfully choreographed orgies, where Manson would control who did what and with whom.

Another early recruit was Patricia Krenwinkel, a former girl scout from a normal middle-class family. Her expensive education landed her a good job as a legal clerk at a big insurance company in Los Angeles. She met Manson on Manhattan Beach when she was 21 and abandoned everything to be with him, ditching her car and walking out of her job without bothering to pick up her last paycheck.

Leslie Van Houten was just 19 when she dropped out of school. She lived on the streets on a perpetual acid trip until she met Manson. Twenty-year-old Linda Kasabian left her husband and two children and then stole $5,000 from a friend to join The Family. She too began to see her seamy life through a constant haze of LSD. Another redhead – Diane Lake – joined after her parents dropped out to join the Hog Farm commune. Meanwhile, preacher's daughter Ruth Ann Moorehouse married a hapless bus driver so she could leave home and join The Family.

Then there was Susan Atkins, who Manson renamed Sadie Mae Gutz when he made her a fake ID. At 21, she was a topless dancer and bar-room hustler. In that role she became involved with Anton LaVey's First Church of Satan when she played a blood-sucking vampire in LaVey's 'Witches' Sabbath' at Gigi's night-club in North Beach. Later, she became Manson's closest aide, though like the others, she had to share his sexual favours. He promised each girl a baby in return for their devotion, while Susan used the situation to plant her half-baked Satanist ideas into their receptive minds.

One of the few men in the commune was 23-year-old former high school football star from Farmersville, Texas, Charles 'Tex' Watson. He had once been an honours student, but in Manson's hands he became a mindless automaton. Another college dropout, Bruce Davis, joined them, as did Bobby Beausoleil, former guitarist with the Digger band Orkustra and protégé of underground film-maker Kenneth Anger. Anger was a follower of British Satanist Aleister Crowley and one of LaVey's magic circle. Beausoleil played Lucifer in Anger's movie *Invocation of My Demon Brother* and took part in a Black Mass Anger performed on stage at the premiere. However, Beausoleil spoiled the occasion by ripping off some of Anger's camera equipment.

Anger even had a locket made with a photo of Beausoleil on one side and a picture of a toad on the other. The inscription read: 'Bobby Beausoleil – who was turned into a toad by Kenneth Anger'. Two years later Beausoleil was arrested for the Manson murders, while Anger went on to write the best-selling exposé *Hollywood Babylon*.

The Family hung around on the fringes of the movie community. With three girls to every man, they were welcome at any party. Often they would sit in a circle and drop acid, taking a group trip. Family member Paul Wilkins remembered that Manson was always the one who handed out the tabs, taking less than everybody else, so he remained in control.

Dennis Wilson of 1960s Californian band The Beach Boys was particularly fascinated by Manson and his lifestyle. The Family freeloaded on him unmercifully: he put them up, fed them and gave them clothes from his own wardrobe. According to Family member Paul Watkins, Wilson also picked up their medical tab for the treatment of gonorrhoea and paid up $21,000 when a car of his that they borrowed was wrecked.

The Family quickly grew to the point where the bus could no longer contain them. They moved out to a huddle of shacks around Topanga Canyon on the western fringes of Los Angeles. Almost every young hippie drifter on the West Coast passed in and out of The Family at that time, while Joan 'Juanita' Wildebush, Sandra Good, T. J. 'the Terrible' Walleman, Juan Flynn, Cathy Gillies, Brooks Poston and Steve 'Clem' Grogan, Kitty Lutesinger, Cathy 'Gypsy' Share and Stephanie Scram became more permanent members. There were junior additions too.

Susan Atkins gave birth to a son, imaginatively named Zezozece C. Zadfrack, while Mary Brunner had a boy named Valentine Michael after the protagonist hero in Robert Heinlein's 1960s trendy cult science fiction classic *Stranger in a Strange Land*.

By and large, the girls were middle-class dropouts. Susan Atkins was the only one with a criminal record. They brought with them money, cars, daddy's credit cards, everything necessary for The Family to survive. Together they formed the secret core of The Family. To join, they had to meet Manson's hypnotic gaze and perform seemingly impossible tasks. They were taught to think of themselves as élite and to regard the outside world as hostile, threatening and beneath contempt. With their means of support in the outside world surrendered, Manson controlled them with threats of expulsion and occasionally, death.

During his time in Los Angeles, Manson stayed close to the Process Church. When it courted pop stars such as John Phillips of The Mamas and the Papas, so too did he. To accommodate the ever-growing Family Manson traded the VW for an old school bus, which was painted black. It was adorned with Bobby Beausoleil's painting of the Baphomet or the Goat of Mendes – the devil figure thought to have been worshipped by the Knights Templar and popularised by Aleister Crowley. In an attempt to avoid trouble with the police, the words 'Holywood [sic] Film Production Company' were painted on the side.

When Process Church broke up, Manson and his followers headed for the desert. Through contacts in San Diego, The Family got permission to stay out on the Spahn Ranch in the Santa Susana Mountains, an old movie set where Westerns had been filmed, owned by 80-year-old George Spahn. He was virtually blind. In return for being allowed to live there free, the girls cooked and cleaned for him – and, according to some accounts, provided him with sexual favours. Lynette Fromme later told prosecuting attorney Vincent Bugliosi that she was in love with Spahn and would have married him, had he proposed.

To enhance their counter-culture status, The Family collected food thrown out by supermarkets to feed themselves. This was supposed to show how wicked and wasteful the 'capitalist' world was. The effect was marred somewhat by the fact they picked up the discarded food in a Rolls! They freed themselves from the other constraints of straight society by hustling dope, 'borrowing' credit cards and 'liberating' cars and other valuables. Meanwhile family member Cathy Gillies rented The Family's second home, the Baker Ranch in Coyote Canyon, using Dennis Wilson's collection of gold records as a deposit.

Surrounded by compliant sycophants, the drug-addled Manson began to build huge delusions, fuelled by Susan Atkins' cursory study of Satanism and the teachings of the Process Church. She convinced him that his own name, Manson, was significant. In her twisted logic, Manson, or Man-son, meant Son of Man or Christ. According to her, he was also the Devil. Manson began to see himself as the gnostic deity Abraxas – a rooster-headed god figure with serpent's feet in whom light and darkness, good and evil, are supposed to be unified and transcended. He also called himself both Christ and Satan, and said that after the apocalypse, the coming black-white war, he – 'the Beast of the bottomless pit' – would bring salvation.

When Manson first heard The Beatles' *The White Album*, released in the US on 25 November 1968, he believed the tracks were full of messages directed at him and his Family. 'Sexy Sadie', he thought, was aimed at Susan Atkins, who he had already renamed Sadie. 'Piggies' sneered at the establishment and the word became very much part of The Family's vocabulary. 'Blackbird' was a call for black people to revolt, while 'Revolution 9' was aural chaos. But to Manson, 'Revolution 9' meant Revelations, Chapter 9.

Although illiterate until his early twenties, Manson had been brought up with a thorough knowledge of the Bible. Chapter 9 of the Book of Revelations talks of the coming of Appollyon, the Exterminating Angel. Manson saw himself in this way too. In addition, Verse 21 of Chapter 9 reads: 'Neither repented they of their murders, nor of their sorceries, nor of their fornications, nor of their theft.'

Blissfully unaware that a helter-skelter was a harmless British funfair ride, he interpreted the track 'Helter Skelter' as heralding the beginning of what he saw as an inevitable race war. The blacks would rise up and wipe out the 'piggies' – the police, authority figures, the rich and the famous, and what Manson called 'movie people' who – although they partied with him – had plainly failed to recognise his cinematic potential. Throughout this cataclysm, Manson would wait in safety in the desert. Once the blacks were in charge, he reasoned, being inferior, they would find themselves incapable of intelligent rule so they would have to turn to him and ask him to take over as world ruler.

The only problem remaining was how to provoke this Armageddon. To this end, Manson tried to recruit violent biker groups such as the Straight Satans and later, turned to violence himself. On 1 July 1969, he shot a black drug dealer named Bernard 'Lotsapoppa' Crowe over a deal that went wrong. Manson boasted that he had killed Crowe. In fact, Crowe was not dead, merely wounded, but when it was reported that the body of a dead Black Panther (the African-American organisation set up to promote black power) had been found dumped in Los Angeles, Manson and The Family became paranoid, believing the Panthers were out to get them.

'Almost immediately it seemed that all kinds of blacks started showing up, renting horses,' said Tex Watson. 'He was convinced they were Panther spies and he started posting armed guards at night and having us sleep scattered back in the hills. If we'd needed any more proof that Helter Skelter was coming down very soon, this was it – blackie was trying to get at the chosen ones.'

Meanwhile, Manson believed anything The Beatles could do, he could do better. He fancied himself as something of a pop star and took one of his feeble compositions to successful West Coast musician Gary Hinman. It was then that he learned that Hinman had recently inherited $20,000. He sent Mary Brunner, Susan Atkins and Bobby Beausoleil to Hinman's house on Old Topanga Canyon Road to steal the money and to kill Hinman for refusing to put Manson at the top of the charts. The three Family members argued with Hinman for about two hours, then Bobby Beausoleil lost his patience and pulled The Family's gun, a 9 mm Radom pistol. He handed it to Susan Atkins and began searching the house.

With Beausoleil out of the room, Hinman tried to escape. He struggled with Susan Atkins and the gun went off. The bullet ricocheted round the kitchen and embedded itself under the sink. Hearing the shot, Beausoleil ran back, grabbed the gun and beat Hinman about the head with it. The intruders called Manson, who drove over to the house. Manson took a sword and cut Hinman's ear. He then told Beausoleil to find the money. The girls were to clean up Hinman's wounds and to bring him out to the ranch. Leaving his followers to carry out orders, Manson left.

Mary Brunner stitched up Hinman's ear with dental floss, bandaged his other wounds and gave him something to drink. With Hinman tied up on the hearth-rug, Beausoleil and Atkins ransacked the house but the money was not there. All they found were two pink slips – the ownership documents to two cars. Under threat of death, Hinman signed them over. At dawn the following morning, he managed to reach the window and screamed for help. Beausoleil panicked and stabbed him twice in the chest and left him to bleed to death.

Susan Atkins dipped her finger in Hinman's blood and wrote 'political piggie' in blood on the wall. She also drew a cat's paw, a crude version of the logo of the Black Panthers. The three of them then bundled up bloodstained clothes and bandages, anything that might tie them to the murder. They tried to wipe their fingerprints off everything they had touched during their long stay at Hinman's house. Then they left, locking all the doors behind them, but they began to worry that Hinman was not dead, so they climbed back into the house through a side window and smothered him for good measure. Following this, they hot-wired his VW van and drove to the Topanga Kitchen, a nearby café, where they celebrated with coffee and cherry cake. Afterwards they drove back to the Spahn Ranch to tell Manson what they had done.

Hinman's body was found by friends on 31 July 1969, four days after he was murdered. The Los Angeles Sheriff's Office – which deals with crime outside the metropolitan area – was called in. Sergeant Paul Whiteley and Deputy Charles Guenther were assigned to the case. The investigation started out easily enough: the killers had not done a good job of cleaning up and they found Beausoleil's fingerprints in Hinman's house. On 6 August, they picked up Beausoleil. They found the knife used to kill Hinman and a T-shirt drenched in his blood in Beausoleil's car. He was convicted of murder and went meekly to jail without implicating Atkins or Manson.

This loyalty impressed Manson not at all. He now aimed to get his dire compositions recorded by record producer Terry Melcher, the son of Doris Day, to whom Dennis Wilson had introduced him. Melcher was a big player in the music industry but failed to see potential in Manson's material. Determined on revenge, Manson formed his followers into death squads. They dressed in black and trained in the arts of breaking and entering abandoned buildings. These exercises were known as 'creepy crawlies'.

As part of their training, Manson told them they were to kill anyone who stood in their way.

On 8 August 1969, Manson called his followers together and announced: 'Now is the time for Helter Skelter.'

A death squad was despatched to Melcher's remote home at 10050 Cielo Drive in Benedict Canyon in the Hollywood Hills, but he had moved. This did not matter to Manson. The people he saw going in and out of the house were 'movie types'. Their slaughter would act as a warning. He sent Tex Watson, Susan Atkins, Patricia Krenwinkel and Linda Kasabian to the house armed with a .22 Bluntline Special revolver, a knife and a length of rope.

According to Watson, Manson told him: 'What I want... I want you to go to that house where Melcher used to live. I want you to take a couple of the girls I'll send with you and go down there... and totally destroy everyone in that house, as gruesome as you can. Make it a real nice murder, just as bad as you've ever seen. And get all their money.'

The women were instructed to do as Watson told them. They were told what to do with their victims: 'Pull out their eyes and hang them on the mirrors.' And they were to write messages on the walls in their blood, specifically 'Helter Skelter' and 'Rise'. Manson was insistent. As they set off, he told the girls again: 'Remember to leave a sign, something witchy.'

The house at the end of Cielo Drive was indeed occupied by 'movie people'. Film director Roman Polanski, who had rented it, was away shooting a movie in London but his wife, movie star Sharon Tate – who Manson had seen on a previous visit – was at home. She was eight months pregnant. Coffee heiress Abigail Folger and her boyfriend Polish writer Voytek Frykowski were visiting. So too was Tate's friend, celebrity hairdresser Jay Sebring.

Manson's death squad parked their white-and-yellow Ford outside 10050 Cielo Drive and waited while Tex Watson shinned up a telegraph pole and cut the phone lines. Kasabian lost her nerve at the last minute and stayed outside. Tex Watson, Susan Atkins and Patricia Krenwinkel pushed open the wrought-iron gates. At that moment a white two-seater Nash Ambassador came down the driveway. It was driven by 18-year-old Steven Parent. He had been visiting the caretaker. Brandishing the .22, Tex Watson leapt into the headlight beams and screamed for the driver to stop. He thrust the gun into the car window. Steven Parent begged for his life, but Watson pumped four bullets into his chest.

Patricia and Susan scouted around the house, but could find no way in so Watson started cutting his way through the screen on the window of an empty room in the front. Once inside, Manson's disciples found Voytek Frykowski asleep on the couch. He woke to find a .22 in his face and asked what they wanted.

'I am the Devil,' replied Watson. 'I am here to do the Devil's business. Give me your money.'

He told Susan Atkins to get some towels to tie Frykowski up. On her way back from the bathroom, she saw the others talking in a bedroom. She reported back to Watson, who told her to go and get them. Susan Atkins told Sharon Tate and her guests that the house was simply being robbed and no harm would come to them. While she was tying them up, Jay Sebring broke free and made a lunge for the gun. Watson shot him in the armpit and then stabbed him four times.

Fearing they would all be killed, Frykowski attacked Watson, who beat him to the ground with the pistol butt. He hit him so hard that the walnut grip of the pistol broke in two. Frykowski staggered to the door, screaming for help. In a frenzied attack, the girls stabbed him to death: there were 51 stab wounds on his body.

Frykowski's gallant stand put some fight in the others. Abigail Folger made a break for it, but Krenwinkel caught up with her halfway across the lawn. She was knocked to the ground and Watson stabbed her to death. Sharon Tate begged for the life of her unborn child but Susan Atkins showed no mercy. While Patricia Krenwinkel held Tate down, Atkins stabbed her 16 times. Her mutilated body was tied to Sebring's corpse. Watson then went around kicking and stabbing the lifeless bodies. The killers spread an American flag across the couch and wrote the word 'pig' on the front door in Sharon Tate's blood. They changed their bloody clothes, collected their weapons and made their way back to the Spahn Ranch, disposing of the evidence on the way.

'I felt so elated,' said Susan Atkins. 'Tired, but at peace with the world. I knew this was just the beginning of Helter Skelter. Now the world would listen.'

Later that night, Manson and another member of The Family returned to Cielo Drive to look for Susan Atkins' knife and clean up. They wiped Steven Parent's car clean, then removed the fingerprints in the house with the towel used to tie up Frykowski, leaving it draped over Jay Sebring's face. Back at the ranch, Manson got high on marijuana and read the reports of the murders in the newspapers as if they were reviews. To celebrate this great victory, he had an orgy with his female followers but soon craved more blood.

On 10 August, Watson, Kasabian, Krenwinkel and Atkins set out again. This time Manson accompanied them. Leslie Van Houten and Steven 'Clem' Grogan came along for the ride. Manson randomly selected a house in the Silver Lake area of Los Angeles: 3301 Waverley Drive. He took a sword and the .22, walked up the drive to the long low house and broke in. The house belonged to 44-year-old grocery store-owner Leno LaBianca and his 38-year-old wife Rosemary, who ran a fashionable dress shop. They woke to find Manson holding a gun in their faces. He tied them up and told them they would not be harmed; he only intended to rob them. Then he took the money that Mr LaBianca had left on the night-stand and Mrs LaBianca's purse.

Tex Watson later admitted to being with Manson and followed his instructions to gag Mr and Mrs LaBianca with wire from a lamp and put pillowcases over their heads. Leaving Watson with the weapons, Manson left the house, saying: 'Make sure the girls get to do some of it, both of them.'

Outside, Manson told Leslie Van Houten and Patricia Krenwinkel to go into the house and kill the LaBiancas. He said he was going to the house next door to murder its occupants. Instead, he drove home.

When the girls arrived, Watson asked: 'Did he say to kill them?'

They nodded.

Leno LaBianca began screaming: 'You're going to kill us, aren't you? You're going to kill us!'

Watson later said that he knew from the look on Van Houten's face that she did not want to kill the LaBiancas: 'But like all the rest of us, she must have felt she owed it to Charlie to do whatever he asked, since he'd given himself so totally for us. Katie [Krenwinkel], on the other hand, began to look through the kitchen drawers for knives with positive relish.'

Mr LaBianca continued to shout. Watson said he was surprised that the victim could talk so much with the wire and pillow material in his mouth. He sent the girls into the bedroom to attend to Mrs LaBianca and went about his murderous business once more.

'I walked back to the sofa with the bayonet and the horror began all over again,' said Watson. 'I drove the chrome-plated blade down full force. "Don't stab me anymore," he managed to scream, even though the first thrust had been through his throat. "I'm dead, I'm dead..." The shiny bayonet plunged again and again.'

Then Watson and Krenwinkel stabbed the helpless Mrs

LaBianca 41 times while chanting a mantra. They wanted Van Houten to join in. Reluctantly, she stabbed Mrs LaBianca 16 times in the buttocks, though she was already dead.

Krenwinkel went into the living room to find that Mr LaBianca was, miraculously, still alive. Watson used the bayonet again, repeatedly, remembering Manson's words that he should make it 'as gruesome as you can'. He then carved the word 'WAR' on the belly. Krenwinkel stabbed the dead man 14 times with an ivory-handled carving fork, which she left sticking out of his stomach, completing the grotesque tableau with a small steak knife in his neck.

The girls used the victims' blood to write more revolutionary slogans on the walls – 'Death to pigs' and 'Rise' in the living room and 'Healter [sic] Skelter' on the door of the refrigerator. Then the three killers took a shower together. They had something to eat and went home.

Meanwhile, Manson had delivered another death squad to its target. He dropped off Susan Atkins and Linda Kasabian at the Venice Beach home of an actor friend of Kasabian, who he described as another 'piggy', then drove himself back to Spahn Ranch. However, Kasabian knocked on the door of the wrong apartment. Abandoning the murder plan, Susan Atkins defecated in the stairwell and they left.

When Sergeant Whitely and Deputy Guenther – the men from the Los Angeles Sheriff's Office who had put Bobby Beausoleil away – read about the Tate murders, they saw similarities with the Hinman case, particularly the writing in blood on the walls. They knew Beausoleil could not have been directly involved in the Tate murders because he was in custody at the time but they always suspected he had not acted alone and they knew he hung out with a weird bunch of hippies at the Spahn Ranch. Those who had been with Beausoleil on the Hinman murder could be responsible for the Tate murders too, they figured. Whitely called Sergeant Jesse Buckles, who was on the team handling the Tate case at the Los Angeles Police Department, and told him of his suspicions but Buckles dismissed the idea. He did not even report it to superior officers. After all, the LAPD already had their man.

The Tate murders had been discovered the following morning by Mrs Winifred Chapman, the housekeeper who lived out, but the young caretaker William Garretson, who lived in the guest house in the back garden, slept through the murders and claimed he had not heard anything. He was dazed, confused and very frightened. The police leaned on him hard, but they could not break him and there was nothing beyond the circumstantial evidence that he was on the property at the time to link him to the murders. Then, when reports of the LaBianca murders came in, Garretson had to be released. Plainly he could not have killed Mr and Mrs LaBianca while in custody.

By this time, Los Angeles was in panic. A gang of maniacs was on the loose. Poolsides emptied, gun sales soared and security firms were run off their feet... The pressure was on to make a quick arrest.

The most promising lead in the Tate case was drugs. It was well known that celebrity hairdresser Jay Sebring also supplied his clients with marijuana and other drugs. A terrified Polish friend of Voytek Frykowski told the LAPD that he too was setting up as a drug dealer. However, the Tate case was clearly linked to the LaBianca case, also under the LAPD's jurisdiction. They were middle-aged and eminently respectable, no drugs connection there. But could this be a Mafia connection? Leno LaBianca was a keen gambler and racehorse owner. This line of inquiry also led nowhere. Sharon Tate's husband Roman Polanski, who had been away filming in Europe at the time, returned and told the police: 'If I'm looking for a motive, I'd look for something that doesn't fit your habitual standard.'

It was prophetic, but unhelpful.

It was not until 15 October, over two months after the

murders, that one of the LaBianca team at the LAPD thought of checking out similar cases that might have been handled by the Los Angeles Sheriff's Office. Unlike the Tate team, they were immediately interested in the Hinman killing. However, Whitely and Guenther had not been sitting on their hands. On 16 August 1969, the Los Angeles Sheriff's Office raided the Spahn Ranch, looking for stolen cars and credit cards. Ten days later, Donald 'Shorty' Shea, a Spahn Ranch stuntman and horse wrangler, was murdered. Manson suspected Shea had tipped off the police and set up the raid. It is possible he knew something about the Tate and LaBianca killings. Manson was also angry that Shea, a white man, had married a black woman.

It soon became clear to the killers that their senseless slaughter had not set off Helter Skelter, the great revolutionary race war, as expected. Instead, it simply provoked a police crackdown. Clearly, the killers were now in danger and The Family began to break up.

'When they catch me, it's going to be like feeding me to the lions,' said Manson, exhibiting for once considerable insight. 'They're going to put me far away because I have no family, no one that will help me.'

Some of The Family fled to the Barker Ranch. That too was raided on 12 October – the local Inyo County Police were looking for stolen cars and illegal firearms. They arrested 24 Family members, including Manson himself. Others had scattered. It took three days to search the huge ranch properly. When the police approached their hiding place, Kitty Lutesinger – five months pregnant with Bobby Beausoleil's child – and Stephanie Scram stumbled out of a dry gully. Frightened, they begged for police protection.

As several of The Family members gave the Spahn Ranch as their address, the Inyo County Police called the Los Angeles Sheriff's Office. Whitely and Guenther had been looking for Kitty Lutesinger in connection with the Hinman murder, so they drove up to interview her. Kitty was eager to help: she said that she had heard Manson order Bobby Beausoleil and Susan Atkins to go to Gary Hinman's house and get money from him. This tied him to the Hinman case. She also said that she had heard other Family members talking about a man being grabbed by the hair and stabbed in the legs. This was not Hinman, who had no wounds on the legs but it could have been Frykowski.

Meanwhile, Susan Atkins had taken off alone. She had returned to prostitution to support herself and was already in jail. When interviewed, she admitted to being at Hinman's house when he was murdered. She was booked on suspicion of murder and sent to the Sybil Brand Institute, Los Angeles county jail.

The police already had one of the murder weapons in their possession. The .22 Bluntline Special used to killed Steven Parent had been thrown out of the car by the killers on their way back from the LaBianca murders. It was found on a Los Angeles hillside by ten-year-old Stephen Weiss, but the police just tagged it and filed it away in a manila envelope. Its significance was only recognised after Weiss's father read a description of the gun used in the Tate killings in the *Los Angeles Times*. Meanwhile, the LaBianca team set their intelligence-gathering team onto gleaning any information they could about Manson and his followers. Eventually, they pulled in Danny de Carlo and Al Springer of the bikers' gang Straight Satan – they had a lot of circumstantial and hearsay evidence concerning Manson and the murders. And Terry Melcher told the police that Manson had been to 10050 Cielo Drive when he had lived there. The net was closing.

In jail, Susan Atkins could not keep her mouth shut. She began bragging to cell-mate Ronnie Howard and another prisoner called Virginia Graham about the killings. And she said she planned to do unspeakable things to Elizabeth Taylor, Richard Burton, Frank Sinatra, Tom Jones and Steve

McQueen when she got out. They grew frightened and told the authorities. Atkins' so-called hit list was released in the papers, causing a number of celebrities to leave Los Angeles. Faced with the jail-cell confessions, Atkins could not back down. On 5 December 1969, she testified to the Grand Jury, describing what had really happened at 10050 Cielo Drive on the night of 8 August. And she blamed Manson.

The Manson trial began on 15 June 1970. It lasted for nine-and-a-half months, the longest murder trial in America at that time. The transcript ran to over eight million words. Throughout the entire trial the jury – seven men and five women – were sequestered. They were kept in a hotel and supervised by bailiffs for 225 days. There was a vast amount of evidence to gather and a huge number of witnesses to locate and interview. Tex Watson had gone home to Texas and fought extradition. Manson had his own line of delaying techniques. First, he said he wanted to defend himself. His request was refused but the attorneys appointed him by the court were rejected, one after the other. In the end, he was defended by Irving Kanarek, himself a master of delaying tactics. His notorious obstructionism once stretched a simple case of theft until it took up two years of court time.

The defence began by challenging the right of the judge William Keene to preside over the case. The challenge was successful. He was dismissed and replaced by Judge Charles Older. Then the trial was almost over before it started when newly elected President Richard Nixon declared Manson was guilty, overriding the assumption of innocence that is the basis of common law. As the jury was sequestered, it was felt there was no reason to call a mistrial.

The Manson trial was unique. Never in the history of American jurisprudence had someone been charged with mass murder by proxy as there was no suggestion that Manson had actually killed anyone by his own hand. His strategy was to control the entire defence team. As long as he could prevent his followers from saying that he had ordered the murders, he stood a chance of getting off scot-free. His female followers were still largely under his thrall. Susan Atkins, who promised to turn state's evidence and testify against Manson, retracted her earlier statements and faced the charges beside him. Inside court and out, Manson's women pledged to follow him to the end.

On 24 July 1969, Manson appeared in court with a cross carved on his forehead. He had cut it himself with a hacksaw blade. Though he said nothing, he issued a press statement saying: 'I have Xd myself from your society'. A few days later, his co-defendants appeared with the same mark on their foreheads. By the end of the week, The Family women who camped outside the court building had done the same. Manson's X later turned into a swastika.

When Manson turned his back on the judge, so too did his followers. Later he caused uproar by hurling himself at the bench, screaming at the judge that he should have his head cut off.

For their own safety, prosecution attorneys were given bodyguards and walkie-talkies during the trial. Family members made no direct attack on them, but they did attempt a raid on a gun store, which failed. They were apprehended in a bullet-riddled van after a shoot-out with the police. Their plan had been to use the guns to hijack a plane and demand Manson's release.

Manson's strategy of letting his acolytes take the rap failed. Linda Kasabian, who had not actually participated in any of the murders, took the stand as a witness for the prosecution. She said she loved Manson, but then told the court everything she knew about the murders. She had been outside the house during the Tate murders and had heard other Family members talk about the killing of the LaBiancas. More damningly, from the witness box she told Manson: 'I am not like you, Charlie. I can't kill anyone.'

Manson's defence had tried to establish Tex Wilson as the evil genius behind the murders but when he finally arrived from the Texas jailhouse where he had been held during the lengthy extradition battle, the jury saw a good-looking, clean-cut, square-jawed, all-American boy – not an evil genius at all. In his testimony, he too tied Manson to the murders: 'Charlie called me over behind a car. He said for me to take the gun and the knife and go up to where Terry Melcher used to live. He said to kill everyone in the house as gruesomely as possible.'

In what amounted to a threat, Manson told the jury: 'You say there are just a few in my Family – there are many, many more, coming in the same direction. They are running in the streets, and they are coming right at you.'

Then he taunted them with a simple truth. 'I've killed no one,' he said. 'I've ordered no one to be killed. These children who come to you with their knives, they're your children. I didn't teach them – you did.'

No one was fooled. Manson, Beausoleil, Atkins, Krenwinkel, Van Houten and Grogan were all sentenced to death in the gas chamber. But Charlie was not afraid: 'My faith in me is stronger than all your armies, government gas chambers or anything you may want to do to me,' he maintained.

In some ways, he was right. Before the sentence could be carried out, the death penalty was abolished in California. Manson and his followers had their sentences commuted to life imprisonment and they are now eligible for parole. So far, only Steven Grogan has been granted this. Finally, in 1977, he revealed where Donald Shea's body was buried.

Former Family member Lynette Fromme made a half-hearted attempt to get Manson out. In 1975, she pulled a gun on US President Gerald Ford but she did not pull the trigger and succeeded only in putting Manson back in the headlines again.

Manson constantly asks for parole. He does it, not

because he has a reasonable chance of getting out, but because this gains him publicity. He revels in his image as the baddest man on Earth and boasts he is responsible for 35 other murders.

At a parole hearing in 1981, he said that Los Angeles County district attorney Stephen Kay, an assistant prosecutor at the original trial, would be murdered in the car park as he left the building but he was alive and well at the next parole board hearing.

The following year, Manson was transferred to a maximum security cell at Vacaville prison after the authorities learned he was planning an escape by hot-air balloon. A ballooning catalogue, a rope, a hacksaw and a container of flammable liquid were found.

At one parole board hearing, Manson was asked why he unravelled his socks and used the yarn to make into woollen scorpions. He rose from his seat and said quite seriously: 'From the world of darkness I did loose demons and devils in the power of scorpions to torment.'

Parole was refused.

In 1986, Manson's parole request was opposed by California's governor George Deukmejian. In response, Manson read out a 20-page handwritten statement described by those who heard it as 'bizarre and rambling'. Three years later he refused to appear before the parole board because he was made to wear manacles. These, he said, made the board think he was dangerous.

In 1992, his hearing was held within hours of the first execution held in California for over a decade. Of course, Manson's death sentence cannot be reinstated. Nevertheless, he weakened his chances of getting parole when he told the board: 'There's no one as bad as me. I am everywhere. I am down in San Diego Zoo. I am in your children. Someone had to be insane. We can't all be good guys. They've tried to kill me thirty or forty times in prison. They've poured fire over me. They haven't found anyone badder than me because there is no one as bad as me – and that's a fact.'

He might, however, find some competition in this book.

Manson was denied parole for the eleventh time on 23 May 2007. He will not be eligible again for parole until 2012. The truth is, Manson will never be allowed out.

CHAPTER EIGHT

PETER SUTCLIFFE

Almost 90 years after the original Jack the Ripper ended his killing spree, Yorkshire Ripper Peter Sutcliffe picked up where he left off. By the time Sutcliffe was caught, 20 women had been savagely attacked, 13 brutally murdered and a whole community was virtually under siege. In a reign of terror spanning nearly six years, he managed to elude the biggest police squad ever assembled to catch one man.

It started on 30 October 1975 when a Leeds milkman on his rounds saw a shapeless bundle in a bleak recreation ground known as the Prince Philip Playing Fields. With Bonfire Night just a week away, he thought it was a Guy but when he went over to investigate, he found a woman sprawled on the ground, her hair matted with blood, her body exposed. Her jacket and blouse had been torn open, her bra pulled up; her slacks had been pulled down below her knees and in her chest and stomach there were 14 stab wounds.

The milkman didn't see the massive wound to the back of her head that had actually caused her death. The victim had been attacked from behind and two vicious blows delivered by a heavy, hammer-like implement, had smashed her skull. The stab wounds were inflicted after she was dead.

The body belonged to 28-year-old mother-of-four Wilma McCann. She regularly hitchhiked home after a night on the town and had died just a hundred yards from her home, a council house in Scott Hall Avenue. Although her clothes had been interfered with, her panties were still in place and she had not been raped. Initially, there seemed to be no overt sexual motive for her murder. Her purse was missing. So, in the absence of any other motive, the police treated her killing as a callous by-product of robbery.

As the police got to work, they had discovered that, despite having four children, Wilma McCann had never settled into the domestic role of a wife and mother, preferring to spend her evenings in Leeds' many hotels. On the night she was killed, she had left the children in the care of the eldest, nine-year-old Sonia, and went out drinking. As she was making her way home after closing time, a lorry driver stopped to give her a lift, but left her at the side of the road when greeted with incoherent instructions and drunken abuse. Eventually she got a lift from a West Indian man at around 1.30am. At 5am, a neighbour found her two oldest daughters huddled together in the cold at the bus stop. Their mother had not come home the night before and they were hoping she would be on the first bus.

The pathologist's report later revealed that Wilma had consumed 12–14 measures of spirits on the night of her death and traces of semen were found on the back of her trousers and underpants. By the time the coroner returned a verdict of 'murder by person or persons unknown', the police had assigned 150 officers to the case. They interviewed 6,000 lorry drivers, along with another 5,000 householders in the area and anyone with even the remotest connection to Wilma. However, this brought them no closer to finding her killer. Her death left her children devastated. After a troubled childhood, her son Richard ended up in prison on drugs charges. Sonia took to drink and committed suicide in 2007.

The man the police were looking for was Peter William Sutcliffe. The eldest of John and Kathleen Sutcliffe's six children, he was born in Bingley, a dour town just six miles north of Bradford, on 2 June 1946. Unlike his sports-loving father, he was small and weedy as child. A shy boy intimidated by his father's aggressive masculinity, he immersed himself in reading and clung to his mother's skirts.

At primary school he did not mix with the other kids, preferring to seek safety in the corner. His father was so concerned that he would visit the school every afternoon in the hope of getting his son to join in. This failed. The move to secondary school did not help. The young Sutcliffe spent two weeks hiding in the loft of the family home, reading comics by torchlight, until his truancy was reported.

While his younger brothers inherited their father's appetite for life, the opposite sex and the consumption of large quantities of beer, Peter liked none of these things. Although he took no interest in girls, he spent hours preening himself in the bathroom. Later, he took up bodybuilding. He left school at 15 and took an engineering apprenticeship at the mill where his father worked. This lasted nine months. After briefly working as a general labourer, he took a job as a grave-digger at a cemetery in Bingley and regularly joked about having 'thousands of people below me where I work now'. He developed a macabre sense of humour during his three years there. Once he pretended to be a corpse: he lay down on a slab, threw a shroud over himself and started making moaning noises when his workmates appeared. They called him 'Jesus' because of his beard. He also stole rings from those he buried.

At his trial Sutcliffe claimed he had heard the voice of God while he was working at the cemetery. He said he was digging a grave when he heard a voice coming from a cross-shaped headstone. The voice told him to go out onto the streets and kill prostitutes.

Despite Peter Sutcliffe's youthful good looks, girls were not attracted to him. His first girlfriend Sonia was a 16-year-old schoolgirl when he met her in the Royal Standard, his local pub.

A devout Catholic, Sutcliffe was devastated when it was discovered that his mother was having an affair with a neighbour, a local policeman. His father arranged for the children, including Peter and bride-to-be Sonia, to be present at a Bingley hotel for a humiliating confrontation. His mother arrived in the bar believing she was meeting her boyfriend, only to be greeted by her husband and children. He forced her to show the family the new nightdress bought for the occasion. Later that year, 1969, Sutcliffe carried out his first known attack. He hit a Bradford prostitute over the head with a brick in a sock following a row over a £10 note.

After an eight-year courtship, Peter and Sonia married. They spent the first three years of their married life living with Sonia's parents. Later they moved to a large detached house in Heaton, a middle-class suburb of Bradford, which they kept immaculate. By then he had become a lorry driver and had brought himself a white Ford Corsair with a black roof, while keeping his first car, a lime-green Ford Capri GT.

Throughout all this, Sutcliffe was carrying on a double life. His brother-in-law, Robin Holland, would often go out drinking with him in the red-light districts of nearby towns in Yorkshire. While playing the faithful husband at home, Sutcliffe would brag about his exploits with prostitutes to Holland. Eventually, this hypocrisy became too much for his friend and he began to avoid him. Sutcliffe continued to go out with his friend Trevor Birdsall. The two had cruised the red-light districts before Sutcliffe was married; Birdsall had even been waiting in the car on the night in 1969 when Sutcliffe had hit the prostitute with a brick and returned to brag about it. Despite this, Birdsall would remain Sutcliffe's friend until the Ripper was arrested in 1981.

The first attack by Sutcliffe that reached the ears of the police came just under a year after his marriage. The victim was 36-year-old Anna Patricia Rogulskyj, who lived in nearby Keighley. An attractive blonde, she divorced her Ukrainian husband two years before and was expecting to marry her new boyfriend shortly. But on the night of 4 July 1975, she had a row with him. In anger, she walked out on him and went drinking with friends at a club in Bradford.

At 1am, they dropped her home, where she expected to find her boyfriend. He was not there, so she set off across town on foot to his house for a confrontation. She banged on the door, but there was no answer. In frustration, she took off one of her shoes and smashed the glass of a downstairs window. As she stooped to put her shoe back on, Sutcliffe emerged from the shadows and struck her a savage blow to the head with a hammer. Although she was unconscious, he hit her twice more. Then he pulled up her skirt, pulled down her panties and slashed her repeatedly across her stomach with a knife.

The police were mystified for the attack appeared motiveless. Anna's boyfriend and friends were clear of any involvement. There seemed to be no sexual element in the attack and no money had been taken. All they had to go on was the neighbour's vague description of a man in his late twenties or early thirties, about 5ft 8in and wearing a checked sports jacket.

Six weeks later, on 15 August 1975, Sutcliffe and his friend Trevor Birdsall drove to Halifax. In a pub there, they saw 46-year-old Olive Smelt, who was out for a drink with girlfriends, leaving husband Harry at home with their 15-year-old daughter and nine-year-old son. The two men gave the women a lift home. After dropping Olive a short walk from her home, Sutcliffe left Birdsall in the car. He took a short cut and caught up with her and hit her on the back of the head. Striking her again as she fell to the ground, he slashed her back with his knife just above the buttocks. This time he was disturbed by an approaching car. Another victim had survived, but was left understandably traumatised.

Just 12 days later, on 27 August, Sutcliffe attacked 14-year-old Tracy Browne in a country lane near Silsden. He struck her from behind, hitting her on the head five times. Sutcliffe was never charged with this attack, but confessed to it in 1992.

Despite similarities between these attacks, police did not link them for some time and it would be three years until they realised that they were the work of the Yorkshire Ripper. By that time there were at least three more victims.

Three months after Wilma McCann had been murdered, there was a second killing in the area of Chapeltown, the red-light district of Leeds. Not all the women who worked there were professional prostitutes. Some housewives sold sex for a little extra cash. Others, such as 42-year-old Emily Jackson, were enthusiastic amateurs, who did it primarily for fun. She lived with her husband Sydney and their three children in the respectable Leeds suburb of Churwell. On 20 January 1976, Emily and Sydney went to the Gaiety pub on the Roundhay Road, the venue for the Chapeltown irregulars and their prospective clientele. Emily left her husband in the main lounge and went hunting for business outside. An hour later, she was seen getting into a Land Rover in the car park. At closing time, Sydney drank up and took a taxi home alone. His wife, he thought, had found a client who wanted her for the night.

Emily Jackson's body was found the next morning left

under a coat on open ground just 800 yards from the Gaiety. Like Wilma McCann, her breasts were exposed and her panties left on. Again, she had been killed by two massive blows to the head with a heavy hammer. Her neck, breasts and stomach had also been stabbed – this time over 50 times. Her back had been gouged with a Phillips screwdriver and the impression of a heavy ribbed Wellington boot was stamped on her right thigh.

The post mortem indicated Emily Jackson had had sex before the attack, not necessarily with the murderer. Once again, there seemed to be no real motive. The killer left only one real clue: from the mark on her thigh and a footprint nearby, the police could tell that he wore a size seven shoe. Detective Chief Superintendent Dennis Hoban, later in charge of the McCann inquiry, was convinced this was the work of the same man. Emily Jackson's husband Sydney believed he would kill again.

Four months later, another attack took place in Chapeltown. Twenty-year-old prostitute Marcella Claxton was walking home from a drinks party at around 4am on 9 May 1976 when Sutcliffe, who was cruising the area in his white Ford Corsair, spotted her. He pulled up. Marcella explained she was not working that night but she accepted a lift. Instead of taking her home, Sutcliffe drove her to Soldier's Field just off Roundhay Road. He offered her £5 to undress and have sex on the grass. She refused, but got out of the car to urinate behind a tree. He got out too and Marcella heard a thud as something Sutcliffe had dropped hit the ground. He said it was his wallet, but he then walked up behind her and hit her on the head with a hammer. As she lay on the grass, bleeding heavily, he stood nearby masturbating, but he did not kill her. Later he admitted: 'I don't know what it was this time, but I just couldn't go through with it. I could not bring myself to hit her again for some reason or another.'

When he had finished, he tucked a £5 note in her hand

and got back into his car. Her clothes soaked in blood, Marcella managed to half-crawl, half-walk to a nearby telephone box, where she called for an ambulance.

'After I had dialled 999 and was sat on the floor of the telephone box, a man in a white car kept driving past,' she said. 'He seemed to be staring and looking for me. It was the man that hurt me... He got out and began searching the spot where he had left me. He must have come back to finish me off.'

Marcella required extensive brain surgery and 52 stitches to close the wounds in her head. Despite appalling injuries, she gave an accurate portrayal of Peter Sutcliffe, describing her attacker as a young white man with crinkly black hair and beard. She said he had a Yorkshire accent, but did not live in Leeds and drove a white car with red upholstery. However, her attack was not be conclusively linked to the Yorkshire Ripper case until Sutcliffe had been arrested and confessed. In his confession he alleged that Marcella suggested that 'we start the ball rolling on the grass.' He vehemently denied masturbating.

'I didn't want sex with any of them – certainly not that one,' he said. 'Even the police said she were like a gorilla.'

Marcella was educationally subnormal with an IQ of 50 and she was black. The West Yorkshire Police had a terrible reputation for race relations at the time.

For months, Sutcliffe lay low. This may have been because of increased police activity, or because prostitutes were becoming more wary. Or it could have been because he lost his job in March, not because he was not a good worker but because he was constantly late in the mornings after his late-night forays into red-light districts. It was only in October 1976 that he found a new job, driving for a transport company based in the Canal Road Industrial Estate between Bradford and Shipley. Then he went back into action again.

On 5 February 1977, 28-year-old part-time prostitute

Irene Richardson left her tawdry rooming house in Chapeltown half-an-hour before midnight to go dancing. The following morning, a jogger in Soldier's Field – the same public playing field where Marcella Claxton had been attacked – saw a body slumped on the ground. Stopping to investigate, he found Irene Richardson lying face down. Three massive blows had shattered her skull; her skirt and tights had been torn off. Her coat was draped over her buttocks and calf-length boots had been removed from her feet and laid neatly across her thighs; her neck and torso were studded with knife wounds. The attack had been so savage that her intestines spilled out. Later, the post mortem found semen in her vagina, but she had died only half an hour after leaving her lodgings and it was thought that it had come from sexual intercourse prior to the attack.

Tyre tracks were found near the body. The tyres were identified and could have been fitted to any one of 26 models of vehicle. At that time, the road tax office had not computerised its records: the police had to go through the records by hand and drew up a list of 100,000 vehicles in West Yorkshire alone that might have fitted those tyres.

The police now linked the murder of Irene Richardson with those of Wilma McCann and Emily Jackson. They were plainly the work of a serial killer. A parallel with the Jack the Ripper case quickly sprang into the public imagination. The murderer soon became known as the Yorkshire Ripper and came to nationwide attention.

Soon George Oldfield, Assistant Chief Constable at West Yorkshire Police Headquarters in Wakefield, received the first in a series of letters by someone claiming to be the Yorkshire Ripper. He claimed also to have killed Joan Harrison, whose body was found in a garage in Preston, Lancashire, on 20 November 1975. She had been hit over the back of the head with the heel of a shoe and then kicked to dead. The killer made some attempt to hide the body at the back of the garage. He had also pulled her bra back down to cover her breasts, put her trousers back on and then covered her with her coat. Her handbag had been rifled and dumped in a dustbin.

Other clues had been left. One was a deep bite mark above her breast. This showed that the killer had a gap between his front teeth. Semen found in her vagina and anus showed that the killer was a 'secretor' – that is, one of the 80 per cent of the population whose blood group shows up in their bodily fluids. The killer's blood group was B, which is rare outside Asia and found in just ten per cent of the UK's population.

Oldfield dismissed the letter as just another one of the many crank missives he and the newspapers had already received. There were too many differences from the other three murders. However, as more letters came in, mentioning the murder in Preston, the police began to believe that Joan Harrison was one of the Ripper's victims.

With a killer on the loose, the girls of Chapeltown heeded police warnings, moving in droves to Manchester, London and Glasgow. Those who could not travel so far from home began to ply their trade in nearby Bradford, not knowing they were placing themselves in the Ripper's hands.

The next victim, Patricia 'Tina' Atkinson, was a Bradford girl. She lived just around the corner from the thriving red-light district in Oak Lane. On 23 April 1977, she went to her local pub, The Carlisle, where she was well known for her heavy drinking. She reeled out just before closing time and was seen walking towards Church Street. Soon afterwards, Sutcliffe picked her up. Together they walked to his car and he drove the intoxicated woman back to her flat. As she entered the front door, he hit her on the back of the head with the same ball-peen hammer used in the other attacks. Three more hammer blows smashed into her skull before the unconscious body hit the floor. He flung his lifeless victim onto the bed and pulled her clothes off. Then he stabbed her in the stomach seven times with a chisel.

When Tina Atkinson was not seen the whole of the next day, people assumed she was at home, sleeping it off. The following evening, friends dropped round and found the door to her flat unlocked. Inside, they discovered her body on the bed, covered with blankets. The left side had been slashed to ribbons. There was a size seven Wellington boot print on the sheet, tying the murder – if any more evidence were needed – to the murder of Emily Jackson. It was the work of the Yorkshire Ripper.

On Saturday, 25 June 1977, Sutcliffe and his wife Sonia went to view a new home at 6 Garden Lane in the Heaton district of Bradford. Sonia was just ending her teacher training course. Soon she would get a teaching job and she was convinced that they would be able to afford a home of their own. That evening, Sutcliffe dropped his wife off at the Sherrington Nursing Home where she worked nights. With his neighbours Ronnie and Peter Barker, he went on a pub crawl around Bradford, ending up at the Dog in the Pound, where an ex-sailor in drag worked behind the bar. At closing time, they went to get some fish and chips.

It was well past midnight when he dropped the Barker brothers at their front door, but instead of going home, Sutcliffe drove off down the main road towards Leeds. At around 2am, he spotted a lone girl wearing a gingham skirt in the streetlight of Chapeltown Road. Sixteen-year-old Jayne MacDonald had just started her first job in the shoe department of a local supermarket. That night she was happy and she had kissed her father goodbye before leaving their home in Reginald Terrace, Chapeltown to go out dancing.

After the dance, Jayne went with friends to buy chips in the city centre. Engrossed in conversation, she missed her last bus. At 11.50pm, she began walking home with Mark Jones, a young boy she had met earlier that night. He said his sister would give Jayne a lift home, but when they got to the house his sister was out. Mark continued walking Jayne home. They stopped for a brief kiss and a cuddle, but at the Florence Nightingale pub, they went their separate ways. It was 1.30. At 1.45, she stopped at a phone box near Dock Green pub at the corner of Beckett Street to call a taxi, but could not get through. Then, as she passed the Hayfield pub and turned left down Reginald Terrace, Sutcliffe had already parked his car. He got out and began to follow her down the quiet side street.

Coming up from behind, he hit Jayne on the head with his hammer, then dragged her 20 yards into an adventure playground, where she was found lying face down by children the next day. He had hit twice more. Then he pulled down her halterneck top to expose her breasts, pulled up her shirt and stabbed once in the back and repeatedly through the chest. The Ripper's trademarks were unmistakable.

For once, the dead woman was not a prostitute. This gave new impetus to the investigation. By September, the police had interviewed almost 7,000 residents in the area and had taken 3,500 statements, many of them from prostitutes working there. Still they were no closer to capturing the killer.

Two weeks after the killing of Jayne McDonald, Sutcliffe left Sonia at home with her parents and headed for the red-light district of Bradford. That night – Saturday, 9 July 1977 – Maureen Long from Farsley, near Leeds, was also spending the night in Bradford. After visiting various pubs, she met up with her estranged husband. Then she moved on to the Bali Hai discotheque, where she drank and danced until 2am.

She then planned to go to her husband's home in Laisterdyke and was waiting in the queue at a taxi rank when a white Ford Corsair drew up. The driver was Peter Sutcliffe, who offered her a lift. He drove her to Bowling Back Lane. When she got out of the car to urinate, he struck her a massive blow to the back of the head. As she lay on the ground, he ripped open her dress and stabbed her repeatedly in the abdomen and back. But the barking of a dog interrupted his frenzied attack. Leaving his victim for dead, he fled the scene. Alerted by the barking, a night watchman who worked nearby saw a car leaving the scene at high speed. He noted that it was 3.27am. However, he misidentified the car as a Ford Cortina Mark II.

The following morning, two women living in a nearby caravan heard cries for help. They found Maureen Long lying seriously injured on the ground. She was rushed to hospital and underwent emergency surgery. By some miracle she survived, but the description she gave of her assailant was too hazy to help the inquiry.

The investigation staffing was increased to 304 full-time officers who had soon interviewed 175,000 people, taken 12,500 statements and checked 10,000 vehicles. The problem was that they had no idea of the type of man they should be looking for. Certainly no one suspected 31-year-old long-distance lorry driver Peter Sutcliffe who, on 26 August 1977, moved into his new home with his wife Sonia, who was about to start her first teaching job. The neighbours found Sutcliffe polite and mild-mannered. He was a hard-working and trusted employee, a good son and a seemingly loyal husband, the sort of man who did jobs around the house or tinkered with his car at weekends. Nothing about him suggested he was a mass murderer.

Those who knew Sutcliffe would have been surprised if they had seen him out picking up prostitutes but he continued to do so regularly. On Saturday, 1 October 1977, he spent the day working on his new red Ford Corsair, having sold the white model the day before. That evening, he decided to give his new car a test drive. Heading for Manchester, he took a hammer that the previous resident had left in the garage with him.

At 9.30pm, 20-year-old Jean Jordan climbed into Sutcliffe's car not far from her home in Moss Side. Four years before, she had run away from her home in Scotland. Arriving in Manchester, she met Alan Royle and had moved in with him. Two years later they had their first child; two years after that, their second son was born. On the evening of 1 October, Alan had gone out. He returned to find the children in bed, but Jean gone. He assumed that she had decided to go out with her girlfriends. In fact, she was moonlighting as a prostitute and out looking for business.

Jean had been haggling with another client when Sutcliffe turned up. He wanted her because, he said, she was 'slim and not bad looking.'

'She told me she was going with the other man until she saw me,' Sutcliffe said. 'I suppose this was the biggest mistake she ever made.'

Jean took £5 in advance and directed Sutcliffe to some wasteland two miles away, on Princess Road, Chorlton, near the Southern Cemetery that was used by prostitutes and their clients. They were a few yards away from the car when Sutcliffe smashed a hammer down onto Jordan's skull. He hit her again and again, 11 times in all, and then dragged her body into some bushes. However, another car arrived and he was forced to make a quick getaway.

As he drove back to Bradford, Sutcliffe realised that he had left a vital clue on the body: the £5 note he had given Jean Jordan was brand new. It had come directly from his wage packet and could tie him to the dead girl.

For eight long days, he waited nervously. He scanned the press, but there was nothing about the body. She was not even reported missing because her common-law husband assumed she was making an unannounced trip to Scotland to visit relatives. Finally, Sutcliffe thought it was safe to risk returning to Moss Side.

He decided the house warming party that he and Sonia were hosting on Sunday, 9 October, would be an ideal opportunity to return to Manchester and retrieve the note. When the party ended around midnight, he drove his parents to their home in Bingley and then headed for Manchester. The traffic was light and he reached the outskirts of Manchester in three-quarters of an hour. Fifteen minutes later, he was parked by the Princess Road allotments and heading into the wasteland to find Jean Jordan's body.

Her body was where he had left it, but despite a frantic search he could not find her handbag. In frustration, he turned his attention to the corpse, which he felt was mocking him. Frenzied, he attacked the body with a knife, stabbing and slashing it. When the gas that had built up in her stomach vented through a gash in her torso, the stench caused him to vomit, but he continued to attack. Sutcliffe used a large piece of glass with a cutting edge to mutilate the victim's body in a way unseen in previous Ripper killings. He even tried to cut off her head to hide it, so that the police would not recognise the hammer blows that were his signature. Perhaps they would not realise that the Yorkshire Ripper had crossed the Pennines, but might think that there was a new maniac at large.

However, the glass was not sharp enough to decapitate the corpse so he tried to saw the head off with a hacksaw blade. This failed too. Now fearing almost certain capture, he kicked the body in frustration before driving back to Bradford. When he arrived home, he was surprised to find there was not much blood on his clothing. He left his trousers in the garage, disposing of them later by burning them with some garden rubbish.

The following day, an allotment owner found Jean Jordan's naked body. It had been badly mutilated and there was a coil of intestine wrapped around her waist. Most of the top clothing was badly bloodstained and crawling with maggots, as was a nearby depression under a privet hedge where the body had lain beneath a wooden door. Clearly the murderer had returned to the scene and pulled the body out from where he had concealed it, stripping away the clothing and mutilating it.

Sutcliffe's initial hammer blows had flattened Jean Jordan's head, leaving her face unrecognisable. When he had returned nine days later, he had stabbed her 18 times in the breasts and chest, in the stomach and around the vagina. Some of the gashes were eight inches deep.

When reports of the murder of the unidentified woman were published in the newspapers, Alan Royle telephoned the police to say that he suspected it might be his common-law wife, Jean Jordan. He was able to make a preliminary identification from her clothing but the final identification could only be made from a fingerprint she had left on a lemonade bottle before leaving home for the last time.

Five days after the body was discovered, another allotment holder found Jean's handbag in some long grass underneath a fence, some 189 feet away from where the body had lain. The handbag was open and it appeared to have been searched. However, a £5 note and a £1 note were discovered in a small side pocket, which seemed to have been missed. The notes were wet, but when the £5 note was dried it was clear that it was freshly minted.

Serial number AW51 121565 put it among a batch sent to the Shipley branch of the Midland Bank. The consignment had then been split up to be distributed to local businesses to pay their workers on Friday, 30 September. This put the note in the heart of Yorkshire Ripper country on the day before Jean Jordan died. Still, it could have passed through three or four pairs of hands before it reached hers.

In the following three months the police interviewed 5,000 men. One of them was Peter Sutcliffe. However, he had an alibi for the night Jean's body had been disturbed. He had been at a house-warming party. After leaving Sutcliffe's well-appointed new house, detectives filed a short report which left him free to go about his gruesome business.

While the interviews were still going on, Sutcliffe struck again. This time he returned to the Chapeltown district of Leeds. On the evening of 14 December, 25-year-old Marilyn Moore had left a friend's house near the Gaiety pub and was walking along Gipton Avenue, Chapeltown when she saw a car drive slowly by in a way that suggested the driver was a possible client. When she turned into Leopold Street, she found the car parked at the junction with Frankland Place and a man standing beside the driver's door.

He was about 30 and 5ft 6in tall with a stocky build, dark wavy hair and a beard, and he appeared to be waving to someone in a nearby house. Sutcliffe had seen her refuse to get into a car before and this was a ploy to reassure her. As she walked by, he asked if she was doing business. After agreeing on a price of £5, they headed for a place about a mile-and-a-half away that Sutcliffe said he knew. On the way, he told her that his name was Dave and said that he had been waving goodbye to a sick girlfriend. It was plain that he knew the area well and mentioned two other prostitutes, Hilary and Gloria, both of whom were known to Marilyn.

Sutcliffe drove to Scott Hall Street and headed up a muddy track towards some waste ground behind a mill. They were about 200 yards from the Prince Philip Playing Fields, where Wilma McCann had been murdered some two years before. When they had parked, Sutcliffe suggested they have sex in the back seat. Marilyn agreed, but when she got out she found the back passenger door was locked.

As Sutcliffe came round to open it, he swung at her head with a hammer but he lost his balance slightly and caught her only a glancing blow. She screamed and held her head in her hands. A second blow knocked her to the ground. As she fell, she grabbed at his trousers.

'Dirty prostitute bitch!' shouted Sutcliffe as he hit her again. But her screams had set a dog barking. Sutcliffe returned to the car, spinning the wheels as he raced away.

Again he had left his victim alive. Marilyn gradually got herself to her feet and staggered towards the road to find a phone and get help. On the way, a couple noticed her and phoned an ambulance. She was rushed to Leeds Infirmary for emergency surgery to relieve the pressure on her brain caused by a depressed fracture of the skull. She had been hit eight times with the hammer and there were bruises to her hands and arms, where she had tried to protect her head.

Due to the severity of her head injuries, the police thought that her description of the suspect might not be reliable, though it turned out to be very accurate. However, it transpired that she had telephoned the police three times before to say that she had seen the Yorkshire Ripper. She also said that she thought he had a Liverpudlian accent.

She misidentified his car as a Morris Oxford, though the tyre tracks were consistent with those found at the scene of Irene Richardson's murder. There was no doubt that the Yorkshire Ripper had been the one who attacked her. After he was finally arrested, he admitted the attack. More were to follow.

On the night of 21 January, 22-year-old Yvonne Pearson left her two children in the care of a 16-year-old neighbour and went to the Flying Dutchman pub. She left there at around 9.30pm, telling a friend that she was going to 'earn some money.'

Yvonne had fallen on hard times. She had once been a high-class call girl servicing rich businessmen in most of Britain's cities, but now she was due in court in five days' time on a charge of soliciting. This would not be her first offence and there was a chance that she would go to prison.

That night Sutcliffe had been helping his brother Mick to move his parents into a new home near the Bingley centre. He refused to stay for a drink – Mick and his father John had assumed that he wanted to get home to Sonia. However, Sutcliffe headed straight for the red-light district of Bradford. As he was driving down Lumb Lane, a car backed out of a side street, causing him to brake sharply. When he screeched to a halt, a blonde dressed in a black sweater and black trousers tapped on the window and asked if he wanted business.

'On reflection it was a very fateful moment for her, me just slowing down as she came along,' he later admitted. 'This was one time when I was genuinely going home as it happened, but I still had a hammer in the car on the floor, under my seat. I told her to get in.'

Yvonne directed Sutcliffe to piece of waste ground at the back of Drummond's mill, where his father worked. They agreed a price of £5 and she asked: 'Shall I get in the back?'

When she got out, she found the back door locked. Sutcliffe went round to help her. Then, as she got in, he hit her over the head twice with a heavy walling hammer. She fell down and started to moan loudly. He dragged her by the feet about 20 yards to where an old settee was lying on its back.

Almost immediately, another car appeared and pulled up alongside his. To stop her moaning, Sutcliffe grabbed handfuls of horsehair from the sofa and began stuffing them into his victim's mouth, while holding her nose. After a while, he let go of her nose to see if she was still making a noise. She was, so he grabbed it and held it again, terrified of being discovered.

After what seemed an inordinately long time, the other car pulled away. By then, Sutcliffe was seething with rage and determined to take it out on Yvonne. He pulled off her jeans and began kicking her head and body. Although she was already dead, he later claimed that he apologised to her. He said it would be all right – she could get up. Of course she didn't.

Sutcliffe then put together a makeshift grave by turning the settee on top of Yvonne. He said he was very distraught and in tears when he left her: 'This was the first time I had apologised to someone I had killed.' He even claimed to have stopped on the way home to try and work out why he had done this particular killing – 'My mind was in a turmoil.'

For weeks, he scanned the papers and found it hard to believe that the body had not been found. Then he read a story that Yvonne Pearson was thought to have moved to Wolverhampton. She had been reported missing the following Monday, but the police suspected she may have disappeared to avoid the impending court appearance. Nevertheless they checked her whereabouts with other police forces and searched derelict areas but no information was forthcoming.

Even though Sutcliffe later claimed to have been distressed by the murder of Yvonne Pearson, he struck again just ten days on, long before her body was found. His next victim was 18-year-old Helen Rytka, who shared a miserable room by a flyover in Huddersfield with her twin sister Rita. Concentrating on the car trade, the two worked as a pair in the red-light district around Great Northern Street.

The Yorkshire Ripper murders scared them, so they had devised a system which they thought would keep them safe: they based themselves outside a public lavatory. When they were picked up separately, each took a note of the number of the client's car. They each gave their client precisely 20 minutes, then returned to the toilet at a set time, but their system went terribly wrong.

On the snowy night of Tuesday, 31 January 1978 Helen arrived back at the rendezvous five minutes early. At 9.25pm, a bearded man in a red Ford Corsair offered her the chance of a fast £5. She thought she could perform her services quickly and make it back to the rendezvous before her sister returned, but Rita never saw her alive again.

Sutcliffe had already picked Rita and her sister out: 'One

day I had to make a delivery in Huddersfield in the afternoon. I noticed a few girls plying for trade near the Market Area,' he said. 'Two or three nights later I decided to pay them a visit. The urge inside me to kill girls was now practically uncontrollable. I drove to Huddersfield in my red Corsair one evening. When I got to the red-light area, I came across one or two girls walking round the street. I stopped and asked one girl if she was doing business. She said yes, but I'd have to wait as her regular client was picking her up at any minute. She was a half-caste girl. I drove off, and after going about 50 yards round the corner I saw another half-caste girl. I stopped and asked her, and she got in.'

Helen took her client to nearby Garrard's timberyard, some 80 yards away.

'On the way to the yard we passed the half-caste girl I had tried to pick up. She told me that it was her sister,' he said. 'She told me she shared a flat with her sister, but she was quite willing to have sex in the car. She said it would cost £5.'

When they pulled up in the woodyard, he gave her the £5 and Helen undid her trousers ready to have sex straightaway.

'It was very awkward for me to find a way of getting her out of the car,' Sutcliffe admitted. 'We were there five minutes or more, while I was trying to decide which method to use to kill her. Meanwhile, against my wishes, she was in the process of arousing me sexually. I found I did not want to go through with this, so I got out of the car on the pretext of wanting to urinate.'

He didn't urinate, but managed to persuade his victim to get out as well, saying that they would be better off having sex in the back of the car. As she was getting in, he seized his chance and swung at her head with his hammer.

'Unfortunately, during the downward swing the hammer caught the top edge of the doorframe and gave her a very light tap on her head,' he said.

Apparently she thought he had struck her with his hand. 'There's no need for that,' she said, plainly frightened. 'You don't even have to pay.'

He expected her to immediately shout for help as there were a couple of taxi drivers chatting with each other about 40 yards away. He hit her again, a 'furious blow', and she crumpled like a sack; he dragged her out of sight of the taxi drivers and pulled off her jeans and panties, and then flung himself on top of her, covering her mouth with his hand.

'I told her if she kept quiet she would be all right,' he said. By this time he was aroused. 'I had no alternative than to go ahead with the act of sex as the only means thereby of persuading her to keep quiet, as I had already dropped the hammer several yards away... I just undid my fly; I spread her legs out and did it. It only took a few minutes before I ejaculated inside her. Her eyes appeared to be focusing on me when I was doing it, but she just laid there limp – she didn't put anything into it.'

After he had ejaculated, she began moaning. Though they were out of sight of the taxi drivers, there was a possibility they could hear them.

'I couldn't drive away for obvious reasons, one being that she was still showing signs of life,' he said. He was worried that he was about to be discovered and furious that his victim could not keep quiet. He hit her five times more. The walls of the foreman's shed a few feet away were splattered with blood.

He got out a small knife taken from the kitchen drawer at home and stabbed her in the heart and lungs five or six times. Then he dragged Helen's body into a woodpile and hid it under a sheet of asbestos or corrugated metal. After this, he made his escape.

'I drove straight home,' Sutcliffe said. 'I found that I had some blood on one of my fawn court shoes. I rinsed it off. I had my Levi jeans and I think I had a dark blue pullover on, but I couldn't see any blood on these. I kept the hammer – I'm not sure which one it was – but I don't think it was the walling hammer.'

Back at the lavatory, Rita was desperately worried but fear of the police prevented her from reporting her sister's disappearance for three days. Eventually, a police Alsatian found the hidden body. It had been horribly mutilated – there were three gaping wounds in the chest where she had been stabbed repeatedly. Her bra and black polo-neck were pushed up above her breasts; her socks were left on, but the rest of her clothes were scattered over a wide area. Black lace panties had been found pinned to the shed door the next day by a lorry driver. It was not unusual in that area.

The Ripper's latest victim had disappeared from a busy street. Over 100 passers-by were traced. All but three cars and one stocky, fair-haired man eliminated. The police appealed on the radio to any wife, mother or girlfriend who suspected they were living with the Ripper, but no one came forward.

A few weeks later a passer-by spotted an arm sticking out from under an overturned sofa on wasteland in Bradford's red-light district. He thought it was a tailor's dummy but the putrid aroma sent him rushing for the phone. Further investigation revealed the body of Yvonne Pearson. The killing bore some of the hallmarks of the Ripper. A blow to the head had smashed her skull. Her bra and sweater were pulled up, exposing her breasts, and her chest had been jumped on repeatedly until the ribs cracked. Black flared slacks had been pulled down and horsehair from the sofa was stuffed in her mouth.

Yvonne had spoken of her fear of the Ripper only days before she disappeared. On the night of her death, she was seen climbing into a car driven by a bearded man with black piercing eyes, soon after 9.30pm. But there was a puzzle: the blow to the head was initially thought to have come from a rock, not a hammer. There were no stab wounds. It was inconceivable that no one had found her before with her arm sticking out so obviously. There was also a copy of the *Daily Mirror* tucked under her arm. It was dated 21 February, exactly one month after she had been murdered. Sutcliffe later denied returning to the body.

Two months after Yvonne Pearson's body was found, the Yorkshire Ripper attacked 41-year-old Vera Millward. The Spanish-born mother of seven had come to England after World War II and worked as a domestic help. She lived with a Jamaican and had resorted to prostitution in Manchester's Moss Side to help support her family. A frail, sickly woman, she had just one lung. She had undergone three major operations in 1976 and 1977, and suffered from chronic stomach pains.

On the night of 16 May 1978, she left her home at around 10pm, telling her boyfriend that she was going out to buy cigarettes. Knowing what she really meant, he did not expect to see her for a few hours. On Tuesdays and Thursdays she had a regular client who would usually park outside her flat in Greenham Avenue and flash his car headlights. That night he failed to show up. Vera hung around, hoping to pick up some business. A man driving through the area was the first to come along: Sutcliffe. He had felt the urge to kill again and had taken another trip to Manchester in his red Corsair to cruise the red-light area.

When he got there, there was no sign of any girls so he drove around aimlessly for some time. Then he got lucky.

'I saw a woman obviously waiting to be picked up,' said Sutcliffe. 'It was Vera Millward. I stopped and asked her if she was doing business. She said, "Yes." But it would have to be in the car. The price was £5, she got in and I drove off.'

They drove for about two-and-a-half miles to the Manchester Royal Infirmary and stopped at a quiet spot in a parking compound often used by prostitutes and their clients.

'She got out of my car and went to the back door,' said Sutcliffe. 'I picked my hammer up from under the seat and walked round the back of the car. As she was opening the rear door, I hit her on the head with the hammer and she dived backwards past where I was stood. She was on her hands and knees when I hit her again at least once. She fell flat on her face. I pulled her by her wrists over to the edge of the area, where there was either a fence or bushes.'

A man later claimed to have heard three screams for help from the hospital grounds, but decided they must be from a patient at the hospital.

'I took out my knife I was carrying, I think it may have been the same one I used on Rytka, but I'm not sure,' said Sutcliffe. 'I pulled her clothes up and slashed her stomach either vertical or diagonal; it opened up her stomach. Then I rolled her over onto her stomach and left her lying there. I drove away. I think I had to reverse out to get back again. I didn't get any blood on me on that occasion. I think I was wearing my brown car coat.'

Three months after Vera Millward's death, the police visited Sutcliffe again because his car registration number had cropped up during special checks in Leeds and Bradford. They returned to question him about the tyres on his car. This time they were looking for treads matching tracks at the scene of Irene Richardson's murder, 21 months earlier. As always, Sutcliffe was helpful and unruffled, giving them no reason to suspect him. They never even asked him for his blood group or his shoe size, which was unusually small for a man.

Suddenly the Ripper's killing spree stopped. For 11 months he dropped out of sight. The police believed that he had committed suicide, taking his identity with him to the grave. It was all eerily similar to the sudden end of Jack the Ripper's spree.

But Sutcliffe was not dead. Nor could he contain his desire to murder.

'Following Millward, the compulsion inside me seemed to lay dormant,' he recalled. 'But eventually the feelings came welling up, and each time they were more random and indiscriminate. I now realised I had the urge to kill any woman.'

On the evening of Friday, 2 March 1979, 22-year-old student Ann Rooney was attacked in the grounds of Horsforth College, Horsforth, just outside of Leeds. She was hit on the head three times from behind. Somehow she survived and described her attacker as being in his twenties, 5ft 10in tall, of broad build, with dark curly hair and a drooping moustache. She also identified his new Sunbeam Rapier, which had been seen cruising the red-light districts of Leeds, Bradford and Moss Side. The distinctive semicircular wounds to her head, it was determined, were probably caused by the head of a hammer. However, it would have been a different size from that known to be used by the Ripper, so she was not listed as one of his victims. Later, in Broadmoor, he confessed to an attack on a student around that time, but he said that it was in Bradford, not Leeds.

On the night of Wednesday, 4 April 1979, Sutcliffe had been out drinking with Trevor Birdsall. Shortly after closing time, he had dropped his friend home and drove to Halifax in his sporty Sunbeam. He cruised around the quiet residential district of Bell Hall. In the playing fields of Savile Park, there were a few people walking their dogs. After several circuits of the park, he spotted a young woman walking alone.

Around midnight, he got out of his car and accosted 19-year-old Josephine Whitaker. She had been to her grandparents to show them the new silver watch she had just bought for £60. Her grandmother, Mary Priestley, had been at a church party and had not returned home until late. She invited Josephine to stay the night, but as the case for the girl's contact lenses was at home and she had work the next day, she insisted on walking home. She left at around 11.40pm intending to walk across Savile Park to Ivy Street, where she lived.

'I'd been driving round aimlessly,' said Sutcliffe. 'The mood was in me and no woman was safe while I was in this state of mind. Without realising, or without having a particular destination, I arrived in Halifax late at night... I saw Josephine Whitaker walking up this street. She was wearing a three-quarter length skirt and a jacket. I parked up in this street with terrace houses and started to follow her on foot, and I caught up with her after a couple of minutes. I realised she was not a prostitute, but at that time I wasn't bothered – I just wanted to kill a woman.

'When I caught up with her, I started talking to her. I asked her if she had far to go. She said, "It's quite a walk." She didn't seem alarmed by my approach.'

They had a brief conversation as he walked alongside her.

'I was walking along chatting to her,' he said, 'and she was telling me things which I thought sounded completely innocent – she had been to her grandma's, she had bought her a watch and liked to go horse-riding... We were approaching the open grassland area. She told me that she normally took a short cut across the field. I said, "You don't know who you can trust these days." It sounds a bit evil now.'

He had a hammer and large rusty Philips screwdriver, which he had sharpened into a point, in his pocket.

They started to walk across the playing fields. When they were some 30 or 40 yards from the main road, away from the light of the streetlamps, Sutcliffe asked the girl whether she could tell the time from the nearby clocktower. When she did so, he complimented her on her eyesight and lagged behind, pretending to look at the clock. His motive was more sinister.

'I took my hammer out of my pocket and hit her on the back of the head twice,' he said. 'She fell down and she made a loud groaning sound.'

Her skull had been fractured from ear to ear.

Then Sutcliffe noticed someone walking along the main road. He grabbed his victim by the ankles and dragged her, face down, some 30 feet from the road further into the darkness. She was still moaning as he did so. A man walking by the park at the time of the murder said later that he had heard an unusual noise – 'the type of noise that makes your hair stand on end.'

As he was crouched over the body, Sutcliffe saw other figures walking along the path. One passed within five feet of him.

'As these people were walking on the path, she was still moaning loudly,' he remembered. 'I took my screwdriver – I remember I first pulled some of her clothing off. I was working like lightning and it was all a blur. I turned her over and stabbed her numerous times in the chest and stomach with the screwdriver. I was in a frenzy.'

In fact, he stabbed her 21 times with the screwdriver in the chest and stomach, and six times in the right leg. He also thrust the screwdriver into her vagina.

'After I'd stabbed her, she stopped moaning,' Sutcliffe recalled. 'I left her lying face down. I walked over to the main road, but I thought I saw someone coming up from the bottom, so I went back across the field the way I had come and went to my car. I drove home – I don't think I had any blood on me but my feet were covered in mud. I had my black boots on, which had been worn out and thrown in the bin. I had my old brown coat on that night.'

At 5.30am, a bus driver saw what he thought was a bundle of rags in the park and reported it to his office. An hour later, Jean Markham also spotted what she thought was a bundle of rags – until she noticed a shoe nearby. When she went across the road to pick up the shoe, she realised this was the body of a young woman. Plainly she was dead and so she ran back to her home to telephone the police.

Out on his newspaper round, Josephine Whitaker's 13-year-old brother David was crossing Savile Park. The police activity attracted his attention. It was then that he saw the shoe – it was his sister's. He ran home to tell his step-father and mother. They checked her room. Finding it empty, they too called the police.

It had been 322 days since the Ripper last killed. Now, from the injuries to Josephine Whitaker's body, it was clear that he was back with a vengeance.

Unlike most of his earlier victims, Josephine Whitaker was not a prostitute. She lived at home with her family and worked as a clerk in the headquarters of the Halifax Building Society. From then on, no woman felt safe on the streets after dark.

Two weeks before Josephine died, the police received another letter. It was postmarked Sunderland. Handwriting experts confirmed that it came from the same person who had sent two previous letters purporting to come from the Yorkshire Ripper. This one mentioned that Vera Millward had stayed in hospital. The police believed, wrongly, that this information could only have come from Vera herself. On this basis they leapt to the conclusion that the writer of the three letters was indeed the Ripper.

The letter said that the next victim would not be in Bradford's Chapeltown district as it was 'too bloody hot there' because of the efforts of 'curserred coppers'. This odd misspelling so closely aped the original Ripper's notes that it should have rung warning bells.

Traces of engineering oil had been found on one of the letters. Similar traces were discovered on Josephine Whitaker's body. The police called a press conference and the public were asked to come forward with any information they had about anybody who might have been in Sunderland on the days when the letters were posted. Though the response was overwhelming, all it added up to was more useless information to be checked, analysed and filed.

Then, on the morning of 18 June 1979, two months after Josephine Whitaker's death, a buff-coloured envelope arrived. It was addressed in the same handwriting and contained a cassette tape. On it was a 257-word message in a broad Geordie accent.

A huge publicity campaign was mounted. The public could dial in and listen to the 'Geordie Ripper Tape' in the hope that someone might recognise the voice. Within a few days, more than 50,000 people had called.

Language experts confirmed the accent as genuine Wearside and pinned it down to Castletown, a small, tightly-knit suburb of Sunderland. Eleven detectives were installed in a Sunderland hotel and 100 officers combed the town. Only 4,000 people lived in Castletown, but the police could not find their man – because he was a cruel hoaxer with a cast-iron alibi. Only years later, did they discover his identity. On 20 October 2005, John Humble – an unemployed alcoholic and long-time resident of the Ford Estate area of Sunderland, a mile away from Castletown – was charged with attempting to pervert the course of justice by sending the hoax letters and tape. He was remanded in custody, found guilty and sentenced to eight years in prison.

In July 1979, the police visited Sutcliffe again. Detective-Constable Laptew informed him that his car had been spotted in the red-light district of Bradford on 36 separate occasions. This time Laptew felt suspicious of Sutcliffe, but because all eyes were focused on the Geordie tape, his report was not followed up and Sutcliffe went back to Bradford to claim his eleventh victim.

On Saturday, 1 September 1979, Sutcliffe cruised the streets around Little Horton, a residential area of Bradford. At about 1am on 2 September, he saw 20-year-old student Barbara Leach leaving a group of friends outside the Mannville Arms. She was about to start her third and final year in Social Psychology. Closing time at the Mannville Arms was 11pm, but Barbara and her friends had stayed on to help the landlord collect the empties and tidy up. Their reward was a drink after hours. Though a light rain was falling as they left, Barbara decided go for a walk in the night air. None of her friends wanted to come along.

'I drove past her and turned left into a wide street and stopped on the nearside,' Sutcliffe said. 'I was just going to get out of the car when Miss Leach turned the corner and walked towards the car. She was walking at a very slow pace... She carried on walking past the car. I left the car and followed her for several yards. I had my hammer out and I think I had my big screwdriver with me. When she reached an entrance yard to a house, I hit her on the head with the hammer. She fell down, she was moaning. I took hold of her by the wrists – or was it by the ankles? – and dragged her up this entrance to the back of the house. She kept making loud moaning noises.'

Behind the house he pushed up her shirt and bra to expose her breasts, undid her jeans and pulled them down.

'I remember that I stabbed Barbara with the screwdriver, the same one as Whitaker, and I remember that I put her in the dustbin area and covered her up with something... I think I was wearing my brown coat that night. When I left her, I went to my car and drove away, and went straight home. I remember I later threw the big screwdriver away over the embankment near the lorry park on the west-bound side of Hartshead Service Station.'

Barbara Leach's body was found the following afternoon just 200 yards from the pub. It had been stuffed in a dustbin and an old carpet slung over it. She had been stabbed eight times.

Two high-ranking officers from Scotland Yard were sent to Yorkshire but got nowhere. A task force from Manchester reviewed the £5 note inquiry. They narrowed the field down to 270 suspects, but could get no further.

Like everyone else in Yorkshire, Sutcliffe spoke to his family and friends about the Ripper. He would make a point of picking up Sonia from work to protect her and told a workmate: 'Whoever is doing all these murders has a lot to answer for.' Once his colleagues at the depot made a bet that he was the Ripper, but Sutcliffe just laughed and said nothing.

The Ripper took another break of nearly a year. Then, on Thursday, 18 August 1980, he struck for the twelfth time. The victim was Marguerite Walls, a 47-year-old civil servant. Marguerite had been working late at the Department of Education and Science in Leeds, tidying up loose ends before going on a planned 10-day holiday. She left at 10pm to walk the half-mile home when Sutcliffe spotted her.

'I was on my way to Leeds, with a view to killing a prostitute,' he said. 'I was already in some kind of a rage and it was just unfortunate for her that she was where she was at the time, 'cos I parked the car and got out and followed her along the road.'

Near a driveway with high stone pillars, he hit her repeatedly with a hammer, yelling 'filthy prostitute!' – though it was clear she was not, though he later claimed that she walked slowly like a prostitute.

There was no one else about and so he dragged her inside the gateway into what appeared to be someone's garden. Somebody walked pass the entrance.

'I don't know whether they had seen me or not, because they appeared to look in,' he said. But he was not dissuaded. 'I didn't have a knife on me this time, but I had a length of cord which I strangled her with.'

He knelt on her chest as he strangled her. After she was dead, he stripped her of her clothes, leaving only her tights.

'I was going to leave her in an obvious position for people to see, but round about this time the road outside started to be quite busy with pedestrians going back and forth. I changed my mind and covered her up with some straw instead.'

Her body was found two days later, under a mound of grass clippings in the garden of a magistrate's house. She had been bludgeoned and strangled, but her body had not been mutilated so the police did not realise that she was one of the Ripper's victims. Indeed, when Sutcliffe was first arrested in 1981, he denied killing Marguerite Walls.

'No, that wasn't me,' he told the police. 'You have a mystery on your hands with that one. I've only used the rope once on that girl at Headingley.'

The girl at Headingley was Upadhya Bandara, a later victim.

Three weeks after his first denial, he confessed, explaining: 'I thought that maybe it would be better to sort this out at a later date, when I had cleared up all the other matters.'

On the night of 24 September 1980, Upadhya Bandara, a 34-year-old doctor from Singapore attending a course at Nuffield Centre in Leeds, had been out visiting friends. She was walking home down Otley Road and passed by the Kentucky Fried Chicken Shop where, at around 10.30pm, she noticed a man staring at her. Passing down a dimly lit cobbled alley called Chapel Lane, she heard someone behind her and moved to one side to let them overtake. It was then that she felt a blow on the head. A second blow rendered her unconscious.

'She was walking slowly along like a prostitute,' said Sutcliffe again. 'I hit her on the head with a hammer. I didn't have any tools with me to finish her off, so I used the rope.'

He looped it around her neck and dragged her down the road, but as he did so he heard her shoes making a scraping sound. He pulled off her shoes and chucked them over a wall, along with her handbag.

Valerie Nicholas, whose house backed onto the alley,

heard a noise and came out of her back door to investigate. Disturbed, Sutcliffe fled. Mrs Nicholas called the police and Dr Bandara came round to find officers standing over her, moments after her attacker had left. She gave a good description of Sutcliffe, but as she had sustained no stab wounds and the attacker had used a ligature, the assault was not considered to be a Ripper attack. It was, however, linked to the murder of Marguerite Walls and the police believed they had a new killer on their hands. Sutcliffe later admitted attacking Dr Bandara, but said he 'was overcome with remorse, so I didn't finish her off. I apologised to her and left her there.'

His 'remorse' did not stop him from trying to kill another woman 11 days later, but after Upadhya Bandara, Sutcliffe decided to give up trying to strangle his victims.

'I found that the method of strangulation was even more horrible and took longer,' he said. 'This is when I decided I couldn't kill people like this. I couldn't bear to go through with it again, as there was something deep inside preventing me.'

On the evening of 5 November 1980, 16-year-old Theresa Sykes had gone out to buy cigarettes from a grocery shop in Huddersfield. She was almost home when Sutcliffe emerged from the shadows. He caught up with her and struck her on the head from behind. She turned towards her attacker. As she fell, she tried to grab the weapon, but a second blow aimed by Sutcliffe struck her high on the forehead leaving a half-moon-shaped scar. Her screams were heard by her boyfriend and the father of their three-month-old son, Jim Furey. A fitness fanatic, he came racing out of the house. With Furey in hot pursuit, Sutcliffe fled. Losing his pursuer in the darkness, he hid under a hedge until he felt it was safe to emerge and head for home.

'I attacked her because she was the first person I saw that night,' said Sutcliffe. 'I think something clicked because she had on a straight skirt with a slit in it. She crossed the road in front of me… I followed her down this footpath and hit her a couple of times and knocked her down. But someone started shouting and I ran away and hid in a garden.'

Theresa gave a good description of Sutcliffe but, again, this was not regarded as a Yorkshire Ripper attack. It had taken place unusually early for the Ripper – 8pm. Later the police would change their minds and the time of the attack proved crucial. Eight weeks later, when Sutcliffe was arrested in Sheffield, his alibi did not match with his wife's recollection of the evening.

Twelve days later, Sutcliffe had just finished chicken and chips and was sitting in his car outside the same Kentucky Fried Chicken where he had first spotted Upadhya Bandara when he saw Jacqueline Hill. The 20-year-old English student at the University of Leeds was getting off the bus. It was a rainy Monday night. Jacqueline had been at a probation officers' seminar in Leeds city centre and she was returning home to her student hall of residence just 100 yards up Alma Road. It was 9.23pm as Sutcliffe watched her cross the road. He turned on the ignition and drove up Alma Road, then parked a little ahead of her, waited for her to pass and then got out of his car and followed her.

'As she drew level with an opening on the right-hand side, I took my hammer out of my pocket and struck her a blow on the head,' Sutcliffe said. 'She fell down. She was making a noise.'

Seconds later, another woman walked down Alma Road. Sutcliffe quickly dragged Hill onto the wasteland behind the Arndale Centre. There, he stripped her.

'I pulled Miss Hill's clothes off,' he said. 'I had a screwdriver on me – I think it had a yellow handle and a bent blade. I stabbed her in her lungs. Her eyes were wide open and she seemed to be looking at me with an accusing stare. This shook me up a bit. I jabbed the screwdriver into her eyes but they stayed open… I left her lying on her back with her feet towards the entrance. I think she was dead when I left.'

He had a little trouble with his getaway.

'I went to my car and drove up Alma Road to the top and turned round and drove back down to Otley Road. I remember that when I reached about halfway down, someone walking indicated to me that I was obviously going the wrong way down a one-way street but I carried on into Otley Road and turned left. I turned right at the lights and drove home.'

At around 10pm, a student found Jacqueline's cream-coloured raffia bag in Alma Road, where Sutcliffe had attacked her. There were spots of blood on it and the police were called. They did a cursory search, but found nothing. The following morning, Donald Court, a manager of a shop at the Arndale Shopping Centre, was walking along a ramp leading to a car park when he glanced over the wall and saw the body.

Five-and-a-half years had gone by. Thirteen women were dead and the police seemed no nearer to catching the Ripper. The Home Office appointed a special squad to solve the case. Trevor Birdsall had harboured suspicions about Sutcliffe since his attack on Olive Smelt in August 1975. However, the hoax tape then led everyone to believe that the Ripper was a Geordie and this allayed his suspicions. On 25 November 1980, however, Birdsall sent an anonymous letter to the police saying: 'I have good reason to now [sic] the man you are looking for in the Ripper case. This man as [sic] dealings with prostitutes and always had a thing about them... His name and address is Peter Sutcliffe, 6 Garden Lane, Heaton, Bradford. Works for Clarke's Transport, Shipley.'

But this information simply disappeared into the enormous volume of information already amassed. When nothing happened, Birdsall naturally assumed that the police had investigated Sutcliffe and cleared him. Six weeks after Jacqueline Hill's murder, the special squad came to the same conclusion as the West Yorkshire force – it had no idea how to crack the case. What was needed was a little bit of luck.

In mid-December, a job took Sutcliffe to Sheffield, a city he had not visited before. The shipment he was supposed to collect was not ready and he spent most of the day at the depot there. Two weeks later, he drove to Sheffield again in his new Rover V8 3500.

On Friday, 2 January 1981, 24-year-old Olivia Reivers had left her two children, three-year-old Deroy and Louise, five, at home at around 6pm. She was going to meet up with her friend, 19-year-old Denise Hall, and earn some money walking the streets in Sheffield's red-light district. At 9pm, the two women were in Wharncliffe Road when a brown Rover 3500 stopped. The driver offered Denise £10, but she refused. She did not like the look of him.

On 2 January 1981, Sergeant Robert Ring and Police Constable Robert Hydes started their evening shift by cruising along Melbourne Avenue in Sheffield's red-light district. They saw a couple in a brown Rover parked in the driveway of the British Iron and Steel Producers Association Headquarters and decided to investigate. The driver identified himself as Peter Williams and said that the woman with him was his girlfriend, but Ring recognised her as Olivia Reivers, a convicted prostitute who was on a suspended sentence. She had taken the £10, but when her client had driven her to the place where she conducted her business he could not get aroused and they just sat there chatting.

The driver told the police he wanted no trouble and then he scrambled out of the car and asked if he could relieve himself. He went over to the bushes lining the street and, while pretending to take a pee, dropped a ball-peen hammer and sharp knife which he kept in a special pocket of his car coat. The police did not notice this as

Olivia Reivers was remonstrating loudly with the men who had just saved her life, complaining that they were ruining her livelihood.

By the time the driver strolled back to his car, the police had discovered that the numberplates were false. He was taken to the police station, where he admitted his name was not Peter Williams, but Peter William Sutcliffe.

During his interview, Sutcliffe said his main worry was that the police would tell his wife that he had been picked up with a prostitute. Otherwise, he was calm and forthcoming. He readily admitted that he had stolen the numberplates from a scrap yard in Dewsbury. Still the police did not suspect him of being the Ripper. They even let him go to the lavatory alone, where he hid a second knife in the cistern.

There was no real reason to suspect Sutcliffe but the police had so little to go on that, when any man was caught with a prostitute, his details had to be forwarded to the West Yorkshire Police before he could be released. Sutcliffe was locked up for the night. The next morning he was taken, unprotesting, to Dewsbury police station to be interviewed about the theft of the numberplates.

There, Sutcliffe was a chatty, eager interviewee. In passing, he mentioned that he had been interviewed by the Ripper Squad about the £5 note and that he had also visited Bradford's red-light district. The Rover he had been driving at the time was not on their list of suspect cars, but Sutcliffe mentioned that he was a car enthusiast and had once had a white Corsair.

Dewsbury police called the Ripper Squad in Leeds, where Detective Sergeant Des O'Boyle discovered that Sutcliffe's name had come up several times in the course of the investigation. He drove to Dewsbury. When he called his boss, Detective Inspector John Boyle, in Leeds that evening he told Boyle that Sutcliffe was blood group B – the rare blood group found in the Harrison case. He also had a gap between his teeth. This was sufficient to have Sutcliffe locked in a cell for a second night.

Meanwhile, back in Sheffield, Sergeant Ring heard one of his colleagues casually mention that the man he had arrested was now being interviewed by detectives from the Ripper Squad. Ring rushed back to Melbourne Avenue. Hidden in the bushes there, he found a ball-peen hammer and a knife.

The house was searched. Then, early on Sunday afternoon, Boyle told Sutcliffe that they had found a hammer and knife in Sheffield. Talkative up to this point, Sutcliffe now fell silent.

'I think you're in trouble, serious trouble,' said Boyle.

Sutcliffe finally spoke. 'I think you are leading up to the Yorkshire Ripper,' he said.

Boyle nodded.

'Well,' Sutcliffe said, 'that's me.'

It was later revealed that when Sutcliffe was stripped of his clothes, he was found to be wearing a V-neck sweater under his trousers. The arms had been pulled over his legs, so that the V-neck exposed his groin; the elbows were padded. It is thought that this was to protect his knees as he knelt over his victims' corpses. Though Sutcliffe protested there was no sexual motive for his crimes, the implications of this outfit were obvious.

His confession took almost 17 hours to complete. He said that he had begun killing after a Bradford prostitute cheated him out of £10 in 1969. At that time, he mentioned nothing about hearing a voice from God.

Sixteen weeks later, Sutcliffe stood trial at the Old Bailey. The Crown Prosecution, defence counsel and Attorney General Sir Michael Havers agreed that he was mentally ill, suffering from paranoid schizophrenia, but the judge would have none of that. He told both counsels that the jury would listen to the evidence and decide whether Sutcliffe was a murderer or a madman.

Eventually Sutcliffe pleaded guilty to manslaughter. He was calm and self-assured, even managing a laugh when he recalled that, during his questioning about the size seven Wellington boot imprinted on Emily Jackson's thigh and Tina Atkinson's bed sheet, the policeman interviewing him had not noticed that he was wearing the very same boots. Only belatedly, when he was interviewed by a psychiatrist, did he claim that he had been acting on instructions from God to 'clean the streets of prostitutes'.

The jury found him guilty of 13 murders and he was sentenced to life imprisonment, with a recommendation that he should serve at least 30 years. He was not mad, they decided, but very, very evil.

CHAPTER NINE

DENNIS NILSEN

Dennis Nilsen was born in Fraserburgh, a small town on the bleak northeast coast of Scotland, on 23 November 1945. His father was a Norwegian soldier who had escaped to Scotland after the German invasion of his homeland in 1940; he had married Betty Whyte, a local girl, in 1942. He was a heavy drinker and was away a lot. The marriage did not work out and Betty continued to live with her parents. A few years later, the couple were divorced.

Dennis grew up with his mother, elder brother and younger sister but the strongest influence on his young life was his stern and pious grandparents. Their faith was so strict that they banned alcohol from the house; the radio and the cinema seen as instruments of the Devil and Nilsen's grandmother would not even cook on the Lord's Day and so their Sunday dinner had to be prepared the day before.

The young Dennis Nilsen was sullen and intensely withdrawn. The only person who could penetrate his private world was his grandfather, Andrew Whyte. A fisherman, he was Nilsen's hero. He would regale the little boy with tales of the sea and ancestors lost beneath its churning waves.

When Andrew Whyte died of a heart attack while at sea in 1951, his body was brought home and laid out on the dining room table. Dennis was invited to come and see his granddad. At the age of six, he got his first glimpse of a corpse. From that moment on, images of death and love fused in his mind.

At the age of eight, Nilsen almost drowned in the sea and was rescued by an older boy who had been playing on the beach. Aroused by the younger child's prostrate body, it seems he stripped him and, apparently, masturbated over him. Nilsen woke to find himself naked with a sticky white substance on his stomach.

When Nilsen's mother remarried two years later, she had four more children and little time for him. He withdrew and became a loner. Later he claimed he had no sexual experiences as an adolescent. Although he was conscious that he was attracted to other boys, his relationships remained innocent, though once he took a peep under the covers at his brother, who was sleeping naked.

He left school at 15 and went into the army. After basic training he was sent to the Catering Corps. There, he was taught how to sharpen knives – and how to dissect a carcass. During his life in the army, Nilsen only had one close friend. Plainly he was in love with him, though his object was not gay. However, Nilsen would persuade him to pose for photographs, sprawled on the ground as if he had just been killed in battle. When they parted, Nilsen destroyed the pictures.

Nilsen also began to drink heavily to stave off his feelings of loneliness – though when he was drunk he became even more withdrawn. One night in Aden, he was drunk and fell asleep in the back of a cab. He found himself naked, locked in the boot. When the Arab cab driver returned, Nilsen played dead. Then, as the driver manhandled him out of the boot, Nilsen grabbed a jack handle and beat him about the head. He never knew whether or not he had killed the man but the incident had a profound effect on him. Afterwards he had nightmares of being raped, tortured and mutilated.

After 11 years, Nilsen left the army and joined the police force instead. Part of his training included a visit to a mortuary, where recently qualified constables were initiated in the gruesome necessity of familiarising themselves with viewing post mortems. The partially dissected corpses fascinated him. He did well in the police but his private life was gradually disintegrating. Death became an obsession and he would pretend to be a corpse himself, whitening his skin with talcum powder, painting his lips blue and lying in front of a mirror, masturbating.

Eleven months after Nilsen joined the police, he was on the beat when he caught two men committing an act of gross indecency in a parked car. Unable to bring himself to arrest them, he decided to resign from the force.

He then went to work interviewing applicants at the Jobcentre in London's Charing Cross Road. After becoming branch secretary of the civil service union, he developed increasingly radical political views. Nevertheless his work was good enough to earn him promotion to executive officer at the Jobcentre in Kentish Town, north London.

Despite his professional progress, Nilsen was lonely and yearned for a lasting relationship. Since his teens, he had been aware of an attraction towards other men, but in the army and in the police force he had somehow managed to repress it. Now, at work, he met a young man named David Painter. One night he went back to Nilsen's flat, where he crawled into bed and fell asleep. When he woke up, he found that Nilsen had taken pictures of him sleeping and he became incensed. A fight ensued and Painter was so badly injured that he had to go to hospital. The police took Nilsen in for questioning, but he was released without charge.

In 1975, Nilsen met another young man called David

Gallichan outside a pub. They moved into a flat together at 195 Melrose Avenue with a cat and a dog called Bleep. Gallichan, or 'Twinkle' as Nilsen called him, stayed at home and decorated the flat while Nilsen went out to work. They made home movies together and spent a lot of time drinking and talking. Gallichan denied the relationship was homosexual, but it was not destined to last. After two years, Nilsen threw Gallichan out. He was plunged back into a life of loneliness, which he described as 'a long unbearable pain'. After this, he threw himself into his work and became increasingly more militant, spending his spare time on other people's picket lines to show solidarity. He filled his evenings with television and heavy drinking.

On New Year's Eve 1978, Nilsen met a teenage Irish boy in a pub called the Cricklewood Arms and invited him back to Melrose Avenue. They had been too drunk to have sex. When Nilsen woke in the morning, the boy was lying fast asleep beside him. He was afraid that when he woke up he would leave – and Nilsen wanted him to stay. The boy was undressed and Nilsen was aroused. Their clothes were thrown together in a heap on the floor. Nilsen leant over and grabbed his tie. He put the tie around the boy's neck, straddled him and pulled it tight – 'for all I was worth'. The boy woke immediately and began to struggle. They rolled onto the floor, but Nilsen kept pulling on the tie.

After about a minute, the boy's body went limp but he was still breathing. Nilsen went into the kitchen and filled a bucket with water. He brought it back and held the boy's head underwater until he drowned.

'After a few minutes, the bubbles stopped coming,' Nilsen recalled, 'I lifted him up and sat him on the armchair. The water was dripping from his short, brown curly hair.'

Now he *had* to stay. Nilsen had just killed a man, but he could not even remember his name.

Afterwards, he made himself a cup of coffee and smoked

a number of cigarettes while wondering what he was going to do. Bleep came in from the garden and sniffed at the body in the chair. Nilsen chased the dog away, then sat down again, falling into a deep state of shock. After a while, he removed the tie from the dead boy's neck and sat there staring at him.

Eventually he got up and put a towel over the window. Then he lifted the body up over his shoulders, carried the dead boy into the bathroom and gave him a bath. He washed his hair lovingly, recalling later that it was 'very limp and floppy'.

He dried the corpse, running his hands over the still-warm flesh. Soon he noticed the slight discoloration of his lips and face. He took the corpse into the bedroom and laid it on the bed. It was, he thought, rather beautiful. Nilsen had spent Christmas alone but now, on New Year's Day, he at last had company.

He would, he knew, have to dispose of the corpse sooner or later and so he went to a hardware store and bought an electric knife and a large pot. Back home, he could not bring himself to cut the body. Instead, he dressed it in clean socks and underpants and, for a while, he just lay on the bed holding the dead boy.

Nilsen took a bath. Now naked, he decided to have sex with the corpse. Though he found the prospect thrilling, he could not sustain an erection and so he put the body on the floor and went to sleep. Later he got up and made dinner, then watched TV with the body not far away.

The following day, he planned to hide the body under the floor, but rigor mortis had stiffened the joints, making it hard to handle. So he left it out while he went to work. When the corpse had loosened up, Nilsen undressed it again and washed it. This time he masturbated beside it and found he could not stop playing with it and admiring it.

All the time Nilsen was playing with the corpse, he

expected to be arrested at any moment but no one came. It seemed no one had missed the dead boy. After a week of living happily with the corpse, Nilsen hid it under the floorboards. Seven months later he cut the body up and burnt it in the garden, along with a tyre to mask the smell. Afterwards, he raked the ashes into the ground.

By the time of Nilsen's trial the boy had not been identified and so, although he had confessed, he was not charged with his murder. The boy had not had anything on him that would have identified him, only a latch key which Nilsen had disposed of. Then, in 1990, detectives showed Nilsen a poor photocopy of passport-sized photo of a boy named Stephen Holmes, who had been 14 at the time of the murder. The picture was so poor that Nilsen could not give a positive ID, but in 2005 detectives turned up with a better photograph and Nilsen identified it. Apparently Holmes had been on his way home from a concert when Nilsen had met him. The file was then passed to the Director of Public Prosecutions, but it was not considered in the public interest for Nilsen to stand trial again.

Nilsen's first experience of murder frightened him; he was determined it would not happen again and he decided to give up drinking. But he was lonely – he liked to go to pubs to meet people and talk to them. Eventually he slipped off the wagon. In October 1979, nearly a year after the first murder, Nilsen met Andrew Ho, a young Chinese student from Hong Kong, in the Salisbury, a gay pub in London's St Martin's Lane. The young man offered sex and agreed to be tied up, so Nilsen took him home. During the bondage session, Nilsen put a tie around Ho's neck and warned him that he was playing a dangerous game. He then tried to strangle him, but Ho broke free and went to the police. Nilsen complained that Ho had been trying to rip him off. In the end, Ho decided not to press charges and Nilsen was released.

Nearly a year later, on 3 December 1979, Nilsen met

Kenneth Ockendon, a Canadian tourist, in a pub in Soho. He took leave from work that afternoon and gave Ockendon a sightseeing tour of London. Ockendon agreed to go back to Nilsen's flat for something to eat. After a visit to the off-licence, they sat in front of the television eating ham, eggs and chips, and drinking beer, whisky and rum.

As the evening wore on, disturbing feelings began to grow inside Nilsen. He liked Ockendon, but realised that he would soon be gone as he was flying back to Canada the next day. A feeling of desolation crept over him, the same feeling he had had when he killed Stephen Holmes.

Later that night, when they were both very drunk, Ockendon was listening to music through earphones. Nilsen put the flex of the headset around his new friend's neck and dragged him struggling across the floor. When Ockendon was dead, Nilsen took the earphones off and put them on himself. Calmly he poured himself another drink and listened to records while the body lay on the floor.

In the early hours of the morning, Nilsen stripped the corpse and carried it over his shoulder into the bathroom. When the body was clean and dry, he put it on the bed and went to sleep next to it, caressing it frequently through the night.

In the morning, he put the body in a cupboard and went to work. That evening, he took it out again and dressed it in clean socks, underpants and vest. He took some photographs of it, sketched it and then lay next to it on the bed. Speaking to Ockendon as if he could hear him, Nilsen pulled the corpse on top of him and had sex between its thighs. Later, he hid the body under the floorboards.

For the next two weeks, Nilsen would get Ockendon's body out in the evening and watch TV with the corpse propped up in an armchair next to him. Last thing at night, he would undress it.

'I thought that his body and skin were very beautiful,' said Nilsen. When he was finished, he would dress him in something fresh, put him to bed and say good night. The rest of the time the body was wrapped in old curtains and hidden under the floorboards.

As Ockendon had gone missing from a hotel, his disappearance made the news for a few days. Again Nilsen was convinced he was about to be arrested at any moment. Several people in the pub, on the bus, at the sights they had visited and even in the local off-licence had seen them together but still there was no knock on the door. From then on Nilsen felt that he could pursue his murderous hobby unfettered.

Although plenty of people visited the flat in Melrose Avenue and emerged alive, Nilsen now began to deliberately seek out victims. He would go to pubs where lonely young homosexuals hung out. There, he would buy them drinks, offer advice and invite them back to his flat for something to eat. Many accepted.

One of them was 16-year-old Martin Duffey. After a disturbed childhood, he ran away from home in Birkenhead and ended up in London, sleeping in railway stations. On 13 May 1980, he accepted an invitation to go back to Nilsen's flat and, after two cans of beer, crawled into bed. When he was fast asleep, Nilsen climbed on top of him to trap his arms and strangled him. While he was still barely alive, Nilsen dragged his unconscious body into the kitchen, filled the sink with water and held his head underneath for four minutes.

Nilsen went through the standard procedure of stripping and bathing the corpse, then he took it to bed. He talked to it, complimenting Duffey on his body.

'I talked to him and mentioned that his body was the youngest-looking I had ever seen,' Nilsen said. He took the body to bed, kissed it all over, then sat on the stomach and masturbated over it. Nilsen kept the body in a cupboard for a few days. When it started to swell up, he put Duffey under the floorboards next to Ockendon.

Twenty-seven-year-old Billy Sutherland died because he was a nuisance. He was a prostitute. Nilsen didn't fancy him but after the two men met on a pub crawl, Sutherland followed him home. Nilsen vaguely remembered strangling him, he said. Certainly there was a dead body in the flat in the morning.

Nilsen neither knew nor cared about his victims, the only thing that interested him about them was the bodies, *dead* bodies. The murder routine was always much the same – that part was mechanical – but once they were dead, they really turned him on. Touching the corpse would give him an erection.

Nilsen would never think of his victims' bodies lying around his flat while he was out at work but when he got home in the evening, he could not help playing with them. Thrilled to own their beautiful bodies, he was fascinated by the mystery of death: he would hold the corpse in a passionate embrace and talk to it, and when he was finished with it, he would stuff it under the floorboards.

Often he did not even know his victims' names, or did not care to remember them. His fifth victim was another male prostitute, probably from Thailand or the Philippines; he was never identified. Number six was a young Irish labourer that he met in a bar. Nilsen described number seven as a starving 'hippie-type' found sleeping in a doorway in Charing Cross.

He could remember nothing about number eight except that he kept him under the floorboards until he removed the corpse and cut it into three pieces, then put it back again. A year later, he burned the pieces. The next two victims were young Scottish men that he had picked up in Soho pubs.

His eleventh victim was a skinhead that he picked up in Piccadilly Circus. The youth had a tattoo around his neck saying 'cut here'. Nilsen would later oblige. The skinhead boasted about how tough he was and how he liked to fight but once drunk, he was no match for Nilsen, who hung his naked torso in the bedroom for a day before it joined the others under the floorboards.

On 10 November 1980, Nilsen picked up a Scottish barman called Douglas Stewart in The Golden Lion in Dean Street, Soho. Stewart went back to Nilsen's flat and later he woke to find himself being strangled. He managed to fend off his attacker. Nilsen then threatened him with a carving knife, but eventually let him go. Stewart called the police, but they took no action, dismissing the incident as a domestic tiff.

Some of his murders were terrifyingly casual. Nilsen found one victim, 24-year-old Malcolm Barlow, collapsed on the pavement in Melrose Avenue. Barlow was an epileptic and he said that the pills he was taking made his legs give way. Nilsen carried him home and called an ambulance. When he was released from hospital the following day – 18 September 1981 – Barlow returned to Nilsen's flat to thank him. Nilsen prepared a meal. Barlow began drinking, even though Nilsen warned him not to mix alcohol with the pills he had been prescribed.

When Barlow collapsed, Nilsen could not be bothered to call the ambulance again and strangled him, then carried on drinking until bedtime. The space under the floorboards was now full, so the next morning Nilsen stuffed his body in the cupboard under the sink. With six corpses under the floor and several others dissected and stored in suitcases, he had completely run out of storage space. Now he had to spray the flat twice a day to keep down the flies. A neighbour complained of the insidious smell. Nilsen said that it was the building decaying. He considered suicide, but Bleep came in at the crucial moment, wagging his tail. Nilsen simply spat on his image in the mirror. Instead he decided it was time to move but first he had to get rid of the evidence.

After a stiff drink, Nilsen put Bleep and the cat in the

garden and pulled up the floorboards. He stripped to his underwear and began cutting up the corpses on the stone kitchen floor with a kitchen knife – his butchery course in the catering corps came in useful. He put the internal organs in plastic bags, emptying them out in the garden. Birds and rats did the rest. The other body parts were moved out to the garden shed, or stuffed in a hole under a bush. He used to boil the flesh off heads in the pot originally bought to dispose of Stephen Holmes.

Torsos were kept in suitcases until he could move them. Eventually, parts he could not dispose of in any other way were wrapped in carpet and put on a series of bonfires in the garden. A car tyre was placed on top to disguise the smell. Local children would come to watch the blaze, which would burn all day. Nilsen warned them to keep their distance. On one occasion, as the fire burned down, he spotted a charred skull in the middle but crushed it into the embers. The ash was then raked into the ground.

After Nilsen's flat was vandalised, the move became all the more pressing. When two detectives came round to investigate there were still the remains of two more men under the floorboards, inches from their feet.

Finally, Nilsen was ready to move. The day he was leaving, he suddenly remembered that he had left Malcolm Barlow's hands and arms in the garden. He quickly disposed of them. When the police searched the garden after he was arrested, they found over 1,000 bone fragments.

Nilsen moved to an attic flat at 23 Cranley Gardens. This was a deliberate attempt to stop his murderous career. He could not kill people, he thought, if he had no floorboards to hide them under and no garden to burn their bodies in. During this time, he had several casual encounters at his new flat, picking men up at night and letting them go in the morning, unmolested. This made him elated. Finally he had broken the cycle, or so he thought.

In November 1981, just one month after moving,

Nilsen met student Paul Nobbs in The Golden Lion and invited him back to his flat. They were drunk and Nobbs awoke the next morning with little recollection of the events of the night before. Later, bruising appeared around his neck. He went to University College Hospital, where the doctor said that it appeared someone had been trying to strangle him and advised Nobbs to go to the police, but he was not ready to be outed as a gay and so he decided not to do so.

Following this attempted murder Nilsen picked up drag queen Khara Le Fox, aka Carl Stotter, at The Black Cap, a well-known gay bar in Camden High Street. Nilsen throttled him until he passed out, but while he was trying to drown his victim in the bath, Stotter came to and gasped for air until he lapsed into unconsciousness again. Nilsen thought he had killed Stotter, but Stotter came round when Bleep the dog licked him.

When the victim recovered sufficiently to walk to the Underground, Nilsen accompanied him. As they passed through a wood on the way, Nilsen hit Stotter violently on the head, but again he survived the attack. When the pair parted ways, they agreed to meet up again, but Stotter wisely avoided Nilsen from then on. Due to memory loss resulting from the attack and the alcohol consumed beforehand, Stotter did not realise for several years that he had almost been killed.

One day in December 1981, Nilsen was drinking alone when John Howlett, or 'Guardsman John', as Nilsen called him, came into the pub. They had met before and struck up a conversation. After a while they decided to go back to Nilsen's flat. They had a few more drinks there and then Howlett got into Nilsen's bed. Nilsen asked him to leave, but Howett refused to go, so Nilsen grabbed a loose upholstery strap from an armchair and tried to strangle him.

Howlett was one of the few who fought back. He was strong, but Nilsen had taken a dislike to him and was determined that he should die. There was a tremendous struggle and at one point Howlett even tried to strangle Nilsen. Fearing he might be overpowered, Nilsen beat Howlett's head against the bed head. Eventually he went limp. Nilsen left the strap on his neck and then went shakily into the front room to quieten the dog. When he returned, he noticed that Howlett was still breathing. He tightened the strap around his neck again and held it for two or three minutes, but Howlett's heart was still beating and so Nilsen dragged him into the bathroom and drowned him. Exhausted, he left him in the bathtub for the rest of the night. In the morning he put the body in a cupboard and went to work.

With little storage space in his new flat, Nilsen immediately had the problem of disposing of Howlett's corpse and he had to be quick because he was expecting a visit from a friend. He started cutting it into small pieces, which he flushed down the lavatory. This took longer than he expected, so he began boiling the flesh off the feet, hands and head in the kitchen. Smaller bones were put out with the rubbish; larger ones chucked over the back garden fence into a waste area. Those that could not be disposed of immediately were put in a bag of salt and hidden in a tea chest covered with a red curtain.

A few days later, he met a homeless man named Graham Allen in Shaftesbury Avenue. He took Allen home with him and made him an omelette. Nilsen said that he did not remember killing Allen.

'I noticed he was sitting there and suddenly he appeared to be asleep or unconscious with a large piece of omelette hanging out of his mouth,' Nilsen said.

He thought the man might have choked on the omelette. However, there were telltale red marks around his neck, so Nilsen reckoned he must have strangled him.

He took off Allen's clothes, washed his body in the bath and left it in there for three days before dissecting him.

Then he boiled parts of his body, flushing smaller pieces down the lavatory. Larger bits were stored in the tea chest; others in a plastic sack.

On New Year's Eve, Nilsen invited neighbours up to his flat. They declined as he already appeared drunk. Later they heard him leave and return with someone. They heard a commotion upstairs and then someone came running down the stairs, sobbing, and ran out of the front door. Toshimitsu Ozawa went to the police and told them that Nilsen had approached him with a tie stretched between his hands. He thought Nilsen had intended to kill him, but it was New Year's Eve and the investigation went no further.

The death of his final victim, Stephen Sinclair, upset Nilsen. Sinclair was a 20-year-old drifter and a drug addict, who hung about Leicester Square. They met in Oxford Street on 23 January 1983. Nilsen said he felt sorry for the homeless Sinclair and bought him a hamburger. Some of his mates saw Sinclair go off with a strange man.

Nilsen took him back to Cranley Gardens. They sat and listened to music, while Sinclair shot up. When he slumped in a chair in an alcohol- and heroin-induced stupor, Nilsen went into the kitchen to get some string.

Here we go again, he thought.

The string was not long enough, so Nilsen went into the bedroom and got his one remaining tie. But he did not strangle his victim straight away: he draped the seemingly innocuous murder weapon over the sleeping man's knees, then he poured himself a drink and sat down to contemplate all the suffering in Sinclair's life. He decided to put him out of his misery. Sinclair was in a deep sleep and Nilsen slipped the ligature around his neck to strangle him. The unconscious victim woke, struggled slightly and then went limp.

'Nothing can hurt you now,' Nilsen told the corpse.

When Nilsen removed Sinclair's clothes, he found bandages on his arms. Underneath were scars. Sinclair had recently tried to commit suicide by slashing his wrists with a razor.

After Nilsen bathed him, he put him into the bed. Then he took off his own clothes and placed two mirrors by the bed, so that he could enjoy the sight of the two of them naked together. Later he said that he experienced a feeling of oneness there with Sinclair, as if he had discovered the meaning of life and death.

Nilsen continued talking to the corpse as if Sinclair was still alive. He turned the young man's head towards him and kissed him. His dead lover was about to give the game away, however.

Nilsen left Sinclair's body in the bedroom for a few days covered with a blanket and then he cut off his head, boiled it in the pot and dismembered the body, sketching it as he did so. He boiled the hands and feet as well. Larger pieces were put in plastic bags. Some went into the tea chest; some in a small cupboard in the bathroom. Other bags were scattered around the area, while the internal organs and some of the flesh were flushed down the toilet.

Unfortunately, the drains in Cranley Gardens were not built to handle bodies. A downstairs lavatory would not flush properly. The tenant tried to clear the blockage with acid. Other tenants also began to have trouble with their toilets. When Nilsen was asked about his lavatory, he said it was working properly, but from then on he did not flush it. A plumber was called but he could not shift the blockage either.

The drains at 23 Cranley Gardens had been blocked for five days on 8 February 1983 when the drainage-cleaning company Dyno-Rod sent Michael Cattran to investigate. He quickly determined that the problem was not inside, but outside the house. At the side of the house, he found the manhole that led to the sewers. He removed the cover and climbed in.

At the bottom of the access shaft, he found a glutinous

grey sludge. The stench was awful. As he examined it, more sludge came out of the pipe leading from the house. He called his manager and told him that he thought the substance that he had found was human flesh.

Nilsen and the other tenants were there when Cattran made the call. He mentioned that he might call the police, but it was getting dark and his manager thought it might be better if they took another look the following morning. Nevertheless, Cattran took Nilsen and the other tenants to see the pile of rotting flesh in the drain.

That night, Nilsen sat in his flat, drinking away heavily. He said that he contemplated suicide once again but around midnight, he sneaked downstairs and threw the flesh over the fence. Next morning, Cattran and his boss returned to the manhole, but the sludge had vanished. No amount of rainfall could have flushed it through. Someone had been down there and removed it.

Cattran put his hand inside the pipe that connected to the house and pulled out some more meat and four small bones. One of the tenants in the house said that they had heard footsteps on the stairs in the night and suspected the man who lived in the attic flat had been down to the manhole. They called the police.

Detective Chief Inspector Peter Jay took the flesh and bones to Charing Cross Hospital. A pathologist there confirmed that the flesh was, indeed, human.

The tenant of the attic flat was out at work when Chief Inspector Jay got back to Cranley Gardens, so he waited. Nilsen knew something was likely to happen that night. When he left work, he told a colleague: 'If I'm not in tomorrow, I'll either be ill, dead or in jail.' Both laughed.

At 5.40pm, Nilsen returned home. Chief Inspector Jay met him at the front door and introduced himself. He said he had come about the drains. Nilsen remarked that it was odd that the police should be interested in drains. Surely that was a job for the environmental health officer?

In Nilsen's flat, Jay said that the drains contained human remains.

'Good grief! How awful,' Nilsen exclaimed.

Jay told him to stop messing about. 'Where's the rest of the body?' he asked.

After a short pause, Nilsen said: 'In two plastic bags in the wardrobe next door – I'll show you.'

He showed Inspector Jay the wardrobe. The smell coming from it confirmed what he was saying.

'I'll tell you everything,' Nilsen offered. 'I want to get it off my chest. Not here, but at the police station.'

The police could scarcely believe their ears when Nilsen admitted killing 15 or 16 men – apologising for not being able to tell them the exact number. In the wardrobe in his flat, they found two large black bin-liners. Inside one, they discovered a shopping bag containing the left side of a man's chest, including the arm. A second bag held the right side of a chest and arm. In a third was a torso with no arms, legs or head. A fourth was full of human offal. The unbearable stench indicated the bags had evidently been closed for some time.

In the second bin-liner, were two heads – one with the flesh boiled away, the other largely intact – and another torso. The arms were still attached, but the hands were missing. One of the heads belonged to Stephen Sinclair. Nilsen had severed it only four days earlier and had started simmering it in a pot on the kitchen stove.

Under a drawer in the bathroom, the police found Sinclair's pelvis and legs. In a tea chest in Nilsen's bedroom, was another torso, a skull and more bones.

The police also examined the gardens at 195 Melrose Avenue. They found human ash and enough fragments of bone to determine that at least eight people, probably more, had been cremated there.

At the police station, Nilsen showed no remorse. Asked how he had managed to dispose of the bodies in such a gruesome fashion, he said: 'The victim is the dirty platter after the feast and the washing up is an ordinary clinical task.'

Eventually Nilsen was charged with six counts of murder and three of attempted murder. His solicitor had one simple question for him: 'Why?'

'I'm hoping you will tell me that,' was his reply.

Nilsen intended to plead guilty, sparing the jury and the victims' families the details of the horrendous crimes. Instead, his solicitor persuaded him to claim 'diminished responsibility'.

One of the most extraordinary witnesses at the trial was Carl Stotter. He said that Nilsen had tried to strangle him three times, but somehow his frail body had clung to life. Nilsen had then dragged him to the bath and held him underwater. Stotter had somehow found the strength to push himself up three times and beg for mercy but Nilsen pushed him down again. Thinking he was dead, Nilsen took the body back into the bedroom and smoked a cigarette. Then Bleep, Nilsen's dog, began to lick Stotter's face and he started to revive. Nilsen could easily have snuffed out his life then and there. Instead, he rubbed Stotter's legs to stimulate his circulation. He wrapped him with blankets and nursed him back to life.

Paul Nobbs also testified. He said he had slept at Cranley Gardens one night and woke at 2am with a splitting headache. When he woke again, he found red marks around his neck. Nilsen advised him to see a doctor. At the hospital, he was told that he had been half-strangled. He assumed his attacker had been Nilsen, but did not report the assault to the police, assuming they would dismiss the attack as a homosexual squabble.

On 4 November, 1983, Nilsen was convicted of the attempted murder of Stotter and Nobbs, plus the actual murder of six others. He was sentenced to life imprisonment with the recommendation that he should serve at least 25 years.

He says he does not lose sleep over what he has done, or have nightmares about it. Nor has he shed any tears for his victims or their relatives. He killed men whose names he did not even remember because he was scared of being alone, or to have sex with their dead bodies. That is evil.

CHAPTER TEN

JOSEF FRITZL

Unlike the other entries in this book, Josef Fritzl is not a mass murderer, but he qualifies as one of the world's ten most evil characters because of his complete indifference to those closest to him. While others take their misanthropy out on strangers, his mother, wife and children bore the brunt of his. Fritzl is the Austrian father who for 24 years locked his own daughter up in a cellar, treated her as his sex slave and fathered seven children by her.

Josef Fritzl was born on 9 April 1935 in Amstetten, a small town in Austria. His mother never loved him and only had him to prove that she was not barren. When he was three, Germany annexed Austria in the *Anschluss*. As Hitler drove past Amstetten on his way to Vienna, the entire town turned out to raise their arms in a *Sieg Heil* salute. They made Hitler an honorary citizen of Amstetten. In his thank-you letter, the *Führer* said the town's tribute 'filled him with great pleasure.'

When Josef Fritzl was four, his mother threw his father out. He went to war and his name appears on Amstetten's war memorial. Fritzl later complained that his mother never showed him any love.

'She beat me and kicked me until I was on the floor and bleeding,' he said. 'She told me I was a Satan, a criminal, a no-good.'

Fritzl would have spent much of his youth in a cellar. The railway line through Amstetten took arms and reinforcements to the Russian Front and was regularly bombed by the RAF. There was a concentration camp in the town, which held 3,000 male slave labourers used to rebuild the track. A second camp held 500 women. The extermination camp Mauthausen-Gusen was just 25 miles away and the Nazi euthanasia programme, where psychiatric patients, invalids and the elderly were put to death, was begun at Amstetten's Mauer clinic.

After World War II, Fritzl and his mother were destitute but he did well at school and went on to study electrical engineering at a nearby polytechnic. He took a job in a steel company and began to take an interest in women. At the age of 21, he met 17-year-old Rosemarie. They married in 1956 and had seven children together.

In 1959, they moved into the house at 40 Ybbsstrasse in Amstetten, where his daughter was later imprisoned. His mother moved in with them, but soon she was no longer seen in the streets of Amstetten. The roles were reversed and she grew afraid of her son. When she became ill, she was confined to an attic room. Fritzl then bricked up the window so she could see no daylight. She lived in captivity until she died in 1980, some 20 years later.

In the 1960s, Fritzl began raping women. At the time, he had a wife and four children at home. Only one woman brought charges and, in 1967, he was convicted of rape and sentenced to 18 months in jail. It is thought that he came up with the plan for incarcerating his daughter and using her as his sex slave while in jail. That way, he could live out his evil fantasies in the cellar, while living a normal life upstairs. At the time, Elisabeth was the youngest and he began grooming her.

Fritzl was known to be a strict parent. When he entered the room, his children would fall silent, even if they were in the middle of a game. School friends were banned from the house and they lived in constant fear of being punished. His wife Rosemarie was also intimidated by him and he would deliberately humiliate her in front of others. When she could stand it no longer, she moved out to a guesthouse they owned, but he would not let her take the children with her. Eventually, he forced her to return by burning the guesthouse down. A number of young women were murdered in the vicinity of the guesthouse. Fritzl is suspected.

Elisabeth was the prettiest of his daughters. Although he claimed that she was the apple of his eye, he treated her even worse that the other children. At school, she took care to hide the evidence of the beatings she had suffered from her teachers and school friends. When she was 11, he prevented her from going on holiday with her mother and the other children. Instead, he kept her at home and, she says, started sexually abusing her.

While Elisabeth's older brother and sisters managed to escape their tyrannical father by marrying young and moving out of the family home, Elisabeth was forced to stay behind and endure her father's physical and sexual abuse.

The year after the abuse began, Fritzl asked for permission to turn his basement into a nuclear shelter. This was not unusual. Austria was on the front line in the Cold War. Over the next five years, he transformed the cellar into a bunker. Bomb-proof, soundproof and escape-proof, building inspectors gave the shelter their seal of approval in 1983.

Around this time, Elisabeth began to show an interest in boys. To escape the predations of her father, she ran away from home, several times. Each time, he found her, and with the help of the police, had her returned home.

On 28 August 1984, Fritzl lured his daughter to the cellar on the pretext that he needed help with the steel door that would cut her off from the rest of the world for the next 24 years. After the two of them grappled the heavy door into place, Elisabeth said that her father grabbed her from behind and apparently knocked her out with ether. When she came to, she found that she was handcuffed to a metal pole and remained there for the next two days.

Her father then put her on a 5ft dog leash that allowed her to reach the makeshift lavatory in the corner but otherwise restricted movement. Already the bunker had been transformed into a prison: the heavy steel door was electronically controlled and the small room insulated and soundproofed. For the first few weeks, the terrified teenager was held there in total darkness.

Elisabeth tried to fight back. She began banging on the walls and screamed until she could no longer speak, but no one responded and so she eventually gave up. When she stopped battling her father, the beatings lessened although he kept demanding sex and she was kept on the leash for the next nine months. He only visited her to rape her or give her food to keep her alive; this presented her with a vicious dilemma.

'I faced the choice of being left to starve or being raped,' she later said simply.

She could not remember how many times he raped her. The sex was unprotected and Elisabeth fell pregnant but miscarried in the tenth week of pregnancy. Meanwhile Fritzl told everyone that his daughter had run away from home again. Her mother reported her disappearance to the police, but Fritzl forced his daughter into saying in a letter that she had had enough of living with her parents. She had gone to stay with a friend and if they looked for her, she would leave the country. She had, after all, run away before.

Later, another letter arrived, saying that Elisabeth had joined some religious sect and asked the police not to look for her. They wound down the manhunt, unaware that no sects were operating in Austria at the time. Then, when Elisabeth turned 19, her disappearance was no longer a matter for the police and her file was closed. Although friends who knew her thought it unlikely that she had run off to join a sect, no one dared challenge Fritzl. Her fate was sealed, or so it seemed.

In 1989, after five years of captivity, Elisabeth gave birth to her first daughter, Kerstin. She did this entirely alone, helped only by the medical books her father bought her. Mother and child survived, but Kerstin proved sickly from being deprived of light, fresh air, and proper food and sanitary conditions. The following year Elisabeth gave birth to a son, Stefan.

Only a few feet above their heads, life in the Fritzl family home went on as usual. Fritzl rented out rooms – one even to a childhood friend of Elisabeth's. They heard nothing. Pets were banned after a dog showed great interest in the basement. One lodger noticed that he was being overcharged for electricity as Fritzl had by now installed electric light in the cellar and ran it off his meter. Others were aware of food being stolen, or Fritzl delivering large quantities of groceries to the cellar late at night. The cellar was off-limits to everyone and Fritzl seemed to spend an inordinate amount of time down there. The family were told that his workshop was down there and he was working on the plans of some secret project.

In 1992, another child, Lisa, was born in the cellar. The tiny, padded cell was cramped and the baby cried a lot. Fearing the child might die if she remained in the cellar, Elisabeth was easily coerced into writing a letter in which she stated that she had abandoned the infant for its own good. Fritzl then pretended to find the child and a note on the front doorstep at 40 Ybbsstrasse. Both the police and social services were completely taken in. The handwriting was the same as samples in Elisabeth's school books that Fritzl had retained. It seemed no one thought to ask why a woman who had repeatedly run away from her parents would entrust her daughter to them, and Josef and Rosemarie Fritzl were allowed to keep their grandchild.

After keeping his daughter in a 20-square-metre padded cell for nine years, Fritzl finally took pity on her. Father and daughter began to expand the dungeon, digging out an estimated 116 cubic metres of earth – some 200 tons of it. Somehow, without anyone noticing, Fritzl managed to remove 17 truckloads of earth and rubble, while smuggling in bricks, tiles, wooden wall panels, a washing machine, a kitchen sink, beds and the pipe work to make a rudimentary bathroom. Elisabeth and her two growing children now had living quarters that could almost pass as a squalid flat, only their place had no natural light and the ventilation was so poor that the occupants had to sit or lie down most of the time – there was not enough oxygen to breathe.

In 1994, Elisabeth gave birth to Monika. She suffered from a heart condition, possibly caused by her incestuous heritage. Fritzl took the baby upstairs, leaving her on the doorstep and going through the same charade as before. This time the local paper picked up on the arrival and condemned Elisabeth as a neglectful mother. Everyone sympathised with Rosemarie Fritzl, who had already brought up seven children of her own. Now she was expected to take care of her grandchildren as well.

Two years later, Elisabeth was pregnant again, this time with twins. Again Fritzl left her alone to give birth. One of the children was sickly and when Fritzl returned to the cellar three days later it was dead. The infant had not been named, but has now been called Michael. Fritzl took the tiny body and burnt it in the basement furnace, along with the other household waste. It was for the death of baby Michael that he was later charged with murder, on the grounds that the child would have survived had he arranged proper medical care.

The surviving twin, Alexander, was again taken upstairs to be brought up by the uncomplaining Rosemarie. Once more the police and social services appeared to accept the situation at face value. The Fritzls were allowed to keep the children with no further checks into Josef Fritzl's background – they even received handsome state benefits for caring for their grandchildren, money that was badly needed, as several business ventures went wrong.

Fritzl also had an opulent lifestyle to support. In Amstetten, he played the part of a wealthy businessman: driving a Mercedes, dressing in fine clothes and wearing gold rings on his fingers and a gold chain around his neck. The couple entertained and went on separate holidays. Rosemarie would visit the Mediterranean, while Fritzl went off to Thailand, sometimes for weeks on end. There, he would spend his time with prostitutes, while Elisabeth and the children remained locked in the cellar, depending on the food he had left for them.

While he was away, he was seen to buy sexy clothing for a slim woman. As these clothes were clearly not for the stout Rosemarie, it was assumed Fritzl had a mistress. No one had any idea that it was his own daughter.

In Austria too, Fritzl used prostitutes. He was particularly keen on having sadomasochistic sex in the 'dungeon' – the window-less cellar of a brothel in Linz. Some of the women refused to go with him, they were frightened of him and he was thought to be 'sick' and 'mean'. It was later alleged that he would force his daughter to watch pornographic videos and act out scenes from them, beating and kicking her if she refused. There was no privacy in the cellar, so everything that took place would have been in full view of the children. Inevitably, Elisabeth fell pregnant and gave birth to a son they named Felix. He was to remain in the cellar.

There was no chance for Elisabeth and her children to escape. They were told that the heavy steel door to the cellar was electrified and that, if they tried to escape, they would be gassed. A code was needed to open the door, so if they attacked Fritzl and injured or killed him, they would never get out. While he was away, there was always a danger that he might have an accident, leaving them incarcerated to starve to death. Fritzl later claimed that the lock on the door operated on a timer and would automatically open if he was away for a protracted period, so his daughter and their children would be freed, had he died. No such mechanism was found.

Elisabeth did her best to bring up their children as well as possible in the circumstances. She taught them to read and write with the limited materials Fritzl supplied. He began to spend more time in the cellar with his 'downstairs family', buying the children presents and he had dinner and watched TV with them. They celebrated Christmas and birthdays together. However, he was completely indifferent to their suffering. They grew up physically stunted due to a lack of sunlight, oxygen, good food and exercise; of course they suffered psychologically too.

Even Fritzl knew the situation could not go on forever. When Christmas 2007 arrived, he forced his daughter to write one last letter to prepare the ground for her liberation. It explained that she wanted to leave the cult and to return in around six months' time. Fritzl plainly believed that he had dominated his daughter so completely that she would maintain the fiction that she had spent the last 24 years in some freaky religious cult after he eventually freed her; even the children were expected to remain silent. But his plans were overtaken by events.

The downstairs children had been brought up in the most appalling conditions. Their health had inevitably suffered – they had never seen a doctor, or even a nurse to receive the inoculations all children have. When they got ill, Fritzl treated them with a combination of aspirin and cough mixture. Now the eldest child, 19-year-old Kerstin, became seriously ill. She started to have fits. Blood spewed from her mouth and she fell into a coma. Elisabeth begged her father to take Kerstin to hospital. Reluctantly, he agreed.

On Saturday, 19 April 2008, they carried her upstairs and called an ambulance. While Elisabeth returned to the cellar, Kerstin was taken to the local hospital. She was in a coma and no one could tell what was wrong with her, though it was noted that she had lost most of her teeth and was severely malnourished. An hour later, 73-year-old Josef Fritzl turned up at the hospital. He said that the girl was his 19-year-old granddaughter Kerstin. The unconscious teenager, he said, had been left outside his house. According to him, this was not an unusual event in the Fritzl household and he retold the story of Kerstin's mother Elisabeth running away to join a bizarre religious sect.

Fritzl did not wait around even long enough to hear a diagnosis. Instead he rushed away, puzzlingly saying that the doctors should not call the police. He left a note from her mother, which he said he had found with the unconscious child. It read: 'Wednesday, I gave her aspirin and cough medicine for the condition. Thursday, the cough worsened. Friday, the coughing gets even worse. She has been biting her lip as well as her tongue. Please, please help her! Kerstin is really terrified of other people – she was never in a hospital. If there are any problems, please ask my father for help – he is the only person that she knows.'

There was a curious postscript, addressed to the stricken girl.

'Kerstin – please stay strong, until we see each other again! We will come back to you soon!'

Dr Albert Reiter was in charge of the case. As Kerstin's condition deteriorated, he realised that he would have to get in touch with her mother to find out how the child came to be in such a terrible condition. He broadcast an appeal. Journalists flocked to Fritzl's door only to be unexpectedly seen off by him.

At this stage, the police got involved. They could find no record of Kerstin and no sign of Elisabeth but then they discovered there was not the slightest indication that a religious sect of the type described by Fritzl had ever been active in Austria.

In the cellar, Elisabeth Fritzl saw Dr Reiter's appeal. Eventually she persuaded her father to let her go to the hospital, promising she would stick to the story that she had been with a sect for the past 24 years. Arriving at the hospital, she was arrested.

Kerstin was in such a bad condition that they wanted to question her mother with a view to bringing charges of child neglect. At first, Elisabeth stuck to her father's story that she had been in a cult but from the start, the police thought something was very odd about her. Although she was only 42, she had grey hair, no teeth and a morbidly pallid complexion. She looked like a woman in her sixties who had been locked up in an institution. Plainly she was terrified too.

Suddenly Elisabeth said that she would tell them everything, provided they could guarantee that she and her children would never again have to see Fritzl. This was a shock to the detectives for Fritzl was a pillar of the community. A retired electrical engineer and the owner of a number of properties in town, he had lived there all his life. He had brought up three of her discarded children and had even brought her critically ill daughter to the hospital after she had, apparently, abandoned her. Elisabeth then told them a story that beggared belief.

She said that she had not run away to join a cult and that her father was not the caring family man that he pretended to be. A martinet, he had begun beating her brutally from the time she was old enough to walk. The sexual assaults started when she was 11. She then said that, when she was 18, he had drugged her, dragged her to a concealed cellar in his house, raped her and continued doing so for the next 24 years.

The rapes had resulted in seven children and for nearly a quarter of a century, she and three of the children had lived in a window-less hell under the family home. The children had never seen the outside world, let alone breathed in fresh air; they had never known freedom, nor had any contact with wider society. Apart from their mother, the only other person known to them was their jailer, a man who would alternately play with them or terrorise them. He told them the doors to the cellar were electrified and if they tried to escape, they would be gassed. Their mother was raped by him in front of them and yet, with the boxes of groceries and meals he shoved through a hatch, he was their only lifeline. In truth, the good family man of Amstetten was a fiend, the family home at 40 Ybbsstrasse a house of horrors. It was hard to believe but they could not discount the evidence of their own eyes.

Of course the police had to put Elisabeth's allegations to Fritzl. Initially he refused to talk, even producing the letter from his daughter in which she stated that she intended to return from the religious sect where she had spent the last 24 years in an attempt to deflect her accusations.

Later he even complained that he was disappointed that Elisabeth had seized her opportunity to 'betray' him so rapidly, but the following morning, the police took Josef Fritzl back to his house at 40 Ybbsstrasse. The front was a typical suburban town house on an ordinary street but at the back was an imposing concrete structure, not unlike a wartime bunker. Although set among leafy suburban gardens when all the other gardens were open, the back of Fritzl's house was screened off by high hedges. His garden was the only one that could not be overlooked by neighbours.

At first the police could not find the dungeon where Elisabeth said she had been held – it was so well hidden. Sensing the game was up, however, Fritzl then led them down the cellar stairs and through eight locked doors and a warren of rooms. Concealed behind a shelving unit in his basement workshop was a heavy steel door, just one metre high with a remote-control locking device. After some prompting, he gave the police the code to open it.

Ducking through the first door – just over a metre high – the police found a narrow corridor. At the end was a padded room, soundproofed with rubber cladding, where Fritzl would rape his daughter while the children cowered elsewhere. It was so well insulated that no scream, cry or sob could be heard in any other part of the building. Beyond that was a living area, then down a passage little more than a foot wide – one that you would have to turn sideways in to negotiate – were a rudimentary kitchen and bathroom. Further on were two small bedrooms, each with two beds in them. There was no natural light and little air.

On the white tiled walls of a tiny shower cubicle, the captives had painted an octopus, a snail, a butterfly and a flower in an attempt to brighten their prison. The furnishings were sparse – the police found a toy elephant perched on a mirrored medicine cabinet and scraps of paper and glue that the children had used to make toys. The only other distraction was a small TV providing flickering images of the outside world, which the children had never experienced and for Elisabeth had become an increasingly dim memory. There was also a washing machine and a fridge and freezer, where food could be stored when Fritzl took off on the holidays he denied his captives. The whole scene was lit with electric light bulbs and this was the only source of light although Elisabeth had begged her twisted father to give her vitamin D supplements and an ultraviolet light to prevent her kids becoming deformed. The lights went on and off on a timer to give some sense of day and night, something else the children had never properly experienced.

The police found two children who had survived these appalling conditions, 18-year-old Stefan and 5-year-old Felix. They were in a poor physical state and unused to strangers. They were so lacking in social skills that the police found they were practically feral. Because of the low ceilings in the dungeon – never more than 1.7 metres (5ft 6in) – Stefan was stooped. In excitement, young Felix had resorted to going on all fours. Having never been required to communicate with anyone beyond their immediate circle the police found they had difficulty in talking. Between themselves, they resorted to grunts. For the first time in their lives, they were taken out into the daylight.

Confronted with the evidence, Fritzl confessed that he had imprisoned his daughter.

'Yes,' he told the police. 'I locked her up, but only to protect her from drugs. She was a difficult child.'

While admitting to repeatedly raping her, Fritzl rejected his daughter's claims that he had chained her to the cellar wall and kept her 'like an animal', insisting he had been kind to the 'second family' he kept in the cellar. He admitted that the children were his own, the offspring of his incest with his own daughter. DNA tests confirmed this was the case. However, the police did not understand why he had decided that three of the children – Lisa, 16, Monika, 14, and Alexander, 12 – should live upstairs with him and his wife and go to school, while the other three – Kerstin, 19, Stefan, 18, and Felix, 5 – had to remain downstairs in their prison. Asked on what grounds he had made that decision, Fritzl told police that he had feared the noise of their cries might lead to their discovery.

'They were sickly and cried too much in the cellar for my liking,' he said.

Fritzl was taken to jail in nearby St Pölten. Meanwhile, Elisabeth and the children were taken to the Mauer clinic to be reunited. There, while the world's press besieged the clinic, a team of doctors and psychiatrists began the long task of trying to rehabilitate them. Kerstin eventually regained consciousness and joined them. The prognosis for five-year-old Felix was good. It was thought that he was young enough to recover. Everyone who had contact with Elisabeth remarked on how strong she was, though she can scarcely have come through her ordeal unscathed. Kerstin and Stefan have suffered so badly physically from their privations that there are doubts whether they can ever make a full recovery. All have suffered an insurmountable psychological trauma.

Fritzl remained unapologetic. He sought to justify his incarceration of Elisabeth on the grounds that she was an unruly child and even insisted he was a victim of the situation himself. Besides, he claimed to have been kind and generous to his second family.

'I'm no monster,' he said. 'I could have killed them all then nothing would have happened to me. No one would have ever known about it – I would never have been caught.'

After all, he had saved Kerstin's life, putting himself at risk into the bargain.

'Without me she would not be alive anymore,' he said. 'I was the one who made sure that she was taken to a hospital.'

It did not seem to occur to him that she might not have needed to go there in the first place, had she had not spent the first 19 years of her young life locked in a cellar.

But the truth is, Josef Fritzl is a monster. He robbed his daughter of the best years of her life, subjecting her to repeated rapes, the terrible ordeal of giving birth to her father's children by herself, then watching those that remained downstairs suffer the most squalid conditions and growing up in the most circumscribed surroundings without any chance for life. Admittedly, her own childhood at the hands of her father had been bad enough, but these children had no opportunity to run and play, or even see sunlight. The children who were taken from her and went to live upstairs did not escape his strictures either for they had to cope with the idea that for years their siblings were living in the most awful conditions, just metres below their feet. And Alexander would have to get used to the idea that he had a twin brother whose body was incinerated with the household waste.

The trial of Josef Fritzl began on 16 March 2009. Initially he admitted he was guilty of all charges except the enslavement of his daughter and the death of one of their children by neglect. But after hearing his daughter's video testimony he pleaded guilty to those two charges as well. His lawyer said that her testimony had profoundly affected Fritzl, 'destroying' him emotionally. Was this, finally, recognition of just how evil he was? Or was it a final, desperate attempt to maintain a degree of control? In any case, on 19 March he was sentenced to life imprisonment; the conditions of his incarceration are luxurious compared to those his daughter and their children suffered for 24 years.

Despite his last-minute and very public 'change of heart', Fritzl is not concerned about the suffering he has inflicted on his own children. At least he did not kill them, he maintains. In comparison with what he did, to kill them might well have been merciful. That same mercy cannot be extended to him – there is no death penalty in Austria. Although he will die in prison, nothing done to him can ever suitably redress what he has done to those around him, it is all too easy to recognise that he is one of the world's ten most evil men.

FURTHER READING

Andrew, Christopher M. and Mitrokhin, Vasili, *The World Was Going Our Way: The KGB and the Battle for the Third World*, Basic Books, New York, 2005

Bergen, Peter L., *The Osama bin Laden I Know*, Free Press, New York, 2006

Bilton, Michael, *Wicked Beyond Belief: The Hunt for the Yorkshire Ripper*, Harper Perennial, London, 2006

Blair, David, *Degrees in Violence; Robert Mugabe and the Struggle for Power in Zimbabwe*, Continuum, London, 2003

Brady, Ian, *The Gates of Janus*, Turnaround, London, 2001

Bugliosi, Vincent with Gentry, Curt, *Helter Skelter: The True Story of the Manson Murders*, Arrow, London, 1992

Burn, Gordon, *Somebody's Husband, Somebody's Son: the Story of Peter Sutcliffe*, Faber, London, 2004

Cawthorne, Nigel, *The World's Worst Atrocities*, Hamlyn, London, 1999

The Empress of South America, William Heinemann, London, 2003

House of Horrors, John Blake, London, 2007

Chan, Stephen, *Robert Mugabe: A Life of Power and Violence*, I.B. Taurus, London, 2003

Courtois, Stephane et al., *The Black Book of Communism: Crimes, Terror, Repression*, Harvard University Press, 1999

East, R. and Thomas, Richard J., *Profiles of People in Power: The World's Government Leaders*, Europe, London, 2003

Ellis, Stephen, *The Mask of Anarchy: The Destruction of Liberia and the Religious Dimension of an African Civil War*, Hurst & Co., London 1999

Gekoski, Anna, *Murder By Numbers: British Serial Sex Killers Since 1950; Their Childhoods, Their Lives, Their Crimes*, Andre Deutsch, London, 1998

Girma, Yehwalashet, *The Rape of a Nation*, Minerva Press, London, 1996

Goodman, Jonathan, *Trial of Ian Brady and Myra Hindley: The Moors Case*, David and Charles, Newton Abbot, 1973

Hill, Geoff, *The Battle for Zimbabwe: The Final Countdown*, Zebra, Cape Town, 2003

Hollander, Paul (ed.), *From the Gulag to the Killing Fields: Personal Accounts of Political Violence and Repression in Communist States*, Intercollegiate Studies Institute, Willington, Delaware, 2006

Jones, Barbara, *Voices From an Evil God*, John Blake, London, 1993

King, Greg, *Sharon Tate and the Manson Murders*, Mainstream, Edinburgh, 2000

Livsey, Clara, *The Manson Women: A 'Family' Portrait*, Richard Marek Publishers, New York, 1980

Manson, Charles, *Without Conscience: Charles Manson in His Own Words*, Grafton, London, 1988